AF326586

4197 RANDOM, FUN, AND AWESOME SCIENCE FACTS TO WIN TRIVIA

AN ENCYCLOPEDIA OF AMAZING AND WACKY FACTS ABOUT THE WORLD

PROFESSOR SMART

ALL ABOUT SCIENCE

WHAT IS SCIENCE?

When you hear the word science, you might think of lab coats, astronauts heading into space, digging up fossils in a rainforest, or even studying cells under a microscope. All of these images reflect some aspect of science. However, none of these grasps the entire scope of what science is.

Science is all about observing the world, listening and watching your surroundings, and then recording your findings. Science can be broken down into three major groups: formal sciences, natural sciences, and social sciences.

THE FIRST TYPE OF SCIENCE: FORMAL SCIENCE

Formal science is a branch of science that involves the scientific study of mathematics, logic, statistics, systems and decision theory, and theoretical computer science. Some great examples of formal science include coding on a computer, completing an algebra equation, and analyzing how our society works.

THE SECOND TYPE OF SCIENCE: NATURAL SCIENCE

Natural science is a branch of science that involves the scientific study of natural phenomena such as physics, chemistry, earth science, space science, and biology. Examples of natural science include calculation gravity on another planet, understanding how bats communicate using ultrasonic sounds and discovering new elements that we could use to generate power.

THE THIRD TYPE OF SCIENCE: SOCIAL SCIENCE

Social science is a branch of science that involves the scientific study of how our world works, such as communications, economics, education, geography, history, law, and psychology. Examples of social science include analyzing the stock market's economic health, measuring the impact of education on wealth, and helping others overcome gaming addiction.

ABOUT THIS BOOK

In this book, you will find 4197 random, fun, and awesome science facts. Flip to any random page, and your mind will be blown!

- *Professor Smart*

4197 RANDOM, FUN, AND AWESOME SCIENCE FACTS TO WIN TRIVIA

1. Waterfalls are created when flowing streams erode soft bedrock, revealing hard rock such as granite. Over time, this erosion develops cliffs and ledges.
2. Some of the most well-known constellations are Orion, Ursa Major, and Minor, Zodiac, and Pegasus.
3. Wasps feed on sugar sources from flower nectar, honeydew from insects, and fruit to obtain energy for flight and metabolism.
4. Hydrogen is the main constituent of Saturn.
5. Different names were suggested for Uranus in the past. These include Hypercronius meaning above Saturn, Georgium Sidus, meaning the Georgian Planet and King of England, George III.
6. The original Celsius scale with a boiling point at 0 degrees and freezing point at 100 degrees was reversed in 1744 when the person who invented the Celsius scale, Anders Celsius, died.
7. There are online sites that you can find that lets you view the night sky through a live telescope lens.
8. The distance between Earth and our moon would fit all the planets lined up together.

9. The fourth-largest planet is Neptune.
10. Venus is so bright it can be seen during the day with a clear sky.
11. Mercury is the fastest planet that orbits the sun, taking 88 Earth days to complete one orbit.
12. In the Local Cluster, Andromeda is the largest galaxy, but it doesn't have the biggest mass. The Milky Way is more massive as it contains more dark matter than the Andromeda Galaxy.
13. 5 European explorers and astronomers named 40 out of the 88 constellations (Ptolemy appointed 48). Their names are Gerardus Mercator (Dutch explorer in 1500s), Pieter Keyser and Frederick de Hautmann (beginning of the 16th century). Johannes Hevelius (1690), and Nicolas Louis de Lacaille (French astronomer in 1750s).
14. A baby deer takes its first step about half an hour after it's born.
15. Mice can hear and communicate with each other by ultrasound.
16. Neptune has 14 moons in orbit; the largest one is as large as Pluto!
17. Ceres is the largest asteroid with a diameter of 933 km. It is also a dwarf planet.
18. Penguins have no teeth.
19. Hippos live in Africa.
20. The Internet has domain names including .com, .org, and .gov as well as country-specific ones, for example, .org.au (Australia).
21. Dogs are omnivores, which means that they eat vegetables and meats.
22. Cast iron is an iron alloy with carbon, silicon, and a small amount of manganese. It was once used to build bridges.
23. A compound gas, like CO, is made up of a combination of different atoms.

24. Many tiger subspecies are endangered or extinct from humans who have hunted them or destroyed their environment.
25. Polar bears have long sharp claws, up to 1.97 in (5 cm), to grip the ice and stop slipping and catch their prey.
26. There are three types of satellites used for different purposes. Satellites for communication such as voice, data, and video transmissions, are fixed satellites. This makes up most of the satellites that are sent to space. Some satellites are made for GPS and navigation and positioning. In contrast, many others are used for scientific research such as space observations, earth science, and meteorological data.
27. Wasps are nature's pest controllers. They are important in protecting farm crops and gardens from pests.
28. Humans lie down to sleep, but horses and cows sleep standing up.
29. Scientists believe the size of a koala's brain is smaller than its ancestors as their diet doesn't give them enough energy.
30. Charon is Pluto's largest moon.
31. Crocodiles have a very good sense of hearing and can hear their baby crying out from inside an egg.
32. As well as inventing the first electric motor and generator, Michael Faraday also invented a simple Bunsen burner and coined the terms electrode, cathode, anode, and ion. He discovered benzene and studied the chemical element chlorine.
33. A spiral galaxy has a central bulge that contains a black hole.
34. The moon is moving further away from Earth - 4.6 years ago when it was formed, it was only 22,530 km (14,000 miles) away, but now it is 450,000 km (280,000 mi) away.
35. Every country in the world, except the United States,

Belize, Bahamas, Cayman Islands and Palau, measures temperature using the metric Celsius scale. The Celsius scale says water boils at 100 deg C and freezes at 0 deg C. The United States and the other exceptions uses the Fahrenheit scale which says water boils at 212 deg F and freezes at 32 deg F.

36. In 2013, Felix Baumgartner, skydiver, jumped from the stratosphere 36,576 meters (120,000 feet) above Earth.
37. About 100 satellites are launched every year into space.
38. There are more than 200 billion stars in the universe.
39. The suspension in bicycles helps reduce vibration when riding. Mountain bikes have more suspension to deal with uneven surfaces.
40. Our skin has the important functions of protecting our bones, muscles, and organs inside our body. It also regulates our body heat.
41. A googol is a very large number - it has 100 zeros after 1). Google, the search engine, was misspelled and meant to be Googol.
42. Whales are awesome because they can sing!
43. Thin shaved or powdered magnesium is very flammable. It burns with a brilliant white flame. Larger masses of magnesium doesn't light as easily.
44. Giant galaxies in the universe can be as long as 2,000,000 light-years.
45. More than two-thirds of all galaxies are spiral galaxies. A spiral galaxy has a flat, spinning disk with a central bulge surrounded by spiral arms. As it spins at speeds as fast as hundreds of kilometers a second, it causes matter in the disk to take on a spiral shape, like a cosmic pinwheel. The Milky Way is an example of a spiral galaxy.
46. Gums cover the roots of our teeth.
47. Jupiter has a system of thin rings. Its rings are mainly

dust particles from impacts of comets and asteroids from some of Jupiter's smaller worlds.

48. A rainbow is created from the bending (refraction or reflection) of light in water in the atmosphere. It is a full circle, but we only see an arc of it from the ground.
49. Eris, the dwarf planet, was discovered on 21 October 2003.
50. James Clerk Maxwell proved Saturn's rings are not liquid or solid but small particles in orbit.
51. Isaac Newton saw an apple fall out of a tree, which inspired him to formulate the law of gravity.
52. Astronomers use the Andromeda Galaxy to understand the evolution and origin of galaxies. It is the nearest spiral galaxy to Earth.
53. The US and Russian astronauts keep separate water supplies on the ISS.
54. German inventor, Carl Benz, invented the first modern automobile in 1886, the Benz Patent Motorwagen.
55. When you feel your heartbeat, you are feeling your cardiac cycle. Your heart contracts and pushes blood into your arteries. It then relaxes and expands, filling up again with blood ready to pump out again.
56. Titanium is found in igneous rocks. In the Earth's crust it is the ninth most abundant element.
57. Hedgehogs live up to seven years in the wild.
58. The average mission on a satellite is 3 to 4 years. They are sometimes re-orbited after this time, but most of them are sent to the graveyard orbit.
59. Otters live in waterways and are strong swimmers.
60. Makemake, a dwarf planet, is so far away from the sun, making it very cold with an average temperature of -243.2 degrees C (-405.7 deg F). Scientists think methane, ethane and nitrogen ices cover its surface.
61. During Jupiter's and Saturn's lightning storms, methane

is converted into carbon soot, hardening into graphite, and then diamonds. This means that it rains diamonds, sometimes up to a centimeter (0.39 in) thick, on Saturn and Jupiter.

62. The chemical symbol for helium is He. It has an atomic number of 2.
63. Theoretical astronomy involves using analytical models to study topics such as stellar dynamics, galaxy formation, matter in the universe, the origins of cosmic rays, evolution, general relativity, and astroparticle physics.
64. John Glenn, at the age of 77 years, is the oldest person to go to space. He went as a human guinea pig so scientists could study geriatrics in space.
65. Louis Pasteur is buried in the Pasteur Institute in Paris, after being moved from Notre Dame.
66. The Ford model's T car was the first mass-produced automobile in the world in 1908.
67. The queen bee can lay up to 1,500 eggs a day and more than a million in her lifetime, which can be 2 to 7 years.
68. Facial hair grows faster than body hair.
69. The sixth most common element found in our Universe is iron.
70. An artificial satellite is one that is sent to space to send information back to Earth.
71. An engine provides the thrust needed to overcome drag and enable the wings to create lift in an airplane.
72. The speed of sound is approximately 767 mph (1,230 kph).
73. In the Cancer Constellation, the star Asellus Australis is called 'southern donkey.' In contrast, the star Asellus Borealis is called the 'northern donkey.'
74. Recycling glass releases less carbon dioxide than making new glass.
75. Isaac Newton's mother wanted him to be a farmer.

76. Astronomers mainly work for universities and research institutes. There aren't many professional astronomers than other scientists, but there are many amateur astronomers who often share their findings with the professionals.
77. A total of 4 galaxies can be seen with the naked eye - the Small and Large Magellanic Clouds, the Milky Way and the Andromeda Galaxy.
78. It was possible for travelers to pay for their passage into space at one time, but was stopped in 2011 when the ISS crew was reduced to 6.
79. Alessandro Volta invented the electric battery by experimenting on frog's legs.
80. Pigs are used in many research areas, including organ transplants and plastic surgery.
81. Chlorine is a yellow, green gas, but its compounds usually have no color.
82. The circumference of Mars is 21,297 km (13,233 mi).
83. The armed forces use nuclear reactors to power submarines and aircraft carriers.
84. A stingray's skeleton, just like a shark's, is made of cartilage, not bones.
85. A pumpkin is a fruit and not a vegetable as it has seeds.
86. People breathe in oxygen and breathe out carbon dioxide. Plants breathe in' carbon dioxide and 'breathe out' oxygen during a process called photosynthesis.
87. Bees can detect the Earth's magnetic field.
88. From 1994 to 2011, 3 supernovae have been observed in the Whirlpool Galaxy.
89. Johannes Kepler is most famous for his work on Mysterium cosmographical (The Sacred Mystery of the Cosmos - 1596), Astronomia nova (New Astronomy - 1609), Harmonice Mundi (Harmony of the Worlds - 1619) and Epitome astronomiae Copernicanae (Epitome

of Copernican Astronomy - published between 1618 and 1621).

90. The World Wide Web was invented in 1989 by an English physicist Sir Tim Berners-Lee.
91. Hippos can open their mouth wide to 180 degrees as their jaw hinge is set back in their head.
92. The Milky Way and Andromeda Galaxies are getting closer together every day and will merge in about 5 billion years.
93. Beetles are an important part of the ecosystem in which they live because they feed on plant and animal debris.
94. Over 700 different species of venomous snakes live on Earth.
95. Pigs eat animals and plants.
96. About two-thirds of all titanium is used to build aircraft. Titanium is also used in building racing cars and motorcycles as it's light but strong.
97. A toad swallows its prey in one piece as it has no teeth to chew it up.
98. An observatory is a remote location that has at least one large telescope.
99. Galaxies sometimes merge to form a bigger one, or they destroy each other.
100. Stephen Hawking wrote the book "A Brief History of Time" that won a Guinness World Record for being a best seller for four and a half years. In this book, Hawking wrote about the Big Bang Theory and discussed time, space, and black holes.
101. Seals can sleep underwater.
102. Peacocks make a low-frequency sound (infrasound) when they vibrate their feathers. People can't hear the sound.
103. The two true camel species are the dromedary, a single-humped camel that lives in the Middle East and Africa,

and the Bactrian, which has two humps and lives in central Asia.

104. Like Saturn's moon, Enceladus, Eris is thought to be one of the most reflective dwarf planets in the solar system.
105. Mass extinction of dinosaurs occurred about 65 million years ago when dinosaurs became extinct.
106. Although titanium was discovered in 1791, it was not purified to 99.9% until 1910 by a New Zealand chemist, Matthew Hunter. The Hunter process is named after him.
107. Almost anyone who travels into space can be called an astronaut or a cosmonaut.
108. Eris, dwarf planet, rotates on its axis every 25 hours (similar to Earth's 24 hours). It orbits the sun every 557 years.
109. In Australia, Uluru is made up of approximately 50% feldspar, 25-35% quartz, and 25% rock fragments.
110. Ancient civilizations once thought meteors were a sign of anger from the gods or gifts from angels. In the 1600s, many people nicknamed them thunderstones as they thought they came from thunderstorms.
111. A solar eclipse will usually alternate with a lunar eclipse.
112. If we break a bone, it will re-grow and repair itself.
113. Inside a submarine, the moisture breathed out by its occupants must be removed. A dehumidifier stops the moisture from condensing on the walls and equipment inside the submarine.
114. Eagles have amazing eyesight and can see prey up to 2 miles (3.2 km) away. It is 4-5 times stronger than a person's eyesight.
115. A killer satellite was designed to destroy warheads.
116. Mount Rushmore is 60 feet (18 m) high. Each of the President's eyes measures 11 ft (3.3 m) wide, their noses 20 ft (6 m) long, their mouths 18 ft (5.5 m) wide, and the

total height of their head is about the height of a six-story building.

117. Scientists believe that Haumea collided with a large object billions of years ago, resulting in two moons being formed.
118. Bees can be grouped into nine families.
119. With the naked eye, the ISS can be seen worldwide, appearing as a slow-moving, bright white dot in the night sky.
120. As of 2013, Anatoly Solovyev holds the record from having made the most spacewalks - 16 spacewalks over 82 hours and 22 minutes.
121. As a star is getting to the end of its life, it changes color, density, and size.
122. Titanium is 60% denser than aluminium but more than twice stronger.
123. Squirrels, chipmunks, prairie dogs, and marmots all belong to the Sciuridae family.
124. The beaver is nocturnal and becomes active at night.
125. Reptiles are cold-blooded and rely on the environment to warm them up.
126. The Oort Cloud is a theoretical cloud beyond the edge of our solar system.
127. The most deadly tornado was recorded in Bangladesh in 1989, killing about 1,300 people.
128. Chameleons do not change color for camouflage. They change color as a means of communicating with other chameleons and also to regulate their body temperature.
129. When the air around lightning heats up and expands faster than the sound speed, thunder is produced.
130. To date, NASA knows no astronaut that has had sex in space! Getting pregnant would also be very dangerous in space.
131. A search engine is the easiest way to find information on

the web. Google and Yahoo are examples of search engines.

132. Hans and Zacharias Hannsen invented the microscope in 1950. In 1674, Antonie van Leeuwenhoek became the first person to see a live cell through a microscope.
133. The Hubble Space Telescope is named after the American astronomer, Edwin Hubble, who was the first to see galaxies beyond the Milky Way. An asteroid and a moon crater have also been named after him.
134. Different astronomers have different hypotheses about what will happen to our universe. The first is that it will eventually collapse into something else. The second is to keep expanding and growing forever until everything is so far apart that the universe will die. The third is that we have a flat universe that will stay the same and continue indefinitely. The last scenario is known as 'the Goldilocks effect' as everything is 'just right.'
135. New stars are being formed at the center of the Whirlpool Galaxy at a fast rate due to its interaction with its companion M51. This is expected to last no more than another 100 million years.
136. Horses are herbivores which means that they eat plants.
137. Ceres was discovered by an Italian astronomer Giuseppe Piazzi on 1 January 1801, searching for a star.
138. Hammerhead sharks live in schools of more than 500 sharks. The dominant female swims at the center of the school.
139. An anableps is a four-eyed fish that can see above and below the water at the same time.
140. The Mississippi River and Missouri Rivers join to make the longest river system in the USA and North Americal.
141. Neptune's atmosphere comprises mainly hydrogen and helium and some methane.
142. The Triangulum Galaxy actively creates stars that are

scattered around the spiral arms. The rate of star birth is much higher than that of the Andromeda Galaxy.

143. The largest chameleon in the world, Parson's chameleon, can grow up to 27 inches (69.5 cm) long.
144. Due to their size, the larger icy objects in the Kuiper Belt are known as dwarf planets. They are larger than asteroids and too small to be a planet.
145. The largest living structure on Earth is the Great Barrier Reef, off Queensland's coast in Australia.
146. A white hole looks like a black hole, spinning with dust and gas rings around the event horizon. However, they differ to black holes as they spit something out instead of absorbing everything that goes into it. Nothing can go into a white hole.
147. Like cows and sheep, sloths have four chambers in their stomach to help digest the food they eat. It can take a month for them to digest a meal. As it takes so long, they don't have much energy left for moving around.
148. Some bacterias, such as salmonella and E-coli, grow faster in space.
149. Galileo Galilei discovered Ganymede, one of Jupiter's moons, on 7 January 1610.
150. Nickel is found in the Earth's core, but it is rare in the Earth's crust. After iron, it is the most abundant element in the core.
151. Uranium was the metal that helped the discovery of radioactivity.
152. The "Karman Line," 100 km (62 miles) above sea level, is scientifically accepted as the edge of space. This means 532 people from all over the world have reached outer space (as of June 2013).
153. The moon contains small amounts of water.
154. Two men from each of the six different Apollo missions

have walked on the moon, including Neil Armstrong and Buzz Aldrin.

155. Guinea pigs are crepuscular i.e.; they are most active during dusk and dawn.
156. Walt Disney created a cartoon dog called Pluto in 1930 and named it after the planet (it was a planet at the time!)
157. Digital televisions became possible in the 1990s when inexpensive, high-performance computers became available.
158. At 4,700 m (13,123 ft) high, the tallest mountain on our moon is slightly over half of Mt Everest's height.
159. There are a few words for a group of flamingos. They can be called a pat, stand, flamboyance, just to name a few.
160. The body of a badger is built for digging. They have a stocky body with short legs, broad feet, and long claws used to dig underground burrows called setts. A sett can be a maze of tunnels and chambers where up to six badgers can sleep.
161. In 1959, the first US monkeys who survived a trip to space, on a Jupiter rocket, were Able and Miss Baker.
162. Supernovas can create shock waves strong enough to trigger new star formations.
163. British chemists, Sir William Ramsay and Morris Travers discovered krypton, neon, and xenon in 1898.
164. In the PC game Descent, one of the secret levels takes place on Ceres.
165. Iron is a chemical element and also a metal.
166. Some bats 'hibernate' during winter. This is known as 'torpor,' where they can lower their body temperature, metabolic and heart rates and slow their breathing.
167. About 21 million light-years from Earth sits the Pinwheel Galaxy.
168. Electricity is made when electrons move from one atom

to another. It is the "flow of electrons" through a conductor like a wire.

169. When uranium atoms are split apart to form smaller atoms, it releases energy. This process is called nuclear fission and can produce heat and electricity. France, Japan, and the US make the most nuclear power in the world.
170. A toucan has short wings, so it can't fly very far.
171. Large bridges started to use wrought iron in the 19th century. They were replaced by steel as it was a much stronger material.
172. People in Africa and Central and South America eat grasshoppers! They are an excellent source of protein.
173. The camel's hump gets smaller when it uses its stored fat. When they find food and water again, the hump fills back up with fat.
174. Our skull or cranium, which protects our brain, is made up of 22 bones fused.
175. Emperor penguins are threatened to become extinct due to climate change impacting the sea-ice environment where they live.
176. The different types of teeth in our mouth have different functions. We bite food with our incisors and chew it up with our molars.
177. Earth has a powerful magnetic field caused by its nickel-iron core together with its fast rotation.
178. The Spitzer Space Telescope can no longer take pictures under extreme temperatures as it has run out of liquid helium.
179. The chemical symbol for sulfur or sulfur is S with an atomic number of 16.
180. Richard Assmann and Leon Teisserenc de Bort are considered early pioneers of aerology (the atmosphere).
181. Engineers and people who design sports equipment use a

range of technology for their designs, including computer modeling, nanotechnology, and robots.

182. Pure titanium is a transition metal and can bond easily with other elements.
183. A male duck is called a drake, a female duck is called a hen, and a duck is known as a duckling.
184. A marine biologist is a scientist who studies things that live in oceans.
185. Acoustics is the scientific study of sound waves.
186. Bees communicate by performing a 'waggle' dance. Through this choreographed dance, they can tell other bees the direction, distance, and value of foraging resources. When swarming, scout bees dance to communicate potential resting places they have found.
187. An airplane is an aircraft with fixed wings. Engines propel it through the air for transportation, recreation, research, and military uses.
188. Crocodiles have the strongest bite of all animals in the world. Their jaw can apply 5,000 lbs (2,268 kg) per square inch of pressure, compared with a person's jaw, which can apply about 100 lbs (45 kg) of pressure per square inch.
189. Scientists once thought that Earth was the center of the Universe until Copernicus proposed that the sun was the center. Due to the universe expanding equally at all places, there is no center!
190. Snow hydrology is the scientific study of how snow and ice are made, disperses, and moves.
191. A crater, 9.5 km (6 mi) wide, covers most Phobos (one of Mars' moons). It was named Stickney, after the wife of the person who discovered it, Chloe Angeline Stickney.
192. Chinese and Islamic astronomers recorded a supernova that could be seen in the daytime in 1054.

193. Mercury's orbit around the sun ranges from 46 to 70 million km (28.5 to 43.5 million mi) from the sun.
194. Scientists believe the universe is flat, even though the planets aren't.
195. The largest snowflake in the world was 15 in (38.1 cm) wide and 8 in (20.32 cm) thick. It was found in Montana in the US in 1887.
196. Stars not only move around the center of the Milky Way, but they also move up and down.
197. The Russian satellite Sputnik was the first human-made object that went into space.
198. Makemake, dwarf planet, was discovered just before Easter and so was named after the god of fertility from Rapa Nui, natives of Easter Island. Before publicizing the discovery, the project team used a secret codename "Easter Bunny."
199. The brightest galaxy in the M51 group is the Whirlpool Galaxy.
200. A dam is built to contain water flow, often together with a hydroelectric power plant for electricity.
201. The average length of an adult's small intestine is 23 feet (7 m).
202. An electric current running through a surrounding coil creates an electromagnet. Hydroelectric dams make electricity using electromagnets.
203. A quadcopter is a drone controlled by four rotors.
204. The last supernova of four supernovae that have been found in the Pinwheel Galaxy was recorded in 2011.
205. The hair in a giraffe's tail is ten times thicker than a human hair.
206. There are over 340 species of hummingbirds in the world.
207. Charon, Pluto's largest moon, has grown bigger in the past as its surface stretched.

208. Nitrogen gas is used to keep packaged foods fresh, as an alternative to carbon dioxide for storing beer and electronic parts.
209. The sun makes energy by fusing hydrogen nuclei into helium.
210. In 1964 the first black hole Cygnus X-1 was discovered.
211. Laika was the name of the first creature (dog) to go into space in 1957. It survived a week in Sputnik 2 and died when the spacecraft burned up on re-entry into the Earth's atmosphere.
212. The Hubble Space Telescope can see more than the naked eye - it can also see ultraviolet and near-infrared.
213. In a vacuum, there are no particles to vibrate, so there is no sound.
214. Jupiter has the shortest day of all the planets.
215. While most planets don't have seasons, Uranus does.
216. In 1925 the Tri-State tornado traveled through Missouri, Illinois, and Indiana, destroying more than 219 miles (352 km) and killing 695 people along the way.
217. Carrots are an excellent vitamin A source, vital for healthy vision, bones, teeth, and skin.
218. Melanism, the mutation that makes jaguars look black, only affects about 6% of the big cats.
219. An audiologist is a person who conducts hearing tests.
220. The biggest reflecting telescope used for observing space is the Hubble Space Telescope.
221. Fossils are usually excavated from sedimentary rocks.
222. The lightest planet in our solar system is Saturn.
223. The mass of the sun is approximately 1% oxygen.
224. About 3,400 workers built the Empire State Building, of which five died during the construction.
225. Female grasshoppers are larger than male grasshoppers.
226. Duck quacks echo, but it's hard to hear the echo because of the quack's tone.

227. Wild sloths sleep about 10 hours a day. Sloths in captivity sleep up to 15 hours a day.
228. When you breathe in helium, it makes your voice sound higher. This is because helium is less dense than air. Inhaling too much helium is dangerous.
229. Television sets transmit moving images in black and white and color. They can also produce sound.
230. Insects, birds, and bats are all capable of powered flight. The only mammal that can sustain level flight is the bat.
231. Ernest Rutherford is also known as "The Right Honourable Lord Rutherford of Nelson" and the "First Baron Rutherford of Nelson".
232. Biology is the study of life and how organisms relate to their environment.
233. The largest impact crater on Callisto, one of Jupiter's moons, is Valhalla, with a diameter of about 1900 km (1190 miles). The second-largest impact basin is Asgard, with a diameter of 1600 km (994 mi). Valhalla and Asgard are both locations where Odin and other gods ruled (Norse mythology).
234. Tigers are strong swimmers. They can swim up to 3.7 miles (6 km).
235. The moon has three types of rocks, all found on Earth - basalt, anorthosite, and breccia.
236. The sand's temperature where turtles lay their eggs decides the sex of the turtle that will hatch. Cooler sand can result in male turtles.
237. Koalas share the same ancestors as wombats, so they are closely related.
238. The ISS travels at an average speed of 27,724 kilometers (17,227 mi) an hour.
239. Refractor telescopes should only be under 1 meter (40 in) long to make it easy to use.
240. For a geyser to form, it requires water, intense heat, and

cracks in the ground. Water seeps into the ground and heats up as it comes into contact with magma heated by magma in volcanic areas. The boiling water then rises back to the surface and erupts into the air through the ground's cracks.

241. The red kangaroo is the largest marsupial on Earth.
242. To avoid the devastating impact of an asteroid collision with Earth, scientists have proposed that we could use nuclear explosions to break it up into smaller pieces.
243. Jupiter has 79 moons orbiting it, currently the largest number of confirmed moons surrounding any planet in our solar system. The four largest, Ganymede, Callisto, Io, and Europa, all named after Galileo Galilee, are called the Galilean Moons. Saturn is waiting for some newly discovered moons to be confirmed, and it will then become the planet with the most moons.
244. You can see larger objects through a magnifying glass due to its convex shaped lens.
245. There are more than 1,000 species of bats in the world.
246. Primates are often used in scientific experiments as they are very similar to humans.
247. The Kuiper Belt is thought to have been created at the same time as our solar system.
248. Some sloths sleep in one tree all their life.
249. A meerkat uses its tail to balance to stand upright.
250. Meerkats are the size of squirrels.
251. Occasionally scientists have observed strange colored lights on the moon, which are thought to be escaping gases from inside the moon.
252. Mercury's surface has wrinkles from the planet cooling and contracting over time.
253. There are three groups of mammals - monotremes (echidna and platypus), marsupials, and placentals (dogs, people).

254. NASA is developing a nuclear-propelled rocket to go to space, which would mean that it would reach Mars in half the amount of time.
255. The moon is getting further and further away from Earth by about 1.5 in (3.8 cm) every year.
256. You can hop from lily pad to lily pad on giant water lilies in the Amazon as each lily pad is large and strong enough to hold your weight!
257. In 1996 the Hubble Space Telescope found a thin layer of oxygen on Ganymede, Jupiter's moons. The thin atmosphere is not enough to sustain life.
258. The scientific study of the brain or nervous system is called neuroscience.
259. The sun is 400 times the size of our moon, which is 400 times closer to Earth. For this reason, we can see solar eclipses on Earth.
260. Animals in danger of becoming extinct are on the endangered species list. Whales and tigers are examples of endangered animals.
261. One of Saturn's moons, Pan, absorbs some of the material making up Saturn's rings, making it walnut-shaped.
262. A troglobite is an animal that only lives in caves. They have unique characteristics, such as no pigment colors and no eyesight or eyes as they live in the dark.
263. Lipstick contains fish scales.
264. Ancient sloths were much bigger than the sloths of today and could grow to an elephant's size.
265. President Woodrow Wilson started the National Advisory Committee for Aeronautics (NACA) before NASA came about in 1958.
266. Humans are the main risk to leopards, destroying much of their natural environment. They are sometimes caught for their bones and whiskers, which some cultures use to heal the sick.

267. Hydroelectric power or energy uses the power of moving water to create electricity. The largest hydroelectric power station in the world is the Three Gorges Dam in China.
268. Electrical activity in the heart makes it a contract.
269. Penguins mainly live in the Southern Hemisphere, including New Zealand, Australia, Antarctica, South Africa, and Argentina.
270. A panda is a type of bear.
271. Russia plans to send humans to Mars from 2040 to 2045.
272. Clyde Tombaugh was 24 years old when he discovered Pluto.
273. Earth's rotation is slowing down gradually, decelerating at about 17 milliseconds per hundred years. This means our days are getting longer. However, it could take up to 140 million years before our 24 hour day becomes 25 hours.
274. The fastest train in the world is the Shangai Magrev in China, which travels at 267 mph (429 kph).
275. The melting point of uranium is 2,075 °F (1,135 °C), and its boiling point is 7,468 °F (4,131 °C).
276. A helicopter is an aircraft that can take off and land vertically. Spinning rotors provide the lift and thrust of helicopters.
277. The box jellyfish can kill a person with its poison if not treated. It is thought to be the deadliest marine creature in the world.
278. Titanium's best properties are resistant to corrosion, even in seawater and chlorine, and it is strong and lightweight. It is stronger than steel and less than half its weight.
279. A virus causes the common cold.
280. The widest section of the Great Wall of China is about 30 ft (9 m).
281. The Gentoo Penguin is the fastest - it can swim up to 22

mph (36 kph). Most other penguins swim about 4- 7 mph (6 - 11 kph).

282. As well as being an artist, Leonardo da Vinci drew many inventions that were not made at the time due to limited technology. These included an underwater breathing apparatus, a life preserver, a diving bell, a revolving crane, a parachute, a pulley, a method to concentrate solar power, water-powered mills and engines single-span bridges.
283. S Andromedae, a supernova in the Andromeda Galaxy, was recorded in 1885 by spotting it through a telescope.
284. Dogs have extremely good hearing and can hear sounds up to 4 times the distance that humans can.
285. The ancient Romans and Greeks name the moon's phases after three goddesses. In essence, Artemis (Diana) for the new moon, Selene, for the full moon, and Hecate was the moon's dark side.
286. Isaac Newton invented the reflecting telescope during the late 1600s.
287. Insects are the largest group of animals in the world.
288. The heaviest wolf weighed 176 lb (80 kg), double their average weight of 88 lbs (40 kg).
289. At the edges of the rainbow colors, the colors overlap and create white light. This means the inside of a rainbow is much brighter than outside.
290. Albert Einstein is famous for his messy hair. He also never wore socks!
291. Uranium is a naturally radioactive metal.
292. A seal has a thick layer of fat or blubber under their skin, which helps keep them warm.
293. The Pacific Ocean is the largest in the world.
294. The only penguin species that live in the wild in the Northern Hemisphere is the Galapagos Penguin.

295. The colored part of your eye, which controls your pupil (dark hole in the center), is called the iris.
296. Koalas sleep a lot (up to 22 hours a day), and when they're not sleeping, they're eating.
297. The bright moon reflection you can see on a body of water is called moon glade.
298. The cerebrospinal fluid which surrounds our brain protects it from physical harm and infections.
299. Phobos, one of Mars' 2 moons, is not round and is one of our solar system's darkest objects.
300. A very heavy star that has exploded into a supernova can become a black hole.
301. Nikola Tesla registered more than 700 patents in his lifetime. He discovered many more inventions, such as the dynamo and the induction motor, which unfortunately were patented by other inventors.
302. Ceres features in the TV series The Expanse where humans inhabit Ceres.
303. An elephant's trunk has no bone; instead, scientists believe it has 100,000 muscles. A trunk can grow to up to 6.5 feet (2 meters) long and weigh up to 308 lbs (140 kg).
304. Albert Einstein's fascination with science started when he was five years old and was shown a pocket compass. He wanted to know what force made the needlepoint in one direction.
305. Callisto, Jupiter's second-largest moon, has the most craters and dates back to 4 billion years ago when the Solar System was first formed. It is one of the oldest landscapes in our Solar System.
306. Eighteen people have died during four trips into space. Eleven others have been killed while training for spaceflight.
307. In 1972, the last person to step on the moon was Eugene Cernan.

308. Common gases from volcanoes are water vapor, carbon dioxide, sulfur dioxide, hydrogen chloride, hydrogen fluoride, and hydrogen sulfide.
309. The petals of a tulip are almost perfectly symmetrical.
310. Female flamingos mate at the same time, and their chicks are born at the same time.
311. You can eat tulip flowers and use them as a substitute for onion in many recipes.
312. The mass of Neptune is 17.15 times Earth's mass, at 102,410,000,000,000,000 billion kg.
313. Ceres is the closest dwarf planet to Earth.
314. The same side of most moons always faces its planet. This is known as 'tidal lock.' Hyperion, Saturn's moon, is the only exception, and it rotates in different directions due to Titan's gravity.
315. Many unanswered questions stem from astronomy, such as: is there life on other planets, what is dark energy and dark matter, what is the fate of the universe?
316. When you are hungry, your stomach rumbles sound louder because there's no food in it to muffle the sound. These rumblings are also called borborygmi.
317. Martian seasons are extreme because of their elliptical orbit around the sun. When it is closest to the sun, its southern hemisphere experiences a brief scorching summer. In contrast, its northern hemisphere goes through a cold winter at the same time. Then at its furthest point from the sun, the northern hemisphere has a long mild summer while the southern hemisphere goes through a long cold winter.
318. You can combine several reflecting telescopes to make a big super telescope.
319. Static electricity is created when an electric charge builds upon an object. The 'zap' you receive is the discharge of the electric charge by an opposite charge.

320. The famous Italian artist, Leonardo da Vinci, was also an inventor, scientist, mathematician, engineer, writer, sculptor, botanist, writer, and musician.
321. You can trap a laser beam in a waterfall, an example of 'total internal reflection.' When a beam of light hits a spout of water at a particular angle, the light will be reflected rather than passing through the water.
322. The largest impact crater on Mercury, the Caloris Basin, has a diameter of 1,550 km (963 mi). The Mariner 10 probe found it in 1974.
323. Every snowflake is different and has a shape with five points.
324. As of 2013, 76 people visited the ISS on two occasions; 25 people made three trips to the station, and five people have been four times.
325. A group of rhinos is known as a 'clash.'
326. The Russians sent the first space mission to Venus. Venera 3 successfully landed on Venus in 1966 but crashed and could not send any data back.
327. The hurricane's eye is calm and can be 2 - 200 miles (3.2 - 320 km) wide.
328. Osteoporosis, arthritis, and scoliosis are some examples of skeletal disorders in humans.
329. Valles Marineris meaning Mariner Valley, is a huge Martian canyon measuring 4,023 km (2,500 mi) long and 6.4 km (4 mi) deep. It is the longest valley in the solar system and stretches a distance similar to New York to San Francisco.
330. An octopus has eight arms and no tentacles. Arms have suction cups along its length, and tentacles have suction cups only at the tip. Squid and cuttlefish have eight arms and two tentacles.
331. The atmospheres of Venus, Earth, and Mars can generate local weather.

332. The dwarf planet Ceres has similar surface features and a rocky core, to inner planets.
333. The average length of an adult's large intestine is about 4.9 feet (1.5 m).
334. You can measure how much rain has fallen over some time by using a rain gauge.
335. We can only see about 10% of the Milky Way as dark matter makes up the remaining 90%.
336. Thomas Edison helped invent direct currents (DC). Nikola Tesla helped invent AC generators which replaced DC for transmitting electricity over long distances.
337. The constellations that border the Cancer constellation are Lynx, Leo Minor, Leo, Hydra, Gemini, and Canis Minor.
338. The steam-powered tricycle was the first self-propelled mechanical vehicle or the automobile invented in 1769 by Nicolas-Joseph Cugnot.
339. There are over 2,000 species of cacti in the world. They come in different shapes and sizes. The tallest cacti can grow up to 66 feet (20 m).
340. The large hooked beaks and powerful talons help eagles catch their prey.
341. Some fish can swim backward.
342. When you mix oil and water, it will separate.
343. In 2006 the Hubble Space Telescope released the largest and most detailed image of the Pinwheel Galaxy.
344. Ceres has one thing that could sustain life that many other planets don't have: water.
345. The official name for Earth's moon is the moon (with a capital M).
346. When volcanoes are active, they can erupt and release ash, gas, and hot magma.

347. The first African American woman in space was Mae Jemison onboard the Endeavour on 12 September 1992.
348. Extreme sports became popular in the 1990's when ESPN's X Games and dedicated extreme sports channels were introduced.
349. Scientists continue to research the use of magnesium as a treatment for high blood pressure and diabetes.
350. X-ray astronomy is the use of X-ray wavelength to study space objects.
351. Humans have one stomach with one compartment. Some animals, like cows and giraffes, have one stomach that has several compartments. Other animals, like seahorses and platypuses, have no stomachs at all.
352. All horses in the northern hemisphere have their birthday on 1 January. In the southern hemisphere, a horse's birthday is on 1 August.
353. Albert Einstein didn't know how to swim, but he loved sailing.
354. Hyakutake was a long-period comet discovered in January 1996 by a Japanese amateur astronomer, Yuji Hyakutake. Later the same year, the Ulysses spacecraft accidentally traveled through Hyakutake's long tail, about half a billion km (more than 300 million miles) long. Hyakutake was a comet from the Oort Cloud.
355. An adult breathes, on average, 11,000 liters of air a day.
356. The Jane Goodall Institute was established by Jane Goodall in 1977 to support research into conservation programs to protect chimpanzees and the environment.
357. Uranium is not the most radioactive metal; polonium is.
358. A pure gas, like neon, is made up of one atom.
359. Objects in the Oort Cloud travel in all different directions and don't follow a typical orbit around the sun. That's why it's called a 'cloud' and not a 'belt' like the Kuiper Belt.

360. The term for an orbit around Earth is 'geocentric.' An orbit around the sun is referred to as 'heliocentric,' and one orbiting Mars is called 'Areocentric' (after Ares, another name for Mars).
361. A snail has no backbone. Most of its soft body is made up of afoot. Its shell keeps it safe.
362. Zebras are social animals and stay in groups with other zebras.
363. A pig can squeal loud, up to 115 decibels.
364. A kangaroo can jump three times its height.
365. The result of a supernova is a black hole.
366. The largest dinosaurs were the herbivores, and they ate plants.
367. A koala has fingerprints just like we do.
368. Nuclear means something to do with the nucleus of an atom.
369. A bee's antennae are very sensitive, so they're cleaned regularly using their front legs.
370. The longest underwater tunnel in the world is the Seikan Tunnel in Japan, measuring 33.46 miles (53.85 km) long.
371. Geckos don't have eyelids.
372. If you boil water in space, it creates one giant undulating bubble (as compared with lots of little bubbles in boiling water on Earth).
373. Mars' gravity is 37.5% less than Earth's, so if you weighed 45 kg (100 lb) on Earth, you would only weigh 17 kg (38 lb) on Mars! You could also jump three times higher!
374. In 1901, Nikola Tesla first had the idea about wireless technology; however, it was never created or tested.
375. An engineer applies mathematical and scientific knowledge to solve problems. The word 'engineer' comes from a Latin word, which means 'cleverness.'
376. Pulmonology is the study of lightning.

377. The Milky Way is called the Milky Road by the ancient Romans as it reminded them of milk.
378. The USS Nautilus, launched in 1954, was the first nuclear-powered submarine.
379. Otters live in every continent except Australia and Antarctica.
380. In the northern hemisphere, you can find constellations such as Lyra (harp), Orion (hunter), Aquila (eagle), Bootes (Herdman), Perseus (Medusa's killer), Ursa Major (big bear) and Ursa Minor (little bear), Draco (dragon), Andromeda (princess) and Canis Major and Minor (big and small dog).
381. The woolly rhino became extinct about 10,000 years ago.
382. After the sun and the moon, the second brightest object in the night sky is Venus.
383. You can see about 2,000 stars without a microscope and about 50,000 using binoculars. If you look through a 2" telescope, you can see 300,000 stars and much more with a 16" telescope.
384. Your lungs are responsible for carrying oxygen from the air into your bloodstream and getting rid of the carbon dioxide.
385. Human sacrifices have been made to Venus by ancient cultures, such as the Skidi Pawnee Indians of North America.
386. Nikola Tesla had a special ability - he was able to visualize in 3D to see all sides of his inventions before they were created.
387. When they migrate, ducks usually fly at 200 to 4,000 feet (61 - 1,200 m) above the ground. However, they can fly higher, and the world record for the highest flight by a mallard duck was 21,000 feet (6,400 m).
388. The Oort Cloud is made up of hundreds of billions or trillions of icy objects.

389. Jupiter's mass equals 2.5 times the combined mass of all other planets in our solar system.
390. When there are no bright lights around, you may be able to see the Andromeda Galaxy! It is the furthest object you can see with the naked eye.
391. The Milky Way has already consumed smaller galaxies. It continues to pull matter away from the Large and Small Magellanic Clouds.
392. The cheetah is the fastest animal on land and can run up to 70 mph (113 kph). It only takes them a few seconds to reach its top speed.
393. A stalactite hangs from the ceiling of a cavern and is formed by continuous dripping of mineral-rich water. A stalagmite is the formation of mineral deposits from mineral-rich droplets from the ceiling. A stalactite and a stalagmite can join up eventually.
394. In Vietnam, the Cu Chi tunnels were used during the Vietnam war for different reasons, including storing food and weapons.
395. The chemical symbol of neon is Ne with an atomic number of 10.
396. The right side of a boat is starboard, and the left side of a boat is the port side. The back of a boat is called the stern. The hull is the body of the boat.
397. Jellyfish live in saltwater and freshwater.
398. The oldest insect fossil is 396 million years old.
399. Each strand of hair has three layers - the outer cuticle, middle cortex (where the keratin is found), and the inner medulla.
400. Earth's orbit slows down about two milliseconds every 100 years.
401. Scientists believe that beneath Uranus' hydrogen methane atmosphere is a hot ocean of water, ammonia,

and methane, which covers a rocky core. It has no solid surface.

402. A camel has wide feet to stop them sinking into the sand.
403. The atmosphere of Titan, Saturn's largest moon, is almost entirely nitrogen. It is the only moon in our solar system that has a dense atmosphere.
404. Pluto's orbit around the sun is elliptical, traveling at about 16,809 kph (10,444 mph).
405. Our brain is a powerful computer! It controls how we think and acts, and it stores our memory.
406. Hippos are aggressive and unpredictable animals.
407. Gold medals in the Olympic Games are made mainly from silver.
408. An octopus has one main brain and "neurons' located in each of its legs. These leg neurons can work out how to crack open a shellfish while the main brain is doing something else.
409. Capuchin monkeys have been trained as 'helper monkeys' to help people with disabilities, just like guide dogs. Due to risks of transmitting diseases and potential risk of injury to people, primates ceased becoming helpers in 2010.
410. Strawberries have high nitrate levels, which increases blood and oxygen flow to muscles. Research has shown that people who eat strawberries before exercising have high endurance and burns more calories.
411. Scientists debate whether Charon was formed when it collided with Pluto or a collision between Pluto and a Kuiper object (like how Earth and its moon were created).
412. Sea sponges can live for thousands of years. The oldest known sponge lived to 11,000 years.
413. About 8,000 light-years away, you can see the Hourglass

Nebula, which is called this due to it resembling an hourglass's shape.

414. 47% of Earth's crust is made up of oxygen.
415. The sedimentary rock sandstone metamorphosizes into quartzite.
416. Flamingos survive up to 50 years in captivity and only 20 - 30 years in the wild.
417. Ceres is situated between Mars and Jupiter in the asteroid belt.
418. Zinc is resistant to corrosion, so it is useful to coat and protect other metals. Galvanized steel, which is used for pipes, buildings, and cars, is coated in zinc.
419. From Earth, the moon and the sun look the same size as the moon is 400 times smaller than the sun and 400 times closer to Earth.
420. A family of meerkats will always have a guard or 'sentry' on duty to watch out for predators.
421. A carnivorous pitcher plant in Borneo relies on bat poo, which is full of nitrogen to survive.
422. The hedgehog was named because of its foraging habits. It digs under hedges to find food - insects and small animals - and it grunts along the way.
423. There are three types of meteorites - stony, iron, and stony-iron.
424. 75% of all volcanoes can be found in an area around the Pacific Ocean called the Pacific Ring of Fire.
425. The saying' busy as a beaver' comes from beavers liking to keep themselves busy building homes and eating all year round.
426. Ceres can be found in the Asteroid Belt, which is home to many asteroids of different sizes and shapes.
427. A tiger can jump a length of more than 16 feet (5 m).
428. Our brain is very complex, and scientists are learning more about it every day.

429. The greenhouse effect on Earth protects humans and moderates the Earth's global temperature. Without the greenhouse effect, the temperature would be -18 degrees C (0 degrees F) instead of 15 degrees C (59 degrees F).
430. Wind helps make electricity in windmills using wind turbines.
431. Scientists believe the core of the Earth is made up of an iron and nickel alloy.
432. Copper can be found naturally and in minerals such as malachite, cuprite, and bornite.
433. Mars' sunrises and sunsets look blue as there is almost no atmosphere on Mars.
434. The ancient Greeks used to think Mars revolved around Earth as they believed that Earth was the center of the universe.
435. There are six flamingo species on Earth.
436. The Pinwheel Galaxy is about double the size of the Milky Way, but it looks faint as it is so far away.
437. Ducks have excellent eyesight and can see up to 340 deg around them.
438. Magnesium is required for over 300 biochemical reactions in our bodies. Normal nerve and muscle function, a healthy immune system, a steady heartbeat, and strong bones rely on magnesium.
439. Vader Crater is a crater on Charon named after Darth Vader from Star Wars.
440. A snail has two antennae pairs, one with eyes to see and the other to touch, feel, and smell.
441. You can see Saturn without a telescope.
442. Galaxy means 'milky.'
443. Sterling silver is an alloy of at least 92.5% silver and other metals, usually copper.
444. Most reptiles lay eggs.

445. Red blood cells contain hemoglobin and transport oxygen around the body.
446. A modern spacecraft would take approximately 450 million years to fly to the center of the Milky Way.
447. Silver has an atomic number of 47.
448. The color of your skin depends on how your body produces much melanin pigment. Light-colored skin means your body produces small amounts of melanin.
449. Pet hamsters eat seeds, grains, fruit, and vegetables. Wild hamsters also eat lizards, insects, frogs, and other small animals.
450. Three different types of paper can be made into a recycled paper mill broke (paper scrap), pre-consumer waste and post-consumer waste (e.g., used wrapping paper).
451. Scientists think that the Milky Way is absorbing a smaller galaxy known as the Sagittarius Dwarf Galaxy.
452. The first telescopes used by merchants allowed them to see upcoming trade ships, to gain a competitive advantage.
453. English physicist, Robert Hooke, wrote the book Micrographia. This was the first book to show how insects and plants looked through a microscope. It was also the first time the word 'cell' was used.
454. Venus spins in the opposite direction to other planets. Uranus also rotates in the opposite direction.
455. The world's longest suspension bridge is the Akashi Kaikyo Bridge in Japan, spanning 6,529 feet (1,991 m).
456. Our digestive system breaks down the food that we eat so that our body can absorb the nutrients from the food and eliminate the waste.
457. In the southern hemisphere, you can find constellations such as Apus (bird of paradise), Chamaeleon

(chameleon), Tucana (toucan), Lepus (rabbit), Grus (crane) and Hydrus (water snake).

458. The Big Bang theory is based on the inflation theory, i.e., the universe suddenly expanded, doubling in size every 10-34 seconds. The 'bang' explosion lasted about 10 - 30 seconds but it changed the hand-sized universe to one that is now 10,000,000,000,000,000,000,000,000 times bigger.

459. The Milky Way's oldest star was formed just after Big Bang and is over 13.6 billion years old.

460. The diameter of Mercury is 2/5 that of Earth's.

461. Some insects can walk on water, for example, water striders.

462. Worker bees are female, and their job is to collect pollen and nectar, make the honey, clean the hive, and take care of baby bees. They are also responsible for the grooming and feeding the queen bee. They live for one month in summer and nine months in winter.

463. Metals that have a high number of movable atoms (free electrons) are good conductors of electricity: copper, silver, aluminum, gold. Steel and brass are examples.

464. Charon, Pluto's largest moon, is not oblong shaped like Hydra and Nix. Due to its gravity, Charon collapsed into a spheroid shape.

465. It takes Jupiter 12 Earth years to orbit the sun.

466. White blood cells are part of our body's immune system and protect us from bacteria, viruses, cancer cells, and infectious diseases.

467. The refracting telescope is more natural to observe the planets and the moon.

468. Mercury is the smallest planet in our solar system, and Mars is the next smallest.

469. After Albert 11 in 1949, Albert III, Albert IV, and Albert

V were the next three monkeys to go to space, but all died either during the flight or killed on Earth's impact.

470. A person has five basic tastes - sweet, sour, bitter, salty, and savory.
471. Wind direction is the direction that the wind is blowing from.
472. Jellyfish have been used to treat rheumatoid arthritis.
473. From 19 February 1971 to 18 February 1972, it snowed 1,224 in or 102 feet (31.1 m) in Mount Rainer in the Washington State, US. That's the height of a ten-story building!
474. The Pronghorn antelope is the second fastest animal on land and can run up to 60 mph (98 kph).
475. Astronauts must exercise at least 2 hours every day in space to maintain their muscle mass.
476. Astronomers make assumptions about the Milky Way based on their observations about the Andromeda Galaxy. This is because both galaxies are very similar in nature.
477. The toucan's bill is made of keratin, which is very light, so it can't be used to dig or fight.
478. The Eiffel Tower in Paris, France, is 1,050 feet (320 m) high. It was the tallest human-made structure in the world from 1887 until the Chrysler Building in New York was finished in 1928. It was named after the French engineer, Gustave Eiffel.
479. The lens is the part of your eye that helps you focus on objects.
480. Halley's comet could be as close as Venus is to the sun or as far away as Pluto during its orbit.
481. The liver's main job is to make bile (which aids in the digestion and absorption of food) and filter the blood from your digestive system.
482. Physics covers the study of matter, energy, and forces.

483. Tornadoes occur in the USA more than any other country in the world.
484. Hippos have three chambers in their stomach, but they do not chew the cud.
485. NASA's New Horizons spacecraft was launched in 2006 to fly by and study Pluto, which it did in 2015! It also managed to study another Kuiper Belt object called 2014 MU69.
486. In 1967 Louis Washkansky received the first human heart transplant in Cape Town, South Africa.
487. People are now more aware of asteroids after the Shoemaker-Levy Comet collided with Jupiter in 1994. Different Hollywood movies, such as Deep Impact and Armageddon, have also increased public awareness.
488. About 5,000 years ago, the Mesopotamians were the first civilization to build pyramid-shaped structures called ziggurats. The first Egyptian pyramid was built about 4,650 years ago in 2640 BC.
489. Saturn's moon Titan receives only 1% as much sunlight as Earth, although 90% of the sunlight is absorbed by the thick atmosphere.
490. The closest star in the Milky Way to Earth is called the Proxima Centauri. It is over four light-years away (1 light year = 10 trillion kilometers or 5.9 trillion miles).
491. Throughout history, stars have had very important roles. They were used to assist navigation, became part of many religious practices, and used in astrology.
492. Carbon is the sixth most abundant element in the Universe.
493. Hydrogen is the most common element in the Universe. Helium is the second most common.
494. The Apollo 14 commander, Alan Shepherd, hid a golf club on the spacecraft, and he was the first person to play golf on the moon.

495. About 50 tonnes of paint are used every seven years to protect the Eiffel Tower from rusting.
496. The hand portion of the wing of a hummingbird takes up about 75% of the wing. This helps it to hover.
497. Sheep are social and stay in groups called a herd, flock, or mob.
498. The Roman and Greek ancient civilizations thought Venus was two different objects. As Venus is closer to the sun and has a shorter orbit, it overtakes Earth's orbit and can be seen at sunset and sunrise. The Greeks called the two objects Phosphorus and Hesperus, and the Romans gave them the names Lucifer and Vesper.
499. The natural color of your hair is determined by one of two types of hair pigment. If you have a lot of eumelanin pigment in your hair, it will be dark-blond, brown, or black. A lot of pheomelanin pigment in your hair will make it red. If you don't have much pigmentation in your hair, your hair will be blond.
500. An astronaut's helmet has a thin layer of gold to block ultraviolet rays from the sun.
501. A butterfly's life cycle has four stages - egg, larva or caterpillar, pupa or chrysalis or cocoon, and adult butterfly.
502. The feathers of a peacock contain microscopic crystal-like structures that reflect light, making it very colorful.
503. Lignite coal contains 60 - 75% carbon. Anthracite contains over 92% carbon.
504. A shark can give birth to a live pup or lay an egg for it to hatch later.
505. A star only looks like it twinkles due to turbulences in the Earth's atmosphere. It doesn't.
506. Fourteen astronauts were killed in the Columbia and Challenger space shuttles.

507. The Eiffel Tower in Paris is constructed from iron and weighs about 10,000 tonnes.
508. The smallest chameleon in the world, the Leaf chameleon, grows up to 0.5 inches (16 mm), the top of a matchstick's size.
509. Venus has a similar gravitational force as Earth does just slightly less, so you would weigh less on Venus than on Earth.
510. Astronomers believe an explosion called Big Bang created the universe. The Milky Way formed not long after.
511. Earth travels through space at 107,826 kph (67,000 mph), so every hour, you are 107,826 km (67,000 mi) farther away!
512. The chemical element 104 'rutherfordium' is named after the scientist, Ernest Rutherford.
513. You will always find titanium bonded with another element as it doesn't occur naturally in its pure form.
514. Software on the ISS, including 350,000 sensors, was designed to provide health and safety monitoring for the crew and station.
515. About 80% of Earth's atmosphere's weight is located in the closest and thinnest layer, the troposphere.
516. Coal is the biggest source of energy for producing electricity. Burning coal heats the water, which turns to steam, spinning turbines connected to generators.
517. The age of the Milky Way is about 14 billion years.
518. There are different theories about the Big Bang. Some astronomers think that our universe was leftover from another universe. In contrast, others believe that we're just in the transition from something we know nothing about to one that we do.
519. Compared with other mammals the same size, a human brain is three times bigger.

520. At one time, it was thought that comets only passed through the solar system once. Edmond Halley was the first person to discover that comets could have a periodic orbit, and in 1705 he suggested that the comets seen in 1531, 1607, and 1682 were the same Comet. He predicted the next time we would see Halley's Comet was in 1758-1759. He was right but died 16 years before the Comet came around again! Halley's Comet was named in his honor.
521. Platinum was the eighth metal to be discovered, after iron, copper, silver, tin, gold, mercury, and lead).
522. Like Earth, Venus is made up of a core of iron, a rocky mantle, and a crust.
523. The Hubble Space Telescope gets its energy from the sun through solar panels.
524. Scientists believe hippos have been around for 55 million years.
525. When an object travels faster than the speed of sound, it is traveling at supersonic speed.
526. A rainbow is an optical illusion - it is not at any specific point, and you cannot touch it. It depends on where you're standing and where the sunlight is shining.
527. Panthers are mammals that belong to the Felidae family.
528. Many monkeys have tails, and at the tip of their tail, they have a bald spot sensitive to touch, just like our fingertips.
529. The law of conservation of energy states that energy can neither be created nor destroyed. It can only be transformed from one type to another.
530. Fish have a lateral line organ that senses vibrations around them and helps them navigate.
531. As titanium is light, strong, non-toxic, and doesn't react with our bodies, many surgical implants are made from this metal.
532. Zinc can be found in the Earth's crust.

533. Nikola Tesla Street Corner is a landmark place at the intersection of 40th street and 6th Ave in midtown Manhattan, New York, commemorating his New York laboratory site and where he fed his pigeons.
534. After the US dollar, the euro, Japanese yen, and British pound are other currencies that are traded heavily.
535. A stingray camouflages well with the ocean's bottom because of their flat body and sandy color.
536. The eyes of an eagle are large and can occupy 50% of its head.
537. A 'scrubber' is a device that removes carbon dioxide from the air inside a submarine. The carbon dioxide is trapped with soda lime inside the scrubber, which removes it from the air.
538. Penguins are carnivores and eat fish, crab, and other seafood.
539. The first hot air balloon flight with people inside occurred in 1782.
540. In 1807 the first internal combustion engine was installed on a boat. Later the same year, a Swiss inventor installed his internal combustion engine into a vehicle creating the world's the first automobile.
541. Deimos, one of Mars moons, has a radius of 6.27 km (3.9 mi). It is very small, with many craters, and it takes about 30.3 hours to orbit Mars. Deimos shines as bright as Venus in the full moon and becomes one of the sky's brightest objects.
542. Thousands of people die from lightning strikes every year.
543. A leopard hides its prey in trees to stop other animals from taking it. When they're hungry, they return to the tree to eat the prey.
544. Neptune is called after the Roman god of the sea.
545. The name Aristotle means 'the best purpose'.

546. Phobos is moving closer to Mars by about 2 meters (6.5 ft) every 100 years so that it will collide with Mars in nearly 30 - 50 million years.
547. Magnesium has an atomic number of 12.
548. Asteroids are made up of precious and non-precious metals and water.
549. The first time that war stopped construction of the Leaning Tower of Pisa in Italy was nearly 100 years, which allowed time for the soil under it to compact. If the war hadn't stopped construction, the tower would probably have fallen over.
550. Viral diseases, such as measles and polio, decrease, and some vaccines can prevent viral infections such as flu and hepatitis A and B.
551. Chile is currently building two reflecting telescopes that will be bigger than the biggest telescope of today. The Giant Magellan Telescope will have a mirror with a diameter of 24.4 meters (80 ft), and the European Extremely Large Telescope will have a mirror with a diameter of 39.9 m (129 ft).
552. Haumea was given the status of the dwarf planet as it had its gravity. However, it wasn't strong enough to remove similar objects from its region.
553. There are six types of observational astronomy: gamma-ray astronomy, optical astronomy, radio astronomy, ultraviolet astronomy, infrared astronomy, and x-ray astronomy.
554. Uranium is a toxic metal, and exposure can affect the health of our bodily organs. Marie Curie, who discovered polonium and radium, died from radiation damage to her bone marrow.
555. Badgers, otters, ferrets, polecats, weasels, and wolverines all belong to the Mustelidae family.
556. Pluto was considered the furthest and ninth planet from

the sun for 76 years until it was demoted to being a dwarf planet in 2006.

557. The Olympic sport of curling uses a stone made of granite.
558. Two commercial aircraft can fly at supersonic speeds. The Concorde could travel at speed twice the speed of sound. It could fly from New York to Paris is 3.5 hours, a flight that usually takes 7.5 hours. It flew for 27 years and stopped flying in 2003, 3 years after it crashed and killed all people on board in 2000.
559. The part of our body with the most bones is in our wrist, hands, and fingers. There are 54 bones in total that gives us the fine dexterity in our hands.
560. As early as 460 to 370 B.C., Democritus became the first person to suggest that the Milky Way was made of stars.
561. Some bee species are social and live in hives while others are solitary and build their own nest.
562. The sun takes 225 - 250 million years to orbit the Milky Way.
563. Particles of snow and ice bump around in thunderstorm clouds and create electrical charges. Positive charges form at the top of the cloud and negative charges at the bottom of the cloud. A positive charge is then built upon the ground under the cloud as opposite charges attract. Lightning strikes when the ground's charge connects with the charge coming down from the cloud.
564. Mars has a symbol that resembles a shield and a spear from the god of war. The male gender has the same symbol.
565. Blood pressure is the strength of your blood pushing against the walls of your blood vessels. The average normal blood pressure for an adult is 112/64 mmHg.
566. A camel can survive for up to six months without food or

water because they store fat in their humps, turning to water or energy when required.

567. Pigeons can count from one to nine, just like monkeys.
568. Dolphins are very intelligent animals.
569. Leonardo da Vinci means Leonardo "of Vinci", the town in Tuscany, Italy, where he was born. He was an illegitimate child and had no surname.
570. In 1966, the first successful uncrewed spacecraft landed on the moon. It was a Luna space probe belonging to the Soviet Union.
571. The thorns of a rose bush are technical 'prickles.'
572. A reptile has a backbone and dry, scaly skin.
573. Mammals don't lay eggs, but two mammals do - the platypus and the echidna.
574. The scientific name for the tulip is Tulipa.
575. In 1917 Thomas Wright first proposed the idea of a galaxy.
576. There are several theories about how Mars' 2 moons, Phobos, and Deimos, were created. Some astronomers have suggested that Jupiter's gravity pushed them into orbit around Mars. Others think that they were formed when gravity pushed rock and dust together. Another theory is that Mars may have collided with an existing moon, and the debris formed Phobos and Deimos.
577. Snakes have flexible jaws that let them open their mouth wide to swallow their prey.
578. Orthopedics is the scientific study of the human skeletal system.
579. Hamsters are nocturnal and wake up at night to eat.
580. Satellite televisions use broadcasting signals from communication satellites.
581. There are about 34 seal species in the world. Eighteen are 'true seals'(or earless seals), and 16 are eared seals, including seven sea lion species.

582. A dead jellyfish can still sting.
583. Polar bears stay warm because of the thick layer of fat (4.49 in or 11.4 cm) under their skin.
584. SN 1006 was recorded as the brightest supernova in 1006 AD.
585. Charon, Pluto's largest moon, is the largest moon compared to its world than any other moon in the solar system. The second-largest moon, in contrast to its planet, is Earth's moon.
586. The flattest planet in our solar system is Saturn.
587. Silver tarnishes and turns a dull grey color, so it needs to be polished back to its shiny appearance.
588. A famous TV show host, Bill Nye, has applied and rejected many times to be an astronaut with NASA.
589. A square pyramid has a square base and four sides that meet at the top.
590. Protein is required for life. In our bodies, they act as antibodies to help fight bacteria and viruses. They also act as enzymes to carry out all cell functions. Our muscles, organs, and immune systems are made of protein.
591. The Kennedy Space Centre in Florida was the launch pad of all the space shuttles.
592. The M87 galaxy was named after the person who discovered it, Charles Messier. The number refers to the 87th member in his catalog.
593. In Cherokee legend, the Milky way is called 'the way the dog ran away' after a dog who stole some cornmeal and was chased away.
594. A large star won't last long in a spiral galaxy as it continually burns enormous amounts of fuel.
595. A cactus is a member of the plant family Cactaceae. The plural of cactus is cacti.

596. Scientists have not been able to experiment much with radon as it is very radioactive and expensive.
597. 10% of Earth's animal species live in the Amazon rainforest, the largest tropical rainforest in the world in South America.
598. Countries capable of launching satellites include the US, the UK, Russia, China, Israel, India, Ukraine, North and South Korea, France, Japan, and New Zealand.
599. One Neptune year is equivalent to 165 Earth years.
600. Hot liquid rock found inside the Earth known as magma is called lava once it erupts from a volcano.
601. Signals are transmitted through our nervous system at 328 feet per second (100 meters per second).
602. We wouldn't be able to see the moon and its phases if there wasn't a sun.
603. The eight moon phases are New Moon, Waxing Crescent, Crescent, First Quarter, Waxing Gibbous, Full Moon, Waning Gibbous, and Last Quarter.
604. The longest river globally is the Nile River in Africa, measuring 4,132 miles (6,650 km) long. It flows through 10 countries - Kenya, Eritrea, Congo, Burundi, Uganda, Tanzania, Rwanda, Egypt, Sudan, and Ethiopia.
605. A zoologist may be involved in the conservation and protection of endangered animals.
606. Thunder is caused by lightning.
607. A person trained by a spaceflight program to lead, pilot, or be a crew member on a space expedition is called an astronaut or a cosmonaut.
608. Laughing gas used in hospitals and dental clinics as an anesthetic is made of nitrous oxide N2O.
609. Mars was named after the Roman God of war due to its reddish color resembling blood.
610. Cheetahs have excellent eyesight during the day but poor vision at night.

611. When a galaxy merges with another, a galactic merger is formed.
612. Wind provides energy to the sails of a sailboat to move it through the water.
613. Penguins have better eyesight underwater than in the air. They have a see-through eyelid so they can see underwater.
614. Helium is a gas that has no color, taste, or odor.
615. Venus is Earth's closest neighbor and the second planet from the sun.
616. Some jellyfish have no tentacles.
617. The length of Makemake's day, about 22.5 hours, is similar to Earth's.
618. Drones enable scientists to survey the ground for archaeological sites, crop damage, and weather and climate change.
619. Despite its name, Antarctica has no ants.
620. Constellations located in the same area of the sky are sometimes grouped and given a family name after the main constellation in that area.
621. Rhodium is a white silver metal that is very reflective and not corrosive. It is considered a rare and precious metal. 80% of rhodium is produced in South Africa.
622. A hurricane is an area of low atmospheric pressure.
623. Jane Goodall, a famous British anthropologist, gave her research subjects (chimpanzees) names. Usually, they're given numbers, so the researcher doesn't become attached to the subjects. David Greybeard, Gigi, Mr. McGregor, Goliath, and Frodo were some of her chimpanzees.
624. A submarine is a special type of watercraft that can go underwater. It can float on top of the water because of buoyancy forces. It carries ballast tanks filled with air when it floats, making the submarine less dense than the water around it. Submarines dive by filling their ballast

tanks with water, which then makes it denser than the water.

625. You can live with one lung only, but it will restrict your physical activity.
626. Jupiter's rings are thick, colorful clouds of deadly poisonous gases.
627. There is an ISS water recovery system that reduces water delivery dependence by 65%.
628. The sun comprises three-quarters hydrogen and helium.
629. Most octopuses are completely soft and have no skeleton, like other cephalopods such as squid. This means they can squeeze into tight spaces.
630. Three-toed sloths are active during the day, while the two-toed species are active at night.
631. Granite, asbestos, hornblende, feldspar, clay and mica are all silicate minerals.
632. Basketball is a sport that thrives on height. The tallest basketball player's title is shared by two players, Manute Bol from Sudan and Gheorghe Muresan from Romania. At one time together for the Washington Bullets, both played in the NBA and measured 7 ft 7 in tall (231 cm).
633. The winds in a very strong tornado can blow at over 300 mph (483 kph).
634. The largest source of energy in the world used to make electricity comes from coal.
635. Mice love food and can eat up to 20 times every day.
636. Nuclear energy is the energy in a nucleus or core of an atom.
637. Platinum was once called 'white gold' because of its silver-like shine.
638. The Milky Way contains up to 400 billion stars, maybe just as many planets and has a diameter of about 120,000 light-years.
639. Tornado Alley' is an area in the USA where most of the

tornadoes occur. The reason is that the air mass moving northward hits the air mass moving southward from Canada and causes unstable air, usually during late spring and early summer. Oklahoma, Kansas, Missouri, Nebraska, Iowa and South Dakota are most affected by tornadoes.

640. A third of Earth's surface is covered in deserts. Only 20% of these are sand deserts.
641. Apart from being a great astronomer, Edwin Hubble was also a great athlete, boxer, and basketball, football, and baseball player.
642. Sugar, salt and acids dissolve easily in water, unlike oils and fats.
643. Before copper was used over 10,000 years ago, gold and meteoric iron were the only two metals used.
644. To travel from Earth to Charon would take 4.6 light-years. This will equate to 6,293 years if you drove a car at 104 kph (65 mph) or 680 years if you're flying a Boeing 777 going 949 kph (590 mph). It took New Horizons 9 years going at 80,467 kph (50,000 mph), which is the fastest speed for a launched spacecraft.
645. Pioneer 11 in 1979 discovered Saturn's two outer rings.
646. A horse can lie down for short periods; otherwise, their blood flow is restricted, and their muscles and organs may not get enough blood.
647. Waterfalls can be created from erosion, earthquakes, landslides, glaciers, or volcanoes! Any large disruption of land can create cliffs, cracks, or faults in the land's elevation.
648. Sunlight takes 20 times longer to reach Uranus than Earth.
649. Platinum, which has been found to change DNA structure and kill cancer cells, is used to treat cancers.

650. A fish can drown in water if there isn't enough oxygen in the water to survive.
651. 78% of the air that we breathe is nitrogen.
652. To get the nutrients it needs to produce eggs; female mosquitoes drink blood.
653. A constellation is a group of stars in the sky that has been grouped to make a pattern. Patterns include animals, mythological creatures, and objects.
654. A galaxy with no spiral, lenticular, or elliptical structure is called an irregular galaxy. The large and small Magellanic clouds that border the Milky way have no distinctive shape. They are within the gravitational force of other nearby galaxies.
655. When new staff joins NASA, they are asked to identify inaccuracies in the movie Armageddon. More than 168 errors have been found.
656. Before the first practical helicopter was flown in 1939, the vertical flight principle was around 400 BC when Chinese children played with flying bamboo toys that lifted into the air when spun.
657. Watermelons, which are about 92% water, have high amounts of vitamins A, B6, and C, lots of lycopene, antioxidants, and amino acids, all good for a healthy body.
658. An F3 tornado on the Enhanced Fujita Scale means the tornado's winds are traveling at 158 - 206 mph (254 - 332 kph). It can rip trees out of the ground in a whole forest, derail trains and take the roofs off houses.
659. The King Cobra is the longest venomous snake globally, growing up to 18.5 feet (5.6 m) long.
660. Penguins can be gay!
661. The Magellanic Clouds differ from the Milky Way in several ways. Not only do they have a different structure and a lower mass, but they also are rich in hydrogen and

helium gases, and they have tiny metals. In comparison, the Milky Way is 70% hydrogen, and the rest is carbon dioxide, ammonia, and formaldehyde.

662. It's hard to hear thunder when it is more than 12 miles (20 km) away.
663. Giraffes are ruminants and have four stomachs, like cows.
664. 10 asteroids were discovered by 1849, 100 by 1868, 1,000 by 1921, 10,000 by 1989, and 700,000 by 2015.
665. Halley's Comet is now a Kuiper Belt object but thought to have come originally from the Oort Cloud.
666. The number of breaths you take per minute is called your respiratory rate. At rest, a normal respiratory rate in an adult is 12 - 20 breaths per minute.
667. Cataract waterfalls are extremely large and powerful—you do not want to get caught in one of these!
668. Penguins are not just black and white. Many species have colored feathers on their heads or bodies.
669. An octopus has three hearts, two that carry blood to the body and an organ heart that circulates blood to its organs like the heart.
670. Ducks lay more eggs when there is more daylight.
671. Europa, Jupiter's moon, is the smoothest object in our Solar System due to its icy surface with no mountains and only a few craters.
672. A year on Earth is 365.2564 days which means we have an extra day in February every four years. This is called a leap year. Every leap year can be divided equally by four, so you can work out which years are leap years.
673. The first artificial satellite to be launched into space was the Soviet Union's Sputnik 1. It was launched in October 1957.
674. The average distance between Callisto and its planet Jupiter is 1,882,700 kilometers (1,169,856 miles).

675. Some snakes, like the python, can swallow their prey whole and alive.
676. There are about ten quadrillion ants (10,000,000,000,000,000) living at any one time on Earth.
677. The platypus is a strong swimmer that can dive underwater for 30 seconds to search for food.
678. Honey bees live in hives made from beeswax.
679. The melting point of radon is -95 °F (-71 °C), and its boiling point is -79 °F (-61.7 °C).
680. Scientists believe a lemon is a hybrid between a citron and a sour orange.
681. Gravitational energy relates to the gravitational field around Earth. It's the reason a ball rolls downhill faster than uphill.
682. Aluminum bats are not allowed in professional league baseball. The ball can fly faster than if hit with a wooden bat, therefore causing greater injury to a player.
683. The Great Pyramid of Giza, also called the Pyramid of Khufu, is the oldest of the World's Ancient Wonders. For over 3,800 years, it was the tallest human-made structure.
684. Charles Darwin was an English naturalist who is most well known for his theory of natural selection. Often called the 'Father of evolution,' he was born on 12 February 1809 and died on 19 April 1882.
685. The space station offers valuable opportunities for testing spacecraft systems and equipment and acts as a staging base for potential Moon or Mars missions.
686. Water is an essential substance in our world. People have to drink it to stay alive, it is used by farmers to grow their crops, you can cook food with it by boiling or steaming, and firefighters use it to put out fires. Many sports such as surfing and skiing are dependent on water.
687. Ernest Rutherford began his investigation into alpha and

beta radiation the same year that Marie Curie discovered two new radioactive elements, polonium, and radium.

688. A fountain geyser erupts in powerful bursts. A cone geyser erupts as a steady jet of water from mounds or cones of geyserite.

689. Some scientists believe that we could only see the universe under a microscope about 10 - 43 seconds after Big Bang. The number 10 - 43 is equal to 0.00000000000000000000000000000000000000000001, or one 10 million trillion trillionths of a second.

690. A bone fossil doesn't contain any bone. It has the same shape as the original bone or object but contains a rock.

691. Scorpions live on all continents except Antarctica.

692. Most asteroids have irregular shapes and are too small to be affected by Earth's gravity.

693. Charles Darwin, an English naturalist, biologist, and geologist, developed the theory of evolution based on natural selection, also referred to as 'survival of the fittest.' He thought that individuals that best adapted to their environment were most likely to reproduce and survive.

694. Galaxies often interact and can collide with each other. When two galaxies collide, dust and gases flow, intermingle and form new stars.

695. Calcium is the fifth most abundant element in the Earth's crust, making up 3% of soil, air, and oceans.

696. Volcanoes can either be active, dormant, or extinct—be careful around active and dormant ones!

697. Venus is covered with sulphuric acid clouds, which means that it was impossible to view its surface until radio mapping, developed in the 1960s, observed its extreme temperatures and hostile environment.

698. Camels have adapted to their hot, dry environment in which they live in. They have humps to store fat, which they metabolize for food and water. They have a third

clear eyelid and long eyelashes to protect their eyes from blowing sand. They can also close their nostrils during sand storms.

699. With technological advances, astronomers now have powerful telescopes for their research.
700. A cross between a lion and a leopard is called a leopon—a jaglion when a lion breeds with a jaguar.
701. Platinum, iridium, osmium, palladium, ruthenium, and rhodium are all 'platinum metals' that share similar properties. They are often used together to make durable machinery parts and tools, as well as jewelry.
702. The Cancer Constellation has the following main stars: Al Tarif, Acubens, Asellus Australis, Asellus Borealis, and Iota Cancri.
703. There are more than 200 squirrel species in the world.
704. The only planet that we know of that has free oxygen, liquid water, and life is Earth.
705. In Dubai, the Burj Khalifa holds the record for being the tallest building in the world, measuring 2,717 feet (828 m) tall.
706. Zinc is the fourth most common metal we use. Iron, aluminum, and copper are the most common.
707. Just before the Battle of Hastings in 1066, Halley's Comet made an appearance.
708. Hydrogen mixed with air can cause a fire.
709. Pineapples have many health benefits. They contain high amounts of vitamin C and manganese, which help treat heart disease, joint pain, macular degeneration (eyes), and prevent osteoporosis. The high levels of bromelain enzymes they contain help digestion, osteoarthritis, some cancers, and reduce blood clots' risk.
710. A baby koala or joey stays in their mother's pouch for about six months.
711. A famous Albert Einstein quote: "If I were not a

physicist, I would probably be a musician. I often think in music. I live my daydreams in music. I see my life in terms of music.... I do know that I get most joy in life out of my violin."

712. The Cosmic inflation theory attempts to explain the exponential expansion of space in the early universe.
713. Pluto is named after the Roman god of the underworld. His father was Saturn, and his brothers Jupiter was the god of the sky, and Neptune was the god of the sea.
714. The Milky Way is called Akash Ganga in Sanskrit, meaning 'Ganges of the heavens.'
715. Some bats like to live alone, and others are very social living in caves with thousands of other bats.
716. A skyscraper has a skeleton of vertical columns, horizontal and often diagonal beams made of steel in such a way that it distributes the weight safely.
717. Isaac Newton's three laws of motion are: (1) Every object in a state of uniform motion will remain in that state of motion unless an external force acts on it; (2) Force equals mass times acceleration: F=MA and (3) For every action there is an equal and opposite reaction.
718. A high-speed wind on Venus carries its clouds every four days around the planet.
719. Toads are born tadpoles, just like frogs.
720. A polar bear has black skin.
721. Isaac Newton was an /English physicist, astronomer, mathematician, philosopher, and alchemist. He is most famous for his law of gravity and three laws of motions. He also invented the reflecting telescope and 'fluxions' which is known as calculus today.
722. Extreme sports are sports with a high degree of risk or danger. They often involve high speeds, dangerous heights, a high level of physical exertion, and specialized

equipment. Skydiving, BASE jumping, BMX racing, and snowboarding are all examples of extreme sports.

723. Calcium always seems to come in fifth place! It is the fifth most abundant element by mass in the Earth's crust, the fifth most abundant dissolved ion in seawater and the fifth most abundant element in the human body. However, it is the most abundant metallic element in our body, with 99% found in our bones and teeth.
724. A female octopus only mates once in her lifetime. She can lay up to 400,000 eggs, which she then protects until they are all hatched. She stops eating after laying the eggs, and eventually, her body turns on her, and she dies.
725. A hurricane rotates clockwise in the southern hemisphere and anti-clockwise in the northern hemisphere. This is due to the Coriolis force made by Earth's rotation.
726. Alligators can't control their temperature internally, so they bask in the sun when they're cold. When they're hot, they cool off in the water.
727. A koala's sharp claws help them climb trees.
728. A scientist who studies dinosaurs is called a paleontologist.
729. A zebra's ears tell its mood. Upright means they're feeling calm, backward means angry and forwards means they're frightened.
730. Johannes Kepler's work assisted Isaac Newton to develop his theory on universal gravitation.
731. Scientists have identified over 925,000 different species of insects in the world. This number is growing every day as scientists name more.
732. During the mating season, the female leopard rubs her body on leaves and trees for male leopards to smell her scent. She also calls out to males to let them know she's ready to mate.

733. Saturn is named after the Roman god Saturnus.
734. The methane in Uranus' upper atmosphere absorbs the sun's red light and reflects the blue light into space. That's why it looks blue.
735. Platinum is often used in jewelry making because it doesn't tarnish or corrode easily.
736. Deep pressure under the Earth's surface or the extreme heat of magma or friction of tectonic plates can form metamorphic rocks.
737. The melting point of chlorine is -150.7 °F (-101.5 °C), and the boiling point is -29.27 °F (-34.04 °C).
738. A queen bee must lose about one-third of her normal body weight to fly to find a new home when swarming.
739. Seals have four flippers and belong to the family called pinnipeds, which means fin-footed. The walrus and sea lion are also pinnipeds.
740. The High Roller in Las Vegas holds the record for the highest Ferris wheel in the world. It is 550 feet (167.64 m) tall. The Ain Dubai will break this record when it opens in October 2020, at 700 ft (213.36 m) high.
741. One of Jupiter's moons, lo, has many active volcanoes on it, shooting plumes of up to 400 km (250 mi) into its atmosphere. It is considered the most active moon in our solar system.
742. Many turtle species are threatened or close to extinction.
743. The most traded currency is the US dollar.
744. A sea cave is formed by waves and tides eroding sea cliffs.
745. Frozen waterfalls freeze during the winter season, and mountaineers often climb them for fun!
746. Some lizards give birth to baby lizards; others lay eggs.
747. The chemical symbol for carbon is C, and it has an atomic number of 6.
748. The sound a cicada makes is the mating call of the male cicada. The sounds can be as loud as 120 decibels.

749. Our moon is the largest satellite of all planets in the solar system.
750. To honor his contributions to science, Louis Pasteur was awarded the very prestigious Grand Croix of the Legion of Honor.
751. The penguin's 'tuxedo' colors help them camouflage against predators when swimming.
752. A famous Isaac Newton quote: "I can calculate the motions of the heavenly bodies, but not the madness of people."
753. Mars is much lighter than Earth, and it is the last rocky planet from the sun; all other planets after Mars are gas planets.
754. Electricity flows in two ways - a direct current (DC) or an alternating current (AC). Direct currents are found in batteries where the electrons move in one direction. An example of alternating current is the electricity in your home when electrons go backward and forwards.
755. Astronomers have found two bright spots on a crater on Ceres at about 19 degrees latitude, which they do not think came from a volcano. Researchers believe it may be ice or salts.
756. When the Milky Way and the Andromeda galaxy collide in about 2 to 4 billion years, it will form one large elliptical galaxy.
757. Ducks are omnivores, eating both types of meat, such as fish, insects, worms, and plants.
758. The only spacecraft to fly by Neptune is the Voyager 2 in 1989.
759. Scientists believe that the universe will end up in a Big Freeze as the world continues to cool while it expands.
760. The mesosphere is the fourth closest atmospheric layer to Earth and is about 50 to 70 km (31 to 53.5 mi) from the Earth's surface.

761. Arachnophobia is the abnormal fear of spiders.
762. The fear of thunder and lightning is called astraphobia.
763. Some people think that the moon gives off light, but it doesn't just reflect the sun's light.
764. Hummingbirds can flap their wings 100 - 200 times a second.
765. Block (aka sheet) waterfalls descend from wide streams or rivers.
766. Sound moves four times faster through water than through air.
767. Reflecting telescopes uses concave mirrors where one mirror captures an image. A second mirror reflects the image from the first image. This is also called a Newtonian telescope.
768. Modern elevators, required for tall buildings, can travel up to 3,280 feet per minute (1,000 m/min).
769. The distance from Earth to the sun is approximately149,597,891 km (92,955,820 mi).
770. The stars that orbit the Milky Way travel faster, much faster than Earth's orbit around the sun. If Earth traveled at similar speeds to these stars, we would orbit the sun in 3 days, not 365!
771. Nikola Tesla, the famous inventor, was obsessive-compulsive. He was obsessed with the number three; he hated round objects and touching hair. He wouldn't speak with women wearing pearl jewelry. He was obsessed with germs, wore white gloves to dinner, and cleaned his dining room every day with 18 napkins. In the final years of his life, his mental health deteriorated, and he spent much of his time speaking with and feeding pigeons.
772. After iron, oxygen, and silicon, magnesium is the fourth most common element in Earth.
773. Cheetahs are the only big cat species that can't roar.

774. A chameleon can change its skin color, in patterns, from pink to blue, red, orange, black, brown, yellow, purple, and green.
775. Some ants bite and other ants sting. Fire ants, harvester ants, and oak ants are examples of stinging ants.
776. The Sahara desert in Africa is the largest hot desert in the world.
777. Mercury would damage the Hubble Space Telescope if it could view it due to its brightness from being so close to the sun.
778. The first person to drive a car over a long distance was Bertha Benz in 1888. She was the wife of Carl Benz, who invented the Benz Patent Motorwagen(first modern automobile). On the trip, she solved many problems. She invented brake lining when the brakes needed repairs.
779. The Hoover Dam is 726 feet (221 m) high. When it was completed in 1936, it was the largest concrete structure in the world and the largest hydroelectric power station.
780. Seals are carnivorous and eat meat like fish, shellfish, and sea birds. Some seals, like the leopard seal, eat penguins and smaller seals.
781. Albert Einstein won the Nobel Prize in 1921 for his work in theoretical physics.
782. Toucans are very social birds and live in groups of up to 20.
783. The hot air balloon is the first flight technology that carried people.
784. Magnetic objects only respond if they're within the magnetic field, so if the magnet is too far away, move it closer.
785. Platelets are the part of our blood that stops you from bleeding when you cut yourself. This is known as blood clotting.

786. Neon belongs to the noble group of gases that is not chemically reactive. It has no color or odor.
787. Modern cell phones enable the user to complete many tasks, including making and receiving calls, sending emails, taking photos, searching the Internet, and playing games and music.
788. After the World Trade Center's collapse in 2001, the Empire State Building again became the tallest building until 2012 when the new One World Trade Center was built.
789. Our universe contains about 70 thousand million, million, million stars.
790. A shape with eight sides is called an octagon. A shape with 20 sides is called an icosagon.
791. More than 3,000 fish species live in the Amazon River in South America.
792. Meerkats live in underground burrows, which they dig with their strong claws. The burrows stay cool under the hot desert sun and ground.
793. The water cycle involves the movement of water between the ocean, air, and land. The sun melts glaciers (solid water), turning it to oceans and rivers (liquid water), which then evaporates into the air (gas water). When it's in the sky, it cools and condenses back to Earth as rain or snow, and the cycle then starts all over again.
794. A white panther is the result of a color mutation called albinism. White panthers are very rare as the panther cannot camouflage well when hunting, so many ends up dying from starvation.
795. As of January 2019, over 61,000 meteorites have been found on Earth, 224 from Mars.
796. Uluru, also known as Ayers Rock, is a large sandstone rock formation found in Australia, about 280 mi (450 km) away from Alice Springs.

797. Silver is a soft, shiny precious metal.
798. There aren't many Greek pyramids, but the most famous is the Pyramid of Hellinikon.
799. There has not yet been any evidence of life on Jupiter.
800. The dwarf planet Eris was named after the Greek goddess of strife and discord.
801. The largest galaxy that we know of in the universe contains over 100 trillion stars, compared with the Milky Way estimated to have about 400 billion stars. We can only see about 2,500 of these stars from Earth.
802. The scientific name for the inner layer of tree bark is Phloem.
803. In 2004, another dwarf planet now called Sedna was discovered beyond Neptune. Sedna orbited the sun in one of the coldest known regions of our solar system and was aptly named after a goddess who lived at the bottom of the frigid Arctic ocean. Sedna takes 10,500 years to complete its orbit around the sun and never enters the Kuiper Belt. Astronomers have suggested that Sedna is the first observed object that belongs to the inner Oort Cloud.
804. On 14 June 1949, Albert 11 became the first monkey to go to space.
805. Don't take antibiotics if you have a virus as they're only good against bacterial infections.
806. Only two spiral galaxies can be seen with the naked eye from the southern hemisphere - Andromeda galaxy and the Milky Way.
807. The negatives of mobile cell phones include using it while driving, bullying and harassment, students cheating during tests.
808. The word skyscraper is now used to describe a high rise building previously referred to as a type of sail on a sailing ship.

809. A train can have more than one locomotive. Cargo trains have one at the front to pull it, but some have one at the back to help push it along.
810. Hedgehogs that live in cold climates hibernate during winter.
811. In a beaver's home or lodge, they usually build two dens - one for drying off as they enter and the other is dry and where they live.
812. Peahens choose which peacock to mate with by the size, quality, and color of the peacock's train and its sound.
813. There are two types of neurons - sensory and motor. Sensory neurons send messages from our senses - light, touch, and sound - to the Central Nervous System. Motor neurons send messages from our muscles.
814. Dark matter hasn't been measured, but scientists believe it is the glue that holds the universe together.
815. Alexander Graham Bell said the first words over the telephone to his assistant Thomas Watson: "Mr Watson, come here, I need you."
816. Some hummingbirds migrate, usually alone and not in groups like other birds. They can travel up to 500 miles (800 km) at a time.
817. The five different rhinoceros species are the Black, White, Indian, Javan, and Sumatran Rhinoceros.
818. Rockets launch artificial satellites into orbit in space.
819. From the vapor plumes that erupt from Ceres into space, astronomers believe that Ceres may have a subsurface ocean that could support life. Despite this, astronomers are more focused on exploring life on Europa and Mars, more than Ceres.
820. The chemical symbol for uranium is U.
821. The circumference of Mercury is 15,329 km (9,525 mi).
822. The first dwarf planet to be visited by a spacecraft is Ceres in 2015. The spacecraft was called Dawn and was

not manned. On the same trip, Dawn also surveyed a protoplanet Vesta.

823. Ducks' feathers are waterproof.
824. The smallest bird in the world is the Bee hummingbird, which grows to 2 in (5 cm) long.
825. The moon is 81 times lighter than Earth.
826. Deer, moose, reindeer, and elk all belong to the Cervidae family.
827. Ledge (classical & curtain), block (sheet), cascade, cataract, chute, fan, frozen, horsetail, multistep (tiered or staircase), plunge, punchbowl and segmented are all different types of waterfalls!
828. The outermost skin of a chameleon is transparent. Beneath this, there are layers of skins with special cells that contain different pigments.
829. Uranus is the only planet that spins on its side. Its axis of rotation is tilted sideways, so the north and south poles are where our equator is. It rotates once every 17 hours and 14 minutes.
830. 17 and a half days was the longest space shuttle orbit.
831. The word "Friday" means "Venus day."
832. As of 2018, China, Australia, and Russia are the three top gold producers in the world.
833. Many applications on the World Wide Web and the Internet allow you to do so much, including sending and receiving emails, sharing files, and playing video games online.
834. Sound is made up of sound waves. Sound waves vibrate and move through the air or water, which we hear as sound.
835. A star is called a brown dwarf star if it doesn't get hot enough to cause a nuclear fusion at its core. It's not a proper star.

836. Neptune is known as a small gas giant - it contains mostly gas.
837. The ISS was designed to be a laboratory and observatory for space environment research. Crew members could conduct experiments in many scientific fields, including biology, human biology, physics, astronomy, and meteorology.
838. At -40 degrees, the Fahrenheit and Celsius scales are equal.
839. Flowers on sunflowers interlock in spiral patterns. Each floret faces the next by the golden angle of 137.5 degrees. The number of left and right spirals is consecutive Fibonacci numbers.
840. Astronomers can't understand why the universe bends, so if you walked in a straight line out into the universe, you would come back to where you started.
841. The Soviet Yuri Gagarin was the first human in space in the spacecraft Vostok 1 in 1961, followed by American John Glenn Jr. Neil Armstrong was the first person to land on the moon in 1969.
842. In 1976, Viking I produced a photograph of a rock on Mars with a human face. Many people believed that extraterrestrials created the face. The spacecraft 'Global Surveyor' confirmed that the face was an optical illusion. However, the people who believed in the extraterrestrials accused NASA of changing the data.
843. The melting point of magnesium is 1,994 °F (1,090 °C), and its boiling point is 1,202 °F (650 °C).
844. Babylonian astronomers first recorded Venus in the 17th century BC.
845. Astronomers study the Whirlpool Galaxy to understand the structure of galaxies and their interactions.
846. Water boils at 212 deg F (100 deg C) while liquid nitrogen boils at -321 deg F (-196 deg C).

847. Nitrous or NOS is used to increase the engine power and speed of cars in motor racing.
848. The second hottest planet in our solar system is Mercury. Venus is the hottest.
849. The saliva that a mosquito leaves in your skin after they bite you creates the itchy bump. When your immune system breaks down the protein that's in the saliva, the itch goes away.
850. A hurricane is a large rotating storm with super strong winds. Hurricane winds are very strong, blowing at least 74 mph (120 kph). They have an area of low pressure in the center called the eye of the hurricane.
851. Silver has antimicrobial properties i.e., it kills or stops the growth of microorganisms like bacteria. It has been used in wound dressings and gels to treat burns.
852. It's hard to predict when a tornado is coming. Thirteen minutes is the average time between sighting a tornado and when it arrives.
853. Panthers are carnivores and only eat meat.
854. The great white shark is warm-blooded, which differs from other sharks. It has to eat much meat to regulate its body temperature.
855. Ducks preen and remove the dirt and parasites from their feathers. They then spread a waxy oil to waterproof their feathers.
856. The platypus carries its prey in its cheeks.
857. Badgers are social animals and live in groups. A group of badgers is called a cete or a clan.
858. The Pinwheel Galaxy is a beautiful spiral galaxy with a stunning pinwheel structure.
859. In the middle of the Triangulum Galaxy is a nebula made up of a gas and dust cloud where stars are formed.
860. NASA's Pathfinder, launched in 1996, made the first airbag mediated touchdown on Mars.

861. One of the prerequisites for extraterrestrial life is liquid water.
862. Rabbits are very social mammals and live in groups called colonies.
863. Beavers are herbivores and only eat plants.
864. Deep inside Saturn, hydrogen becomes metallic.
865. In the human brain, there are about 100 billion neurons. In the spinal cord, there are about 13.5 million neurons.
866. Trainee astronauts previously needed military jet test pilot and engineering experience. However, these days, high achieving engineering, science, or maths students can train astronauts.
867. The thermosphere, the furthest atmospheric layer to Earth, contains the ionosphere and exosphere and about 0.001% of all greenhouse gases. It can extend out as far as 9,656 km (6,000 miles) into space.
868. Eris is slightly larger than Pluto but smaller than Earth's moon. It was discovered in 2003 and took 557 years to orbit the sun.
869. Because there are more oceans than land on Earth, most meteors fall in the sea.
870. The Giant Pacific Octopus is the largest octopus that also lives the longest. It can grow up to 30 feet (9 m) across and weigh up to 600 lb (272 kg).
871. Just like cats, guinea pigs purr when they are petted or happy. They whistle when they are excited.
872. Toucans have the longest bill of all birds, relative to the size of their body.
873. The four kangaroo species are the red, eastern grey, western grey, and antilopine kangaroos.
874. There is wi-fi on the moon, beamed up from Earth with four infrared telescopes!
875. The Arabian horse has the most endurance of all the horses.

876. Pineapples are the only bromeliad plant that produces fruit.
877. Sports injuries occur from poor training, overuse of certain muscle groups, inadequate warm-up, and cool-downs, blunt trauma accidents, or inadequate protective equipment.
878. The large flower of a sunflower is made up of many tiny blooms or flowers called florets.
879. Haumea is the most recent dwarf planet to be named. There are only five dwarf planets.
880. The right side of your brain controls the left side of your body and vice versa.
881. Some species of the seal can slow their heartbeat down to conserve oxygen so they can stay underwater for longer periods.
882. The temperature of an object is the speed at which its molecules move. The faster they move, the higher the temperature.
883. By organizing the Periodic Table elements by atomic numbers, Henry Moseley saw gaps in the table. He predicted four new elements with 43, 61, 72, and 75 protons. His prediction was proven correct when technetium, promethium, hafnium, and rhenium were discovered later by other scientists.
884. Hares are born with fur and their eyes open while rabbits are born with no fur and closed eyes.
885. An adult wolf's pawprint measures about 5.1 in (13 cm) long and 3.9 in (10 cm) wide. This is a big foot!
886. Triton's (one of Neptune's moon) atmosphere differs from that of other planets. It has a thermosphere instead of a stratosphere.
887. It takes about seven seconds for food to travel from your mouth to your stomach when you swallow.

888. About 500 species of fish can change their sex, often due to changes in their environment.
889. Copper is essential for human health. As our body can't make it, we must get it from our diet.
890. Dams are built for many reasons - generating hydroelectricity, reducing flood risks, irrigation, or a water source for cities.
891. The flames of a fire can have different colors depending on which fuel is burning.
892. Insects have two antennae to smell and feel things.
893. An alligator hunts better in the water than on land because they can swim fast.
894. In the 'Little Boy" that was dropped on and decimated Hiroshima, only 1.38% of the uranium it contained underwent fission. There was 140 lb (60 kg) of uranium in that bomb.
895. Earth's solar system is aged approximately 4.571 billion years.
896. Stars are mostly concentrated in the center of the Milky Way.
897. A sloth can poke its tongue out about 10 - 12 in (25 - 30 cm).
898. About 50 active satellites are considered Medium Earth Orbit satellites, in orbit about 35,786 km (22,236 mi) above the Earth's surface.
899. Over 200,000 people have applied to fly to Mars and never return! Of these, 100 were selected, and 24 will make the trip.
900. The chemical element silicon is a metalloid i.e.; it is semi metal. It looks like a metal but does not conduct electricity easily.
901. The computer of the 1940s took up the size of a large room and used lots of electricity. They were very different from the modern laptops of today.

902. An American poll taken in 2019 showed that 6% of people thought the moon landing was fake while 15% sat on the fence and didn't know if it was false or if it happened.
903. In 1612 Galileo Galilee drew Neptune, but the drawings were of a fixed star and not the planet, so he is not said to have discovered Neptune.
904. Earth has five atmospheric layers. In order from the closest to Earth are the troposphere, stratosphere, ozone layer, mesosphere, and thermosphere.
905. A baby beaver is called a kit. They can swim 24 hours after they are born.
906. When a camel feels threatened, it spits and throws up as a defense mechanism.
907. A shark has excellent hearing and can hear a fish up to 1,640 feet (500 m) away.
908. A reflecting telescope gives cheaper to make and provides a clearer picture than a refracting telescope. However, the optics require much maintenance.
909. An adult snake sheds its skin one to two times a year. A younger snake may shed its skin up to four times a year.
910. A hurricane can create a tornado.
911. Some scientists think that there are only 6 (not 7) colors in a rainbow. They believe that the color indigo is too close to blue.
912. A baby koala is known as a joey, like a baby kangaroo.
913. Charon was first called S/1978 P 1 after it was discovered and is the first object around Pluto.
914. Galileo is often thought of as the inventor of the telescope. However, this is incorrect! Hans Lippershey invented the telescope in 1608. Galileo was, however, the first person to use it to study the night sky.
915. Hurricanes form over warm water in tropical regions around the world. The warm moist air rises over the

ocean and gets sucked into clouds of air. The clouds grow and rotate with the Earth's spin if there is enough warm water to feed the storm, a hurricane forms.

916. A group of chain-like galaxies called Markarian's Chain to sit near the Messier 87 Galaxy.
917. Chameleons change color to signal their intentions to each other. For example, a male chameleon becomes brighter to make it more attractive to females. Females will change their color to accept or reject the male chameleon. They also change color to dark green with blue lines when pregnant.
918. Ailuropoda melanoleuca' is the scientific name for the giant panda.
919. The first coins were made about 600BC, about 2,600 years ago. They were made of electrum, a natural gold-silver alloy.
920. It takes Uranus 84 Earth years to orbit the sun.
921. A bald eagle is also called an American eagle and belongs to the Accipitridae family. They are only found in North America.
922. Waste that can be recycled is collected in different ways in our society. You can drop it off at a specific recycling location, sell it to a buy-back center, or leave it on the curb during a specified period for it to be picked up.
923. A platypus sleeps about 14 hours every day.
924. The Greater flamingo is the tallest flamingo species, growing up to 5 feet (1.5 m) tall and weighing up to 8 lbs (3.5 kg).
925. A hummingbird takes about 250 breaths a minute when it's resting.
926. Triton's (one of Neptune's moon) surface looks like a rockmelon. Its cantaloupe terrain covers most of the moon's western half with craters that are all about the same size so unlikely to be impact craters.

927. A giraffe and a human have the same number of vertebrae in their neck.
928. The process where water is used to produce electricity is called hydropower.
929. Photosynthesis is the process where green plants use sunlight to make food.
930. Bacteria will not grow on copper, so for hundreds of years, parts of boats and ships were built with copper so that barnacles wouldn't stick to them.
931. The word volcano comes from the Roman god of fire —Vulcan.
932. The sun supports all life on Earth through photosynthesis.
933. A reflector is another name for a reflecting telescope.
934. Hares are larger than rabbits, have longer ears, and are less social.
935. Valentina Tereshkova, a Russian, was the first woman in space. In 1963 she orbited Earth for nearly three days on the spaceship Vostok 6.
936. Lead is poisonous if you breathe it in or swallow it. For that reason, it is no longer used to make paint or pesticide.
937. Pluto is the largest dwarf planet.
938. A NASA flight controller, John Aaron, saved Apollo 12 when it was struck by lightning. He also developed a safe way for Apollo 13 to come back to Earth.
939. No person has ever seen a black hole even though we believe they exist.
940. Leonardo da Vinci wrote a collection of scientific writings, the 'Codex Leicester', explaining water movement, fossils, and the moon. Microsoft founder Bill Gates purchased the book in 1994 for nearly $40 million.
941. Platinum, in its natural form, is rare to find. 80% of the world's platinum comes from South Africa.

942. Copper has an atomic number of 29.
943. A sheep has four stomach chambers to help digest their food.
944. Flamingos in the Americas are redder and more orange in color because the food they eat has more beta carotene in it. Lesser flamingos in Kenya are paler and pinker as their food has less beta carotene.
945. A hummingbird is the only bird that can fly backward deliberately.
946. In the human body, bones are held in place by joints, ligaments, and muscles.
947. The dollar signs many countries use $ as their monetary symbol.
948. The job of a queen ant is to lay eggs. The job of the male drone ants is to mate with the queen. Female ants are the workers who find food and care for the queen. This includes building the nest and defending the colony.
949. A lightning rod is a conductor or a metal rod, usually on top of a tall building, that diverts lightning safely to the ground.
950. The International Space Station (ISS) is located in the ionosphere, the first part of outer space.
951. Cheetahs are small and light compared with other big cats. Together with their blunt claws, this means they're not built to protect themselves from larger prey. As a result, they will usually give up its catch when a larger, more aggressive animal threatens them.
952. Multistep waterfalls are also known as tiered or staircase waterfalls. They are a series of mini waterfalls that continuously fall into one another.
953. Lightning occurs more in summer as there are more moisture and instability in the atmosphere than in winter.

954. The Great Wall of China has different sections built over a long period and by different dynasties.
955. The Whirlpool Galaxy is also called Messier 51a, M51a, and NGC 5194. It has a companion galaxy, NGC 5195 that is sometimes just called M51.
956. Most of the Earth's rocky surface comprises sedimentary rocks. At the same time, the Earth's crust is made up of igneous and metamorphic rocks.
957. The Killer Whale or Orca is a type of dolphin.
958. The peacock is the largest flying bird on Earth.
959. Snakes live on every continent except Antarctica.
960. The ph scale measures the acidity of a substance. Pure water doesn't smell or have a taste and has a ph level of 7.
961. Inner planets, i.e., planets closest to the sun, consist mostly of an iron core surrounded by a mantle.
962. The sun has a radius of about 695,508 km (432,168 mi), which is about 109.2 times bigger than Earth's.
963. In 2006 the Venus Express spacecraft found more than 1,000 large volcanoes on Venus.
964. Desertification is the process where fertile lands are turned into deserts due to humans cutting down forests, drought, and climate change. The Gobi desert in China and Mongolia is growing larger due to desertification.
965. Although carbon can form many different compounds, it is not very reactive.
966. Lizards, like all reptiles, are cold-blooded.
967. When subjected over extreme heat and pressure over time, sandstone metamorphizes into quartzite. Mudstone metamorphizes into slate.
968. The upper level of the Earth's crust is 95% igneous rock.
969. Dinosaur comes from a Greek word meaning 'terrible lizard.'
970. Due to its lightness, magnesium is the third most common structural metal used after iron and aluminum.

971. The smallest monkey in the world, with a body as small as 5 in (12 cm) is the marmoset monkey.
972. Beavers build dams from sticks and mud to protect them from predators and to get food easily.
973. Many scientists believe there are many plants, insects, and marine species that have not been discovered.
974. Zebras are herbivores and eat grass.
975. About 70% of zinc in the world comes from mines and 30% from recycling.
976. The world's highest Bungee jump was off a hot air balloon at 15,200 feet (4,633 m). Curtis Rivers in 2002 jumped with a 98 feet (29.8 m) bungee cord, bounced five times, and then parachuted the rest of the way down.
977. Bone marrow produces all red blood cells.
978. The Milky Way was the only galaxy we knew until 1924 when Hubble proved other galaxies in the universe.
979. Tulips grow from bulbs. There are over 3,000 tulip varieties in the world.
980. Coconut water has been used in emergencies in the past as a substitute for blood plasma.
981. There are many ways to gather food, such as farming, hunting, and fishing.
982. Robert Hooke, the English Physicist, invented plant cells and 'Hooke's Law,' the law of elasticity. He is famous for his work in microbiology.
983. If you add a nickel to glass, it goes green.
984. Fish use parts of their body to make low pitched sounds to communicate with each other.
985. The sky is blue because the atmosphere absorbs the real color, purple.
986. An object in the Kuiper Belt or the Oort Cloud is called a Trans-Neptunian object.
987. The oldest Ancient Wonder in the world is the Great Pyramid of Giza.

988. Scientists are unsure why some thunderstorms create tornadoes and others don't.
989. Penguins, like ostriches, emus, and kiwis, are birds that cannot fly.
990. Mercury has a large metallic core, partly molten and partly liquid.
991. Silicon has a chemical symbol Si and an atomic number of 14.
992. Jupiter has sixty-seven known moons. Several of those moons were named after the many lovers of the Roman god Jupiter.
993. Jane Goodall is a British anthropologist, famous for her work with chimpanzees. She discovered how they lived in groups, could make and use simple tools, hunted animals, ate meat, and had different personalities.
994. The dwarf planets, Pluto, Haumea, and Makemake, are all situated within the Kuiper Belt.
995. Snails can live anywhere between 5 - 25 years, depending on their species.
996. The Pinwheel Galaxy has an unusual pattern resembling a pinwheel that scientists believe energetic dust and gas winds created.
997. Mineralogy, hydrogeology, sedimentology, paleontology, marine geology, geochemistry, and geophysics are specialized geology fields.
998. Whales sometimes get lost when they migrate, and they don't realize it until they become beached up.
999. The process of the exchange of carbon between all living things on Earth is called the carbon cycle. Carbon is constantly used, reused, and recycled.
1000. Apple seeds have a small amount of a cyanide compound called amygdalin in them, but you have to eat many seeds for it to affect you.
1001. A koala lives for about 20 years in the wild.

1002. A waterspout is a tornado that is formed over water.
1003. Forensic entomology studies the insects that can be found around a dead body to work out when they died.
1004. When you dip a slice of orange into some baking soda and then eat it, it will start to bubble in your mouth. This is because the citric acid in the orange causes a chemical reaction with the baking soda. This base makes lots of carbon dioxide bubbles.
1005. There are over 2,000 known species of jellyfish in the world.
1006. You can use a lemon to create electricity by attaching two electrodes (different metals) to it. The citric acid in the lemon is an electrolyte that will conduct electricity. One metal will collect an excess of electrons while the other one loses electrons. This positive and negative flow creates electricity.
1007. The lifespan of a bald eagle is about 20 years in the wild.
1008. The type of dam built depends on its purpose and other factors such as the budget available. Masonry, arch-gravity, and embankment dams are some examples.
1009. Sagittarius A* is the name of the black hole in the center of the Milky Way.
1010. Scientists have not been able to agree on why zebras have unique stripes. Some say it helps them stay cool, some say it stops tsetse flies from biting them. Others say it's a means of identification or a form of camouflage.
1011. Sloths climb down from their trees to go to the toilet once every 1 - 3 weeks!
1012. The first component of The International Space Station (ISS) sent to orbit was the Zarya module. It was launched into space on 20 November 1998, on a Russian Proton rocket. Zarya provided propulsion, control of attitude, communications, and electric power.
1013. The thin, cold atmosphere becomes thicker and hotter

approaching Jupiter's core, gradually turning into a thick, dark fog. About 1000 km (621 mi) down in the blackness, pressure squeezes the atmosphere so hard that it becomes liquid.

1014. Most submarines belong to the navy and military forces to protect aircraft carriers, attack other submarines, and surveillance. They are also used for marine research and undersea exploration.
1015. A polar bear can eat 100 lb (45 kg) of blubber in one meal. They depend on a high-fat diet to keep warm.
1016. Mars is 54.7 million km (34 million miles) away from Earth and is our closest neighbor after our moon and Venus.
1017. Male deer fight each other with their antlers.
1018. The Andromeda Galaxy is also known as the Great Andromeda Nebular and Messier 31 or M31.
1019. Rudolf Diesel invented the first Diesel engine in 1892.
1020. A small horse is called a pony.
1021. Never look directly at a total solar eclipse as it can make you blind.
1022. Some asteroids have moons.
1023. Because Pluto is so far from the sun, it is icy. It is a rock with a very thick ice layer.
1024. Beetles are a group of insects in the order Coleoptera. Coleoptera means 'sheathed wing'.
1025. Mars has been around for 4.5 billion years.
1026. Galileo Galilei was the scientist who first used a telescope to look into space where he discovered Jupiter's four largest moons.
1027. The state of an object, gas, liquid, or solid, is determined by its temperature.
1028. An electric circuit has conductors, a switch, a load or resistor, and a power source or cell.

1029. Since its demotion to being a dwarf planet, Pluto now also has an asteroid number 134340.
1030. The polar caps on Mars are mostly made up of frozen water and a thin layer of carbon dioxide. If the chilled water from its southern polar cap was melted, it could cover the whole planet with water about 11 meters or 36 feet deep.
1031. Clownfish are also called anemonefish after where they live.
1032. The fastest sprinting horse is the Quarter horse, which can sprint at 55 mph (88 kph) over a quarter of a mile (0.4 km).
1033. A space shuttle could only be launched in perfect weather conditions.
1034. NASA's Pathfinder' small robot, Sojourner, was the first robot to explore a planet. That planet was Mars.
1035. A DVD is a high-density CD and evolved in 1963. CD stands for Compact Disc, and DVD first stood for 'digital video discs' and later for 'digital versatile discs.'
1036. Astronauts stay on the ISS for about six months before returning to Earth.
1037. A peacock's tail makes up 60% of the length of its body.
1038. The stomach in an adult can hold up to 1.5 liters of food.
1039. A chameleon's tongue can catch its prey, usually large insects, in 0.07 split seconds.
1040. Meteor means 'suspended in air.'
1041. The Spitzer Space Telescope was around 720 million US dollars!
1042. Hippos communicate by grunting. They may also use echolocation (making a noise and then listening for the noise to come back).
1043. The International Space Station (ISS) weighs almost 419,500 kg (925,000 lb).

1044. Fossils can be found all over the world on every continent, including Antarctica.

1045. On 11 December 2017, President Donald Trump signed the Space Policy Directive 1, which instructed NASA to send astronauts back to the moon and eventually to Mars.

1046. Food comes from over 2,000 different plants.

1047. Enzymes break down your food in your mouth and your stomach. In your saliva, enzymes called amylases break down carbohydrates while lipases break down fats. In your stomach and small intestine, proteases break down proteins.

1048. Badgers are nocturnal mammals i.e.; they are active at night.

1049. Hedgehogs that live in deserts will sleep through the heat and drought - this is called aestivation.

1050. Hamster comes from the German word 'hamstern,' meaning 'hoard'. They have large cheeks where they store food until they return to their colony to eat it. Pet hamsters also hoard food under their bed.

1051. In 1824, Megalosaurus was the first dinosaur to be given a proper name.

1052. Capillary action is the liquid movement through another material, for example, water moving up a straw against gravity or water soaked into a paper towel. Water has good capillary action properties.

1053. A cracked egg on land makes a mess but 60 ft (18 m) under the ocean, it looks whole with an invisible egg shell around it. This is because of the water pressure on the egg, which is about 2.8 times stronger than air pressure.

1054. Carl Wilhelm Scheele, Joseph Priestley, and Antoine Laurent Lavoiser are all credited for discovering oxygen between 1770 and 1780. The term 'oxygen' was first used in 1777.

1055. Nine spacecraft have launched missions to the outer

planets of our solar system. All of them have encountered Neptune.

1056. The mass of Mercury,330,104,000,000,000 kg (727,754,745,962,768.25 lb) is 0.055 times Earth's mass.

1057. Our skeletal system (bones) has six main functions. It supports our body, allows us to move, protects our organs, produces blood cells and stores, and releases minerals and fats.

1058. As far as we know, Mars has the longest valley in our solar system. Valles Marineris is more than ten times longer than the Grand Canyon at 4,000 km (2,500 mi).

1059. In San Francisco, the Golden Gate Bridge, built-in 1937, is a suspension bridge measuring 8,981 feet (2,737 m) long. The two main cables are made from 80,000 miles (129,000 km) of wire.

1060. Horses have the biggest eyes compared with any other land mammal.

1061. The queen bee only mates once in her life, with many many drones. She then stores the sperm in a special organ and lays eggs until she runs out.

1062. Albert Einstein was born in Germany, but he gave up his German citizenship when he was 16 and became a Swiss citizen when he was 21. He had no nationality in between.

1063. Scientists don't expect to find any life on Mars, but they are looking for a life that may have existed on Mars a long time ago when it may have been covered with water.

1064. Fireball meteors are hard to see as they often happen during the day and over the ocean.

1065. The Oort Cloud is located beyond the Kuiper Belt, past Pluto. It is a big thick bubble around our solar system filled with comets.

1066. A chameleon's tongue is about twice the length of its body, so it can stick it out a long way to catch its prey.

1067. Earth is made of 32.1% iron, 30.1% oxygen, 15.1% silicon, and 13.9% magnesium.
1068. Hedgehogs can climb trees.
1069. There have been over 2,400 research investigations in the ISS microgravity laboratory.
1070. Crocodiles are reptiles, and they descended from dinosaurs.
1071. The first nuclear weapons were developed and used by the United States in World War II.
1072. The element with the highest melting point (3500 °C or 3773 K, 6332 °F) is carbon.
1073. The cosmic microwave background radiation's temperature is 2.7 degrees Kelvin (-270.45° C, -454.81° F).
1074. Astronomy is useful to determine seasons to assist farmers with when to plant and harvest their crops.
1075. A breeze, gale, storm, and hurricane are all winds at different strengths.
1076. A carat measures the amount of gold in an alloy. Pure gold is 24 carats.
1077. About 95% of a jellyfish's body is made of water. If you remove it from water, it dies.
1078. A dog can hear higher frequency sounds than people, helping warn them about attacks before they happen.
1079. A 'double rainbow' can sometimes be seen i.e., a second fainter rainbow outside the primary rainbow. This happens because light reflects twice inside the water droplets. The second rainbow will have violet as the outside color and red as the most inner color.
1080. The word chlorine comes from the Greek word choros, which means greenish-yellow.
1081. To stay warm, Emperor penguins huddle together in large groups.

1082. Chemical energy is often transformed into heat or light during chemical reactions.
1083. The capybara is the largest rodent in the world. The beaver is the second largest.
1084. Johannes Kepler was an astronomer at the same time as Galileo Galilei.
1085. Frogs don't close their eyes, even when sleeping. They can see in all directions at the same time.
1086. For an artificial satellite to keep its orbit and stay in space, it must travel faster than 28,200 kph (17,500 mph).
1087. Silver doesn't rust, and it is used in jewelry.
1088. Mawsynram in the Meghalaya State of India is the wettest place on Earth with an average annual rainfall of 467 inches (11,871 mm). It is close to the Bay of Bengal. When moisture collects over the Bay, it causes precipitation over the city, resulting in a long monsoon season.
1089. A lizard sheds its skin regularly and grows it back.
1090. Your body carries more bacterial cells than human cells.
1091. Warm air weighs less than cool air, so it keeps pushing through the cool air as it rises. The movement of the air is called wind.
1092. About every 2,000 years, a space object about the size of a football field hits Earth.
1093. The southern hemisphere on Mars, with lots of craters, is very different from the northern hemisphere with fewer craters.
1094. A bald eagle can't smell, but it can taste.
1095. Hedgehogs that live in temperate climates stay active at night all year.
1096. Water expands when it's heated and contracts when cooled except between 32 - 39 deg F (0 - 4 deg C) when it does the opposite. This is because as water freezes, it becomes ice, which takes up more space.

1097. Scientific studies have shown that eating psilocybin mushrooms (magic mushrooms) can be beneficial for depression. It is very expensive to extract the chemical from the mushrooms, so scientists are exploring different ways to produce it.
1098. Some otters, such as river otters, like to live alone while other otters, like sea otters, are very social animals.
1099. The name for a group of tigers is an 'ambush' or a 'streak.'
1100. Scientists believed the Milky Way was the center of our universe about 100 years ago.
1101. The scent of a rose comes from the petal's microscopic perfume glands.
1102. Mars appears to move backward through the zodiac, so the ancient Egyptians used to call it the "backward traveler."
1103. An adult lung's surface area could cover an area of 229 square feet (70 square meters).
1104. Scientists think that there are about 2 trillion galaxies in the observable universe.
1105. Deer have one main stomach and three false ones. They chew their cud just like cows.
1106. Over the years, some foods and cuisines have become popular worldwide, including raw fish from Japan, hummus from the Middle East, curry from India, and tacos from Mexico.
1107. A snake has no eyelid.
1108. Atoms are made up of electrons, protons, and neutrons. Electrons have a negative charge, and protons have a positive charge.
1109. Ceres may have been a planetary embryo that formed 4.57 billion years ago in the asteroid belt.
1110. Prairie dogs are very social ground squirrels that live in large colonies containing as many as 400 million individuals.

1111. An alternating current is used to send electricity over large distances. It is safer and can provide more power.
1112. Pluto's four small satellites that orbit it are called Nix, Hydra, Kerberos, and Styx.
1113. Charon is half Pluto's size, about half the United States' width, and just bigger than India. Because of this, Pluto and Charon are often referred to as the double dwarf planet system.
1114. The launch of the first satellite by the Soviets started the Space Race between the Soviets and the Americans.
1115. Astronaut's vision is blurry in space as without gravity, body fluids in their body increase and puts pressure on their eyes.
1116. A meerkat communicates danger by barking or whistling. Just by their sounds, a meerkat will know if the predator is in the air or on the ground and if it's low or high urgency to hide.
1117. Isaac Newton discovered gravity when he watched an apple fall from a tree.
1118. A pony is a small horse with usually a thicker mane and tail.
1119. A baby hare is called a leveret.
1120. Horses can see in lower light conditions than humans due to a special membrane at the back of their eyes.
1121. Uranus receives about 1/400th of the Sun that Earth gets.
1122. The Sydney Opera House is covered in 1,056,006 tiles.
1123. Saturn has ammonia crystals in its upper atmosphere, so it looks pale yellow.
1124. Dysnomia orbits its dwarf planet Eris every 16 days.
1125. Mice are very clean animals. In the burrows where they live, they have separate 'rooms' for sleeping, going to the toilet, and storing their food.

1126. Crux, also known as the Southern Cross, is the brightest constellation.
1127. The atomic number for iron is 26.
1128. To honor his contributions to British science, a £20 note was made in 1991 featuring Michael Faraday. Ten years later, when the note was withdrawn, the bank estimated it had circulated approximately 120 million bills.
1129. Some believe that one of Jupiter's moons, Europa, may have life.
1130. Henry Moseley, famous for his work on the Periodic Table and created the first atomic battery, died when he was 27 years old, serving in World War I. After his death, the British Government banned all scientists from serving in front line positions in wars.
1131. More than 1,000 species of fish are threatened by extinction.
1132. Callisto takes 16.7 days to orbit Jupiter, a distance of 11.2 million km (7 million miles).
1133. Ripening bananas is a science! When picked, they are placed in rooms at a specific temperature (between 60 - 70 deg C). Ethylene gas is pumped in and out again, triggering the banana to ripen. The banana specialists then wait for the right time to ship it to us, ready to ripen a bit more or eat.
1134. A reconnaissance satellite was designed for military intelligence.
1135. Another name for meerkat is suricate.
1136. A massive bright sphere of scorching gas called plasma held together by gravity is known as a star.
1137. Water can be a solid, liquid, or gas.
1138. Eris is the largest dwarf planet, 27% larger than Pluto, which comes next.
1139. The scientific study of lung diseases is called pulmonology.

1140. Panthers are strong swimmers and climbers.
1141. The Asteroid Belt - where most asteroids orbit the sun - sits between Mars and Jupiter.
1142. Spiral galaxies are listed as type S, with an a, b or c depending on the tightness of the spiral arms and the central bulge's size. A barred spiral galaxy with a long bar in the center has the symbol SB.
1143. Ceres is the largest body in the asteroid belt.
1144. Time is measured in seconds, minutes, hours, weeks, and years. 60 seconds make up a minute, and 60 minutes make up an hour. A day has 24 hours in it. A clock, watch, sundial, or hourglass are all instruments that can measure time.
1145. Some grasshopper species can make noises by rubbing their back legs against their bodies, or snapping their wings when they fly. This is called stridulation.
1146. A blue moon is the second full moon in a calendar month. It comes from an old English word 'belewe' or 'betrayer' as people viewed a full moon before lent was a 'betrayer moon.' 'Belewe' eventually became 'blue.'
1147. The roots of a tree help support it and keep it upright and collect and store water and nutrients from the soil.
1148. Radon is very radioactive. When the radioactive elements uranium and thorium decay, they produce radium. When radium decays, it produces the chemical element radon. When radon decays, it produces more radioactive elements called radon daughters or decay products.
1149. Martians have been written about in many novels. One of the most famous is H.G. Wells' 1898 novel The War of the Worlds, where Martians attempted to take over the world.
1150. Ganymede's (one of Jupiter's moons) surface is 40% dark craters, which scientists believe were caused by the

substantial impact of comets and asteroids about 4 billion years ago.

1151. Grasshoppers jump by pushing their back legs off the ground. They use a catapult mechanism to build up energy in their knees, which helps them jump further.

1152. Breathing high amounts of radon is strongly related to lung cancer. After smoking, radon is the next most frequent cause of lung cancer.

1153. The most common type of cave is formed when natural acids in groundwater dissolve soluble rock, such as limestone.

1154. A locomotive changes chemical energy from the fuel (wood, coal, diesel fuel) into kinetic motion.

1155. Fossils have been found of penguins that were 4.5 feet (1.3 m) tall. This is taller than the tallest penguin of today, the Emperor penguin, that grows to a top height of 4 feet (1.22 m).

1156. A comet is a short-term comet if it has an orbital period of fewer than 200 years. A long term comet has an orbital period of more than 200 years.

1157. A cave is formed by many geological processes such as chemical actions, erosion, volcanic forces, microorganisms, and pressure.

1158. Insects don't have lungs. They have spiracles or holes in their body for breathing.

1159. The space station is nearly four times larger than Mir, the Russian space station, and about five times larger than the US Skylab.

1160. It is believed that the Solar System formed about 4,568 years ago.

1161. Mercury is the smallest planet in our solar system. A Mercury day lasts 176 Earth days.

1162. Oncology is the branch of medicine that studies cancer.

1163. Neuroscience is the study of the nervous system.

1164. Flamingos are water birds with long necks, sticklike legs, pinkish feathers, about 3 - 5 feet (0.9 - 1.5 m) high. They live in shallow lakes, mangroves, and sandy flats.
1165. Radon is one of the densest and heaviest gases under normal conditions.
1166. A geologist must have a strong knowledge of physics, chemistry, biology, mathematics, and computer science.
1167. A cat can see better at night than a person can as it needs six times less light.
1168. Nitrous oxide, an air pollutant, and greenhouse gas have 300 times more impact than carbon dioxide.
1169. In 150 AD, Ptolemy, a Greek astronomer, recorded 48 out of the 88 constellations that are officially recognized by the International Astronomical Union. The name of Ptolemy's book, where he recorded the constellations, is Almagest.
1170. The average size of a male adult hippo is 3,310 lb (1,500 kg).
1171. It doesn't matter whether you store tomatoes at room temperature or in the fridge. Researchers have found that the tomato variety is the most important thing that influences the flavor.
1172. The optic nerve sends information from our eyes to the brain, making sense of the information and allowing us to act appropriately.
1173. Zinc has an atomic number of 30.
1174. The Messier 87 Galaxy has a similar size of 120,000 light-years to the Milky Way.
1175. Vesta, larger than 500 km (310 mi) in diameter, is the only asteroid that you can see with the naked eye.
1176. Two types of terrain exist on the moon. The highlands are the bright terrain as they're higher than 'maria.' The 'maria' have a lower elevation and make up the dark terrain.

1177. Snails are one of the slowest animals on Earth, with a maximum speed of 50 yards per hour (45 meters per hour).
1178. Energy can be transformed from one type to another. For example, windmills capture kinetic energy from the wind and transform it into mechanical energy.
1179. A hummingbird can fly upside down.
1180. The IAU stipulates that Kuiper belt objects must be named after mythological beings. Haumea is named after the Hawaiian goddess of fertility.
1181. At one time, the oldest known map of the moon was drawn by Leonardo da Vinci about the year 1505 until an older one was found, carved into a prehistoric tomb in Ireland that was about 5,000 years old!
1182. In 1781 Sir William Herschel, a British musician and sky watcher, discovered Uranus.
1183. Plunge waterfalls move very fast with a horizontal thrust over the edge.
1184. It is believed that the universe has more stars in it than Earth has sand at its beaches.
1185. A dwarf planet orbits the sun and has gravity and is not a satellite or a moon.
1186. Some astronomers believe that objects sucked into black holes can come out in another galaxy.
1187. Galileo had a refractor telescope that could magnify the image 30 times.
1188. Fossilization involves the dissolving and replacing of original minerals in objects with other rock-like minerals.
1189. The beaver's large front teeth grow throughout the whole life.
1190. Fish don't have lungs. They breathe in oxygen from the water through their gills.
1191. Chlorine is dangerous and poisonous in high concentrations, and it is heavier than air to fill up closed

spaces. Because of these properties, it was used as a weapon in WWI. It was dispersed in low lying enemy foxholes and trenches.

1192. A kangaroo can walk on two or four legs. It's faster when it hops on two legs.

1193. Alexander's band is the name of the dark sky between primary and secondary arc rainbows. It was named after the person who first described it in 200 AD, Alexander of Aphrodisias.

1194. Uranus' seasons can go for 20 years.

1195. Penguins are built to be strong swimmers with their tightly packed wings and torpedo-shaped bodies.

1196. Diamond turns into graphite over time.

1197. It is unclear if the word 'chemistry' comes from the Egyptian word meaning 'earth' or the Greek word meaning 'alchemy - the art of casting together alloys.'

1198. Scientists study glaciers to keep track of global warming as glaciers are very sensitive to climate change.

1199. In Chinese mythology, the gods placed the Milky Way (which they called the Silver River) in the heavens to separate a weaver from a herdsman, a couple in love.

1200. Coconut is not a nut; it is a drupe. A drupe is a fruit with a fleshy outer part with a shell and usually a seed inside. Peaches, plums, and mangos are all drupes.

1201. There is about 1.2 oz (35 grams) of dissolved salt in every pound or kilogram of seawater.

1202. It takes the same time for the moon to rotate on its axis as it does for it to orbit Earth. This means we can only see about 60% of the moon's surface from Earth.

1203. The largest living structure on Earth is the Great Barrier Reef off the coast of Australia. It is over 1,240 miles (2,000 km) long.

1204. Potatoes are best stored at 42 - 50 deg F (6 - 10 deg C) to stop the starch turning into sugar, maintain their vitamin C content, and keep them for longer.

1205. Japan's Shinkansen is fast bullet trains that have carried passengers since 1964.

1206. 3753 Cruithne has its orbit around the sun, but it looks like its following Earth's orbit. It is 5 km (3.1 mi) wide and is occasionally called our second moon.

1207. The fastest planetary winds in our solar system come from Saturn and Neptune.

1208. Wolves have long legs and great stamina and can run at 7.5 - 10 mph (12 - 16 kph) for most of the night.

1209. The branch of physics that studies light is called optics.

1210. Zinc is a shiny bluish-white metal in its pure form.

1211. Jellyfish have a bell-shaped, jellylike body with tentacles hanging underneath.

1212. Glacier activity about 10,000 years ago created Niagara Falls.

1213. One Kelvin is equal to one degree on the Celsius scale. There are no negative numbers on the Kelvin scale as the lowest number is 0.

1214. About 12,500 ant species have been identified out of an estimated 22,000.

1215. 65% of nickel is used to make stainless steel.

1216. Just like fats and carbohydrates, protein is an essential energy source in your body.

1217. A tsunami is a huge wave of water usually caused by an earthquake or a volcanic eruption.

1218. Snakeskins are smooth and dry.

1219. Nikola Tesla is also known as the Father of the Alternating Current.

1220. Frogs survive much longer in captivity as they don't have to face all the wild dangers.

1221. The gravitational pull of the moon has slowed Earth's rotation. Our days used to be shorter.

1222. Scientists estimated that the sun would become a nebula in about 5 billion years.
1223. Thomas Harriot was the first person to draw a moon map as it looks through a telescope.
1224. A horse can gallop at a speed of 27 mph (44 kph).
1225. While there is no evidence of Venus's life, scientists doubt any life could exist due to its high temperature.
1226. Stephen Hawking believed that increasing temperatures cause black holes to shrink and evaporate.
1227. Hippos sweat a red-colored natural sunscreen substance.
1228. The Andromeda Galaxy is 260,000 light-years long.
1229. Stephen Hawking once said, "Earth might one day soon resemble the planet, Venus."
1230. Water is made up of two hydrogen atoms bonded to one oxygen atom.
1231. Penny-farthing was a type of bicycle with a large front wheel. This was popular from 1870 to 1890 and was invented because manufacturers believed the larger the wheel, the further you could travel with just one rotation of the pedals. However, it was very dangerous as when a person stopped the bicycle, their momentum continued and toppled them over the top. The 'safety bicycle' as we know it today, was introduced in 1885.
1232. In the solar system, Eris, dwarf planet, is situated past the Kuiper belt.
1233. Mosquitoes are one of the slowest flying insects with a top speed of 1 - 2 mph (0.6 - 1 kph).
1234. An ocean trench can be up to 35797 ft (10911 m) deep.
1235. Chlorine was discovered first in 1774 by a Swedish chemist called Carl Wilhelm Scheele. He believed it contained oxygen, but in 1810, Sir Humphry Davy proved that chlorine was an element on its own.
1236. A kangaroo stomps its foot to warn other kangaroos if danger is approaching.

1237. You can see the Andromeda Galaxy as part of the Andromeda Constellation in the northern sky.
1238. Butterflies smell with their antennae and taste with their feet.
1239. The Hubble Space Telescope can see and study Neptune.
1240. Nickel is usually combined with other metals to make a useful alloy - brass, bronze, nickel cast iron. These metals include copper, aluminum, lead, cobalt, and gold.
1241. Tomatoes have lots of vitamin C, potassium, and antioxidants, which can help us fight disease, maintain a healthy heart, and reduce the risk of cancers, including prostate, colon, and breast cancers. They also contain lycopene, which is important for healthy prostate glands (in men) and helps fight skin cancer.
1242. Drone bees are the male bees, and their only job is to mate with the queen. Their lifespan is approximately 40 - 50 days.
1243. Black panthers don't exist. They are jaguars or cougars with a black color mutation that changes their golden fur color to black. The black fur then matches their black spots, so they look black all over.
1244. A bicycle uses gears and chains which transmit power or energy to the rear wheel. A cyclist uses a low gear to go uphill and a high gear when going downhill.
1245. Although Callisto (one of Jupiter's moons) is about twice the distance from Earth than the moon, when viewed through a telescope, it is much brighter than our moon due to the sun's reflection of its ice layer.
1246. The fuzzy tail of a comet is called a coma. This happens when the Comet nears the sun, and the sun's heat melts the frozen water from the CometComet's surface.
1247. It is unlikely for a meteor to fall on a human being as they mostly fall into the ocean.

1248. Snow blindness or photokeratitis can happen if you don't wear eye protection in the snow to absorb the snow's ultraviolet rays.
1249. There are 19 constellations in the Hercules family, 10 in the Ursa Major Family, 9 in the Perseus Family, and 5 in the Orion Family.
1250. The Kuiper Belt is a disc-shaped region that extends beyond Neptune. It contains hundreds of thousands of large icy objects bigger than 100 km (62 miles) in diameter and trillions of comets. Pluto is the most well-known object in the Kuiper Belt.
1251. Crocodiles are fast swimmers and can swim up to 20 mph (32 kph).
1252. Earth's powerful magnetic field protects the planet from the effects of the solar wind.
1253. The Great Wall of China was rebuilt and made stronger by stone and brick in the 14th century. The earlier parts of the wall were made constructed of stone, wood, and compacted Earth.
1254. Mice teeth keep growing, so they have to gnaw on things to keep them a manageable length!
1255. Vampire bats feed on blood from other mammals (sometimes humans) and birds.
1256. Halley's Comet is known as a periodic comet, i.e., it orbits the sun in a period that is less than 200 years.
1257. An owl's diet consists of small rodents, frogs, lizards, birds, snakes, and other small animals. Some owls eat insects, and some eat fish.
1258. Not all whales have the same shape or size. There are 79 - 84 different species in the world.
1259. Crabs walk sideways because their legs are on the outside of their body, and their 'knees' bend in that direction.
1260. Pigeons can find their way home. Homing pigeons are

your everyday pigeons that have been bred and trained to find their way home.

1261. Nikola Tesla, who invented the AC (alternating current) electric system, worked with Thomas Edison, who invented the DC (direct current) electric system.

1262. An elemental gas, like H_2, is made up of two or more of the same atoms joined together.

1263. A V-shaped bottom boat will move faster than a flat-shaped bottom boat as the flat bottom has more area in contact with the water and creates more drag.

1264. Depending on what meteors are made up of, they may have different colors.

1265. A helicopter is also called a chopper.

1266. A comet is a material from our solar system that dates back to when the sun and planets were formed. It is not a spacecraft or an alien base.

1267. Lightning is a giant spark of electricity in the atmosphere.

1268. By following other ants' scent, a foraging ant can travel up to 700 feet (200 m) from their nest and find their way home without getting lost.

1269. Hedgehogs have strong hearing and smell senses. Their eyesight is weak.

1270. A Type A spiral galaxy has the most tightly wound arms while the Type C spiral galaxy has very loose spiral arms.

1271. The batfish pretends it's dead when danger is nearby. It lies on its side and keeps still.

1272. Many herbivorous or plant-eating dinosaurs had natural weapons to protect themselves from the large carnivorous or meat-eating dinosaurs. For example, Stegosaurus (herbivore) had spikes on its tail to fight off Allosaurus (carnivore).

1273. A seal uses its whiskers to find its prey underwater.

1274. A hurricane-like vortex covers Saturn's south pole.

1275. The patas monkey is the fastest, running up to 34 mph

(55 kph).

1276. Some cacti have fruit such as the dragon fruit and the nopal.
1277. A black hole 10 billion light-years away contain a giant cloud of water vapor, 140 trillion times the water that Earth has in its oceans. This is the biggest discovery of water found in space.
1278. The three types of squirrels are flying, tree, and ground squirrels.
1279. Neptune has 13 moons, of which Triton is the largest.
1280. Smelling objects differently to the way they should smell is called 'dysnomia.'
1281. Lead has never been used to make pencils.
1282. The black and white color of a giant panda helps it to camouflage in bamboo forests.
1283. The sun has burnt off half its hydrogen store and will continue to burn for another 5 billion years when it will die.
1284. One gram of fat contains 9 kilocalories (calories). One gram of carbohydrate or protein has 4 kilocalories. As fat has more kilocalories than protein or carbohydrate, it is often responsible for weight gain.
1285. Different species of owls make different sounds.
1286. It is thought that dinosaurs became extinct when a 12.8 km (8 mi) long meteor hit Earth.
1287. Nickel is hard and ductile (can be made into a thin wire).
1288. Niagara Falls produces huge amounts of energy.
1289. A seismometer is an instrument that measures the size of an earthquake.
1290. Cathode ray tubes (CRT) in earlier television monitors were replaced by thinner screens using liquid crystal display (LCD) and plasma in the 2000s.
1291. A jaguar can live up to 20 years in a zoo but only up to 15 years in the wild.

1292. A video game is an electronic game that can be played on different platforms, including game consoles, computers, and mobile phones.

1293. Uncrewed spacecraft have reached every planet or its orbit.

1294. When a red dwarf star or a red giant starts to die, it will turn into a small white dwarf star until they stop emitting white light and dies as a black dwarf star.

1295. A banana plant is not a tree as it doesn't have a wooden stem or trunk. It is instead a large herb.

1296. Louis Pasteur was the scientist who invented 'pasteurization', a process where beverages (beer, wine, milk) are heated to high temperatures to kill bacteria that spoils food. He patented this process in 1865, and it's still used today!

1297. Some crabs can shed their legs and regrow them after a year.

1298. A seal is a semi-aquatic marine mammal.

1299. Due to their migration pattern, a Northern Hemisphere whale will never meet or breed with a Southern Hemisphere whale.

1300. An octopus has excellent eyesight.

1301. A female cane toad can lay up to 30,000 eggs twice a year.

1302. Alexander Graham Bell's father gave him his middle name 'Graham' as a birthday present when he turned 11 years old. Alexander had always wanted a middle name to distinguish him from his father and grandfather, both Alexander.

1303. Meteoroids can be as small as dust and as big as 10 meters (32.8 ft) in diameter.

1304. A fire is a combustion reaction when a substance combines with oxygen in the air. A fire needs fuel such as coal or wood, oxygen, and heat to burn.

1305. After mating, a male octopus dies within a few months.
1306. 80% more of Uranus' mass is made up of a hot dense fluid of "icy" materials—water, methane, and ammonia—above a small rocky core.
1307. The eagle is a very strong bird that can carry loads up to 15 lbs (6.8 kg).
1308. You can't always see a tornado, which is essentially wind, and you can't see the wind, but their fast-spinning winds often create a funnel of condensed water, which you can see.
1309. Most parrots are social birds and live in groups known as 'flocks.'
1310. A sloth can sleep hanging upside down from a tree using its sharp claws.
1311. Our solar system moons all have mythological characters' names except Uranus, named after William Shakespeare's plays and Alexander Pope's poem.
1312. The Hubble Space Telescope observed a moon orbiting Makemake in 2015. This moon has a provisional name, S/2015 (136472) 1, and is nicknamed MK 2.
1313. The Martian movie paid homage to the Greek god of war, Ares (known as Mars), when they named Ares 3.
1314. Wild rabbits dig tunnels or 'warrens' where they sleep and nest. There are usually several entrances or exits for a quick escape if necessary.
1315. Fats come in three forms - saturated, unsaturated, and trans fat. Saturated fats, from animals and plants, are unhealthy as they increase blood cholesterol and risk of heart disease. Unsaturated fats, from vegetable oil, in moderation are necessary for good health as they can lower blood cholesterol levels. Trans fats are less common in nature and also unhealthy. They are usually added to processed foods to add flavor.
1316. Saturn has a smaller magnetic field than Jupiter, but its

578 times more powerful than Earth's. The big magnetic fields mean Saturn has high levels of radiation.

1317. A female spider can lay up to 1,000 eggs.
1318. Venus Fly Trap is a plant that can trap an insect by closing its leaves. The insect then dies in the acid in the plant.
1319. In 1927, Stefan Bryla, a Polish engineer, designed the first welded road bridge, the Maurzyce Bridge.
1320. Silver is malleable - one gram of silver can be beaten into a thin leaf to cover more than 50 square inches (127 sq km).
1321. The alpha pair of wolves in a pack always eats first, eating up to 20% of their body weight as they may not have eaten for days.
1322. Television shows such as CSI, NCIS, Law & Order all use forensic science to determine "who did it."
1323. Ceres was named after the Roman Goddess of corn and harvests. The word 'cereal' comes from the same name.
1324. A tigon or liger is a cross between a tiger and a lion.
1325. Tornadoes occur on every continent except Antarctica.
1326. A submarine uses SONAR (sound navigation and ranging) to locate its target. The sub sends out sonar waves, which reflects off the target and returns to the ship. The sub's computers then calculate where the target is. Dolphins, whales, and bats use the same system, called echolocation, to find their prey.
1327. At 40,000 deg C (72,000 deg F), O-type stars are the hottest in the solar system.
1328. Space is completely silent as there is no atmosphere for sound to travel through.
1329. The black hole in the center of your eye is called the pupil. By changing its size, it controls the amount of light that enters your eye.

1330. Sir Isaac Newton was a lecturer at Cambridge University for 30 years, but hardly any student attended his lectures.
1331. A plutoid is also called an ice dwarf.
1332. Construction of the Great Wall of China began over 2,000 years ago.
1333. Alzheimer's disease and Parkinson's disease are diseases of the brain.
1334. A massive group of stars, star clusters, interstellar gas and dust, and dark matter held together by gravity is called a galaxy.
1335. Chinese alligators are an endangered species as much of their natural habitat in China have been converted into rice paddies. Only a few Chinese alligators remain in the wild.
1336. Titan (one of Saturn's moons) is made up of a rocky core surrounded by layers of water ice. Even though ice surrounds it, the core is still boiling and full of liquid water and ammonia.
1337. Hair keeps us cool when it's hot, hot when it's cool and protects us from ultraviolet rays in the sun.
1338. Giant pandas live in cool, wet bamboo forests in the mountains of Central China.
1339. 1991 BA, with a diameter of 6 meters (19.6 ft), is the smallest known asteroid.
1340. Mice have many predators in the wild, so they survive an average of six months. In a laboratory or house, they can live for about two years.
1341. Most asteroids on the path to colliding with Earth are destroyed when they reach our upper atmosphere.
1342. About 14% of the electricity in the world comes from nuclear power plants.
1343. Venus rotates slower than Earth on its axis, so a day on Venus would be equivalent to about 243 Earth days.
1344. Rhinoceros means 'nose horn'.

1345. Otters are endangered for different reasons. They were hunted for their fur in the past. Pollution, global warming, lack of food(fish) due to overfishing in some areas, and exposure to diseases have resulted in otter numbers decreasing.
1346. More than half of the world's species live in jungles.
1347. A comet has two tails - a dust tail that we can see with our naked eye and a plasma tail that can be photographed but unable to be seen without equipment.
1348. The first artificial satellite in the world was Sputnik 1 from the Soviet Union.
1349. The Large Magellanic Cloud is located about 163,000 light-years from Earth, while the Small Magellanic Cloud is further away at about 200,000 light-years.
1350. Honey badgers are brave animals with thick skins and will attack snakes, bees, monitor lizards, leopards, and lions. When attacking the larger animals, they go for the scrotum.
1351. Cascade waterfalls descend over several rock steps and are generally quite safe to swim in.
1352. Air is made up of 21% oxygen, 78% nitrogen, and small amounts of other gases, including carbon dioxide, neon, and hydrogen.
1353. Antarctica was discovered before Uranus.
1354. One kilogram of uranium can produce the same energy as 1,500 tonnes of coal.
1355. The Eiffel Tower is taller in summer as the iron from which it is made heats up.
1356. The boiling point of liquids changes depending on the barometric pressure. For example, water boils at sea level at 212 deg F (100 deg C), and on top of Mt Everest, it boils at 154 deg F (68 deg C).
1357. A group of jellyfish is known as a bloom, swarm, or smack.

1358. An earthquake in the ocean can create tsunamis. The 2004 earthquake near Sumatra Indonesia triggered tsunamis that killed more than 200,000 people across 14 countries.
1359. Venus is closer to the Sun than Earth and takes 225 days to orbit the sun.
1360. Crocodiles are carnivores. They swallow small stones which help grind and digest the food in their stomach.
1361. NASA formed the Planetary Defense Coordination Office to monitor hazardous objects that come within 8 million km (5 million mi) of Earth.
1362. Between 6 Apollo crews, 385 kg (850 lb) of the moon was brought back to study.
1363. The James Webb Space Telescope is scheduled to launch in 2021, replacing the Hubble Space Telescope. It is set to orbit Earth 1.5 million km (2.4 million miles) above Earth.
1364. Eris' moon, Dysnomia, is named after Eris' daughter, the demon goddess of lawlessness, in Greek mythology.
1365. Almost identical solar eclipses happen every 18 years and 11 days. This period is called a saros cycle.
1366. There are over 3,000 octopus species in the world.
1367. Sulfur is necessary for life and is one of the top eight most abundant elements in a person.
1368. Lungfish have gills and lungs and can live out of water for many years.
1369. An adult usually has 32 teeth.
1370. Thunderstorms produce lightning.
1371. The Pinwheel Galaxy is also known as Messier 101, M101, or NGC 5457.
1372. The space shuttle was 56 m (184 ft) long and weighed 2 million kg (4.5 million lb).
1373. Giant storms occur on gas giants; for example, the Great

Red Spot on Jupiter is a gigantic storm about twice the Earth's size.

1374. The most aggressive species of penguin is the Chinstrap Penguin. They have a thin black band under their head, making them look like they're wearing a helmet.

1375. Uranus' thick atmosphere gets extremely dense the deeper you go.

1376. Astronauts live inside pressurized modules on The International Space Station (ISS).

1377. At room temperature, sulfur is a bright yellow flaky crystalline solid. It melts into a blood-red liquid and burns into a bright blue flame.

1378. Different animals have different receptors that sense different things to humans. For example, some snakes have organs that can detect infrared light. Bats and dolphins can pick up sonar sounds, and birds and bees can see ultraviolet light.

1379. When astronauts return from space, they often forget things fall due to Earth's gravity as they are used to objects floating around in space.

1380. A flash flood is an extreme river flood which occurs very quickly, mostly without warning or rain. This result from river blockages such as landslides and glaciers giving way with a sudden release of water that might have built up.

1381. At room temperature under standard conditions, hydrogen is a gas that has no taste, odor, or color. H_2 is the molecular formula of hydrogen gas.

1382. The space shuttle discovery grew roses, and their scent was then used for the smell of a perfume "Zen."

1383. Chronic or repetitive stress injuries occur if a person has played a certain sport for a long period. Tennis elbow, shin splints, and runner's knee are all examples of chronic injuries.

1384. The Honey bee, Killer bee, and Bumblebee are examples

of social bees that live in hives.

1385. Every 200 years, a lunar eclipse will happen three times in the same year.
1386. Scientists think that Venus rotates backward from an asteroid collision in the past.
1387. Eagles belong to the Accipitridae family.
1388. Four times Earth's size, Neptune is a large planet.
1389. The four stages of a mosquito's life cycle are egg, larva, pupa, and adult.
1390. An aurora is created by energetically charged particles colliding with atoms at high altitudes in our atmosphere. The plasma particles come from solar winds and collide with nitrogen and oxygen atoms in our atmosphere, releasing energy as aurora.
1391. Magma is made up of atoms and molecules of melted minerals as magma cools, the minerals from the rock.
1392. A flamingo's legs are often longer than their body - their backward bending knee is their ankle.
1393. More than 3,000 regions of star births are in the Pinwheel Galaxy's spiral arms, the most of all the spiral galaxies.
1394. One Mercury year equals 88 days on Earth.
1395. Although there are more than 4,000 different mineral types, only 30 are commonly found in Earth's crust.
1396. A hummingbird can fly backward.
1397. Mars has been given many names in the past by different civilizations. The ancient Babylonians called it Nergal, which means 'Star of death.' The Hebrews called it Ma'adim, meaning 'One who blushes' and the Greeks and Romans named it after their war gods.
1398. Cumulonimbus clouds most often produce lightning.
1399. Hair fibers can be round or irregular shaped. The hair fibers found in straight hair are round, while those in curly hair are irregular or oval-shaped.

1400. Helicopters can fly safely and with flexibility at the height of 500 feet (150 m). In contrast, special-purpose helicopters can fly up to 10,000 feet (3,048 m). At heights above 14,000 ft (4,267 m), passengers would need oxygen to survive.

1401. There are astronomical catalogs of nebulae such as the Barnard catalog, the Gum catalog, and the Sharpless catalog. They group astronomical objects by type, morphology, origin, detection, or method of discovery.

1402. Once the ISS reaches its end of use, it will use many modules for other purposes and space stations.

1403. There are different types of clouds, including cirrus, cumulus, and stratus.

1404. Graphene, the strongest material in the world, is a sheet of carbon only one atom thick. It conducts electricity better than copper and is ultralight and flexible.

1405. Otters are carnivores and eat meat, mostly marine creatures and frogs, small mammals, and birds.

1406. Mosquitoes transmit diseases such as malaria and dengue fever when they bite people and animals. They cause more deaths than any other animal on Earth.

1407. There are more than one trillion stars in the Andromeda Galaxy.

1408. The large thin ears of elephants contain lots of blood vessels to help regulate their temperature, particularly to cool them down in hot climates.

1409. On 18 March 1965, Alexei Leonov from Russia was the first person to perform a spacewalk on the Voskhod 2 mission.

1410. Earth takes 23 hours, 56 mins, and 4 seconds to rotate around its axis (not 24 hours), i.e., one day is 4 minutes shorter than we think.

1411. Saturn's moon Titan has slightly higher surface pressure than Earth.

1412. There are about 15 hedgehog species in the world.

1413. The temperature on the surface of Saturn is -139 deg C (-219 deg F).

1414. Satellites are programmed to avoid meteors, so they will not be hit and be destroyed.

1415. A toucan's favorite meal is a fruit; occasionally, it eats insects, smaller birds, and small lizards.

1416. Plants have been around on Earth for about 400 million years.

1417. A famous Albert Einstein quote: "I am enough of an artist to draw freely upon my imagination. Imagination is more important than knowledge. Knowledge is limited. Imagination encircles the world."

1418. Badgers are grouped as Melinae (Eurasian badgers), Mellivorinae (Honey badgers), and Taxideinae (American badgers). These groups make up 11 species of badger.

1419. Meerkats belong to the mongoose family and are the only one that doesn't have a bushy tail.

1420. Aristotle founded formal logic, pioneered zoology, and helped develop the scientific method.

1421. The Hubble Space Telescope can capture colorful images of space objects such as dying stars or other galaxies.

1422. Luna 1, the first space probe sent to the moon, missed it by about 5,000 km (3,000 mi).

1423. Clownfish have a very close relationship with sea anemone. Sea anemone benefits from clownfish who eat parasites and dead tentacles off the sea anemone attracts prey and gives them nutrients from their droppings. Clownfish benefit as they are protected from other prey by the sea anemone's venomous tentacles to which clownfish are immune.

1424. The inventor of the Super Soaker water squirt gun was

Lonnie Johnson, a NASA scientist.

1425. The slowest fish in the world is the dwarf seahorse, which swims at 0.01 mph (0.01 kph).

1426. When the core of a star collapses after a supernova explosion, neutron stars are created. They may be small (about 10 km (6 mi) in radius, but they can spin very fast at about 600 - 712 times per second.

1427. All spiders make silk, but not all spiders make webs.

1428. Uranium has three naturally occurring isotopes. The most stable is Uranium-238, which accounts for more than 99%. Uranium-235 and uranium-234 make up the rest.

1429. Titanium dioxide (as E171) is often added to food products such as chewing gum and marshmallows, to whiten them.

1430. The indigenous South Americans eat guinea pigs, sacrifice them to their Gods, and make medicine.

1431. Helicopter pilots need a constant control of the helicopter to hover in the same place and offset gusty winds.

1432. About once weekly, the sun rises and sets on Pluto.

1433. A baby alligator is called a hatchling. As soon as it is born, it can hunt for its food.

1434. The nearest cluster of stars in the solar system is the Beehive Cluster in Cancer constellation. The name was given as it resembled a swarm of bees.

1435. Leonardo da Vinci studied the human body's anatomy and created hundreds of drawings to explain his thinking. 'The Vitruvian Man' is a drawing that describes the relationship between human proportions and geometry.

1436. A human baby is born with about 300 bones. Some bones join together as we grow, and an adult ends up with about 206 bones in their body.

1437. All the planets together make up 0.14% of our solar

system, of which 99% would be from Jupiter, Neptune, Uranus, and Saturn, the gas giants.

1438. The core of Saturn and Jupiter are rich in iron.

1439. Charles Darwin's natural selection process often called the 'survival of the fittest, ' explains why organisms change and adapt over time. Organisms that have weaker genes or qualities do not survive. Over time, they are eliminated while those that survive to pass on their traits to the next generation and the future generations can adapt to their environment.

1440. Rocks are classified based on the way they are formed. Igneous rock is formed when magma cools and solidifies. Sedimentary rock is formed when sediment is deposited over time. Metamorphic rocks are formed under extreme pressure and heat.

1441. The heart's four chambers are the left atrium, right atrium, left ventricle, and right ventricle. Four valves make sure that blood only goes in one direction through the chambers.

1442. About 2,600 BC, Stonehenge was built and may have been the first space observatory every.

1443. A geneticist is a biologist who studies genetics.

1444. Aerospace, biomedical, chemical, civil, computer, electrical, mechanical, and software engineering are engineering branches.

1445. Trees can be deciduous or evergreen. A deciduous tree loses its leaves for part of the year, and an evergreen tree has left all year round.

1446. Weather radar shows the movement of precipitation, the type of precipitation, for example, rain or snow, and the weather forecast.

1447. Tulips are native to mountainous regions, so they need a period of cold dormancy. This is called vernalization.

1448. A full moon appears bright but reflects only about 7% of the sun's rays.

1449. Asteroids are blown-out comets! When the ice melts, only the solid material remains.

1450. The first telescopes invented were all refracting telescopes and used glass lenses.

1451. Nose plastic surgery is called rhinoplasty.

1452. The densest planet in the Solar System is Earth.

1453. Germany is closing down all their nuclear power plants and moving towards fossil fuels and renewable energy sources.

1454. There are about 30 clownfish species. They come in different colors - pink, red, yellow, black, brown, and multi-colored.

1455. A hamster has a short tail, stubby legs, and small ears.

1456. When mating, capuchin monkeys urinate on their hands and then rub it on their fur to attract females.

1457. The polar ice caps on Mars are made up of frozen carbon dioxide (dry ice).

1458. Otters love playing. The slide-off embankments into the water, chase their tails and wrestle with each other.

1459. You can find pure elemental sulfur near hot springs and volcanic areas.

1460. On average, a lunar eclipse happens 2 to 3 times a year.

1461. Guinea pigs, also known as cavies, are domesticated rodents.

1462. It can take about an hour for total daylight to come back after a total solar eclipse.

1463. The Whirlpool Galaxy is about 43% of the size of the Milky Way.

1464. Each type of plastic has an identification code or number. Polyethylene (PET), which is used to make plastic bottles and other things, is number 1. Polyvinyl chloride (PVC) is number 3 and used for pipes, hoses, medical devices, and plumbing parts.

1465. Copernicus suggested that the sun was the center of the universe after Europa and three other Galilean moons, Lo, Ganymede, and Callisto, were discovered.
1466. A magnet is an object that can pull another object towards it.
1467. Polar bears are the top of their food chain in the Arctic! There are no other predators except other polar bears!
1468. On 6 March 2009, NASA named a space mission after Johannes Kepler, a famous astronomer. The Kepler mission used a high tech space telescope to look for planets like Earth in our solar system.
1469. Cygnus, the Swan constellation, is about 1,000,000 times bigger than the sun and is the biggest star in our universe.
1470. Computer programs carry out instructions such as adding numbers together.
1471. A camel has oval-shaped red blood cells, which helps blood flow when they haven't eaten for long periods.
1472. Squirrels can run as fast as 20 mph (32 kph).
1473. Polar bears live in the Arctic, near the North Pole. They live in five countries - Alaska, Canada, Norway, Russia, and Greenland.
1474. A nuclear submarine can stay underwater for weeks because the nuclear generator doesn't require oxygen like a diesel engine in a diesel submarine.
1475. Lb', the abbreviation for pound, means 'balance' from Libra, an astrology sign.
1476. In 1919, Ernest Rutherford transformed nitrogen atoms into oxygen atoms by bombarding nitrogen with alpha particles. This was the first deliberate transformation of one element into another.
1477. All the 12 people who have walked on the moon have said moon dust smells like gunpowder.
1478. The driest place on Earth is the Atacama Desert in South America.

1479. A group of meerkats is called a mob, gang, or clan.
1480. Sea otters always carry a favorite stone with them.
1481. For a star or an object to leave the Milky Way, it must have enormous energy and speed.
1482. Depending on how complex a computer program is, many programmers can develop the software program.
1483. Louis Pasteur established the first Pasteur Institute in France, dedicated to researching health and infectious diseases. There are now 32 Pasteur Institutes in 25 countries across the world.
1484. Paper wasps or Polistes use their sense of smell and eyesight to seek out caterpillar prey.
1485. The images on a television screen refresh so fast that it looks like smooth movements.
1486. A lunar eclipse lasts longer than a solar eclipse.
1487. The full-body swimsuit was very popular in the 2008 Olympics, where 23 world records were broken by swimmers who wore the suits. The swimsuit was scientifically designed by NASA and Speedo and made with ultrasonically welded seams, which reduced the drag in the water. As not all athletes wore the suits, they were banned as they gave the swimmer who did wear them more.
1488. High-speed Eurostar passenger trains travel at speeds of up to 99 mph (160 kph) through the underwater Channel Tunnel that connects England to France.
1489. Red blood cells move oxygen around your body.
1490. Charge coins and cards were used before the first credit card launch by the Bank of America. The BankAmericard was first launched in September 1958. In 1966 the Barclaycard became the first credit card to be launched outside the USA in the United Kingdom.
1491. Alexander Graham Bell had other inventions besides his telephone. One of them was an electromagnet, which he

invented to locate bullets in war veteran's bodies. He used it to try and find the bullet in President James Garfield after he was shot.

1492. Rabbits only eat plants.
1493. To keep their wings flapping, hummingbirds visit thousands of flowers every day to drink enough nectar for their metabolism. They can drink up to 10,000 calories of nectar every day.
1494. Rhinos are herbivores which means that they eat plants.
1495. The IAU accepted the name Eris on 13 September 2006.
1496. The only spacecraft to visit the Pluto system is the NASA spacecraft, New Horizons.
1497. Large amounts of hydrogen are found in giant gas planets and stars, powering stars through fusion reactions.
1498. Zinc can be recycled.
1499. A flood is a temporary covering of normally dry land by water.
1500. The scientific name for sunflower is Helianthus. It is the only flower with 'flower' in its name.
1501. From our viewpoint on Earth, Jupiter seems to move slowly in the sky, taking months to move from one constellation to the next.
1502. After Jupiter (63 moons) and Saturn (61 moons), Uranus has the most number of moons (27 moons).
1503. A person's hair has a lifespan of between two to seven years.
1504. 99% of the human body is made up of hydrogen, nitrogen, carbon, and oxygen. The hydrogen atoms came from the Big Bang, and the nitrogen, carbon, and oxygen were made from burning stars.
1505. More comets impact Jupiter than any other planet in our solar system.
1506. You can hear thunder as a low rumble or a loud cracking noise.

1507. Eris' (dwarf planet) temperature is about -217 to -242 degrees C (-359 to -405 degrees F).
1508. An adult male sheep is called a ram.
1509. Neptune's thin rings comprise ice particles and dust, possibly covered with a carbon type substance.
1510. A black hole absorbs light and everything else in space.
1511. The largest hurricane is Typhoon Tip, which occurred in the northwest Pacific in 1979. It was 1,379 miles (2,220 km) in diameter, almost half the width of the USA.
1512. Scientists believe that the universe that we can observe is about 13.8 billion years old.
1513. Uranus is pronounced 'YOU-ra-nus' not 'YOUR-anus.'
1514. Passenger trains with self-propelled carriages are more energy-efficient than ones with a single locomotive at the front.
1515. Lemons, which are high in vitamin C, can prevent scurvy (vitamin C deficiency). Scurvy is common with sailors who don't have enough fruit and vegetables when they're at sea for long periods. The British Navy still carries enough lemons to give their sailors lemon juice per day to prevent scurvy.
1516. A baby hedgehog is a hoglet.
1517. A toad can excrete poison from their skin if they are being threatened. Some species are more toxic than others.
1518. Dogs are often trained to compete in shows of agility, obedience, racing, and sled pulling.
1519. Only telescopes that detect radio waves, infrared light, and x-rays can study the Milky Way as optical telescopes can't see through the dense gas and dust.
1520. The shape of a flamingo's beak helps them filter mud and silt from their food. They dig the mud with their feet and then scoop up food with their beak.

1521. Magnesium's good mechanical and electrical properties make it a preferred material for electronic devices.
1522. Sheep, antelope, cattle, muskoxen, and goats are all mammals and even-toed ungulates. Their hooves are split into two toes.
1523. As of December 2019, Saturn has 53 confirmed moons and 29 awaiting more information to be verified. If all of them are approved, Saturn will have the largest moons relating to one planet in our solar system.
1524. To the Greeks, the Milky Way was known as the Milky Circle. They believed that the goddess Hera was surprised to find another woman suckling Hercules while she slept.
1525. The Magellanic Clouds belong to the Local Group and orbits the Milky Way.
1526. Stalactites and stalagmites are a build-up of calcite.
1527. It's impossible to have thunder without lightning, but you can have lightning without thunder as the thunder may be too far away for you to hear.
1528. A specific type of green algae, Trichophilus, often grows on sloth fur. This helps them camouflage from predators.
1529. In New York, the Brooklyn Bridge was the longest suspension bridge in the world until 1903 when the Williamsburg Bridge was built 4.5 feet (1.3 m) longer. The Williamsburg Bridge was the first suspension bridge over 1,000 ft (305 m) to have steel towers.
1530. The speed of wind in a tornado is usually less than 100 mph (161 kph).
1531. Silver is the best reflector of visible light and often used to make mirrors.
1532. Kangaroos only live in Australia.
1533. The oldest standing stone segmental arch bridge is the Zhaozhou Bridge in China. It was built over 1400 years ago in the year 605 AD.

1534. Spiders are mostly not venomous, and death from spider bites are rare.
1535. Nikola Tesla had a photographic memory.
1536. Stephen Hawking was diagnosed with amyotrophic lateral sclerosis or Gehrig's disease when he was 21. This affected his ability to voluntarily control his muscles and reduced his ability to move and speak over time.
1537. Ledge (aka classical or curtain) waterfalls descend vertically over a cliff and maintain partial contact.
1538. Scientists believe that planting lots of trees can help tackle climate change by removing CO2 from the air. Trees breathe in carbon dioxide and breathe out oxygen. People breathe in oxygen and breathe out CO2.
1539. A rhinoceros can weigh more than 2,200 lb (1,000 kg).
1540. The rate of skin cancers increases because the atmosphere's ozone layer is decreasing and unable to absorb the ultraviolet rays from the sun.
1541. In its pure elemental form and its sulfate form, sulfur is not toxic. Its compounds, carbon disulfide, hydrogen sulfide, and sulfur dioxide, however, are toxic.
1542. All reptiles, insects, arachnids, amphibians, and fish are cold-blooded.
1543. As of 2020, Germany has had 108 Nobel Prize winners. Albert Einstein received the Prize for physics in 1921.
1544. The Kuiper Belt contains frozen gases, including methane, ammonia, nitrogen, and water.
1545. Scientists believe Olympus Mars, a volcano on Mars that is billions of years old, is still active.
1546. Mice are nocturnal animals and become active at night.
1547. Radon is a radioactive gas that has no color, odor, or taste.
1548. Scientists believe that Mars is probably the most 'liveable' planet in our solar system.
1549. Millions of meteors enter the Earth's atmosphere every day.

1550. Twenty-two thousand workers helped build the Taj Mahal in India from white marble. It took 17 years to complete.
1551. The Andromeda and Milky Way galaxies may interact with the Triangulum Galaxy. It may break it apart, turning it into an even larger elliptical galaxy!
1552. Penguins can lower their heartbeat to five beats per minute to save oxygen from staying underwater longer when they dive for food.
1553. Even though he is well known for his work in nuclear physics, Ernest Rutherford was awarded the 1908 Nobel Prize in Chemistry "for his investigations into the disintegration of the elements, and the chemistry of radioactive substances."
1554. A whale often looks like it's smiling. This is because the blubber in their head gives their lower lip an arch, which stops their face muscles from reaching the water's surface.
1555. Horses, donkeys, asses, and zebras are all from the same Equidae family.
1556. A 50 kg (110 lb) person on Earth would weigh 1.5 kg (3.3 lb) on Charon. A 50 kg (110 lb) on Charon would weigh 1,751 kg (3,853 lb) on Earth.
1557. Sudan, Africa, has many Nubian pyramids which are smaller and steeper than the Egyptian pyramids.
1558. Astronaut means 'star sailor.'
1559. Hippos have very thick skin, about 2 in (6 cm) thick, which protects them from predators.
1560. Cattle have one stomach with four compartments that break down their food.
1561. A snowboarder and ice skater glide on a thin layer of water created when their board or skates melts the surface beneath them.
1562. The 17 species of hedgehog are found in Europe, Asia,

Africa, and New Zealand.

1563. Chlorine is the first gas chemical to be used in war.

1564. NASA hopes a human-crewed mission to Callisto may be possible in the 2040s.

1565. The descent module of Mars 2, a space probe launched by the Soviet Union in 1971, separated from the orbiter module about 4.5 hours before it reached Mars. The descent module malfunctioned and crashed, becoming the first human-made object to touch Mars.

1566. Mars' moons are named after the twin gods for Panic and Fear, who fought with Mars.

1567. There are four chemical groups of carbohydrates - monosaccharides and disaccharides (simple carbohydrates) and oligosaccharides and polysaccharides (complex carbohydrates).

1568. Supernovas can be created by nuclear reactions or when stars collapse after running out of fuel.

1569. Some marsupials, such as the short-tailed opossum, don't have pouches.

1570. Going to the center of our Milky Way galaxy would take longer than humans have existed on Earth!

1571. Scientists believe algebra, the Ancient Egyptians used arithmetic and geometry about the year 3000 BC/

1572. Mice and rats are different rodents. A mouse has large floppy ears, long thin hairy tail, and a triangular-shaped nose. A rat is bigger than a mouse, can be dark grey or black in color, and their tail usually has no hair.

1573. Both Buzz Aldrin and Neil Armstrong were initially quarantined for 21 days when they returned from the moon so that they didn't bring any disease back to Earth. At the time, astronomers didn't know there was no life on the moon.

1574. Copper was named from the Latin word for Cyprus' Cuprum' where the ancient Romans mined their copper.

1575. Dinosaurs are extinct, so the only way to learn about them is by studying fossils. Fossils are what's left of animals, plants and their parts from a past geologic age.
1576. Some people believe that the Wise Men saw Halley's Comet and not the Star of Bethlehem when Jesus was born.
1577. The largest tree in the world is the Giant Sequoia in California's Sequoia National Park. It is about 2,000 years old and has a diameter of 25 feet (7.7 m), and it is 275 feet (83.8 m) tall. Many scientists believe it is the largest living organism in the world.
1578. Some astronomers think that there were many big bangs in the past before the one we know about, and the only reason we're here is that we could exist it this universe!
1579. Chlorine is the second lightest halogen gas. Fluorine is the first.
1580. Polar bears have big paws, up to 11.8 in (30 cm) wide to walk on thin ice.
1581. Callisto, Jupiter's second-largest moon, has an interior ocean made of water and ammonia. Its surface comprises water and carbon dioxide ice, rocks, and silicate dust and hydrocarbon compounds.
1582. About one septillion snow crystals drop from the sky every winter.
1583. Jaguars are strong swimmers.
1584. Earth's core has enough gold to cover the entire surface of the planet.
1585. Alexander Graham Bell's father and grandfather were both speech therapists.
1586. Male mosquitoes live up to 5 days. Females can live up to 2 months, depending on their species and if a predator comes along.
1587. The dwarf planets, Eris and Pluto, are both smaller than Earth's moon.

1588. Sheep were one of the first animals to be domesticated.
1589. A person loses 50 - 100 strands of hair every day.
1590. Uranus is named after the Greek god Ouranos. All other planets are named after Roman gods.
1591. Flying foxes and Old World fruit bats belong to the group of bats called megabats. Flying foxes are the largest bats.
1592. Ernest Rutherford had 11 siblings.
1593. Although not bones, scientists include our teeth as part of our skeletal system.
1594. Anti-venom is used to treat venomous snake bites.
1595. Gold looks transparent when it is made into a very thin sheet.
1596. 2002 AA29 is one of Earth's co-orbital satellites with a diameter of 60 meters (196 feet) and makes a horseshoe-shaped orbit around Earth. It gets closer to our planet every 95 years and maybe a good space mission in the future.
1597. Cattle have about 22,000 genes, 80% of which are shared with humans. They share about 1,000 genes with dogs and rodents.
1598. The surface of the sun is 11,990 times bigger than Earth's.
1599. When a cat hunts, it makes very little noise and can sneak up on their prey as they can put their back paws where their front paws were.
1600. Hippos are semi-aquatic mammals, spending time in water and on land.
1601. A lion can live in the wild for about 12 years. They rest up to 20 hours every day.
1602. Television stations sell blocks of broadcasting time to advertisers to fund their programs.
1603. Snakes are carnivores and only eat meat.
1604. The gravitational pull of the moon creates our tides.
1605. There are over 28,000 butterfly species in the world.

1606. The jaguar was used as a symbol of strength by the Maya and Aztecs.
1607. TV broadcasts are transmitted at specific frequencies, like radio.
1608. Most insects come from eggs.
1609. Koalas only eat leaves from 40 - 50 types of eucalypt trees.
1610. Shin splints, muscle cramps, tennis and golf elbows, and sprained ankles are common sports injuries.
1611. Johannes Kepler, the astronomer, became interested in astronomy when he was very young, more so after he saw the Great comet of 1577 and a lunar eclipse in 1580.
1612. Peacocks like to sit on top of buildings and trees, but they build their nests on the ground.
1613. Hair grows everywhere except on your palms (hands), soles (feet), and lip.
1614. Crabs can walk forwards, but they're much faster walking sideways.
1615. A bumblebee's buzzing noise is not just the flapping of their wings but also the vibration of their wing muscles, which helps shake the pollen off flowers onto the bee's body.
1616. In January 2020, scientists identified a fossil of a scorpion that lived 437 million years ago. They believe the animal, which is also the oldest known scorpion, could have lived in oceans and land. This gives them information on how an animal can transition to living only on land.
1617. Albert Einstein is famous for his theory of relativity $E = mc^2$ (the energy of a system is equal to its mass multiplied by light squared).
1618. When the moon is in the New Moon phase, it doesn't show in the sky (no moon) as the sun is shining on the other side.
1619. There are more than 100 rose species in the world. Most

of the flowers have five petals or a multiple of 5 except the species 'Rosa sericea, ' which has four.

1620. Black leopards have dark spots and are sometimes confused with panthers.

1621. A person can hold an alligator's jaws shut with their own hands as the muscles that open the jaw of an alligator are very weak.

1622. In ancient times, Venus had different names. The Egyptians referred to it as Bonou, which means 'bird,' to the Chinese it was the Tai-pe or 'the beautiful white one' and to the Chaldeans, 'the bright torch of heaven.'

1623. Protons and neutrons stick together close to an atom's nucleus while the electrons spin around the nucleus. The positive charge of protons stops the negatively charged electrons from spinning away.

1624. Ernest Rutherford is a New Zealand born British scientist famous for his work in radioactivity. He is often called the Father of nuclear physics.

1625. Nitinol is a nickel-titanium alloy that can remember its previous shape. You can bend it (at very high temperatures), then cool it and make a shape. When you reheat it, it goes back to its original shape.

1626. The gravity on Mars is about 37% of the Earth's to jump three times higher on Mars.

1627. Asteroids are also known as minor planets or planetoids.

1628. Earth only has one natural satellite, the moon.

1629. Neptune's rings are not complete, so they are often called 'arcs.'

1630. Scientists have found fossils that show that the ancient platypuses were twice as large as the platypus of today.

1631. Pigeons have amazing memories.

1632. The majority of meteors are the size of a pebble.

1633. Earth only has one moon.

1634. Louis Pasteur, the French chemist, and microbiologist are most famous for discovering vaccinations, pasteurization, and proving that germs cause disease.

1635. Our moon's diameter is 3,475 km (2,159 mi), four times smaller than Earth's diameter.
1636. The Sombrero Galaxy is a lenticular (lens-shaped) galaxy in the Virgo constellation.
1637. The Andromeda Galaxy is named after Andromeda, the mythological princess.
1638. The Spitzer Space Telescope was predicted to survive around 2.5 years in space, but it lasted for more than 11 years!
1639. Venus's temperature is boiling and can go up to 471 degrees C (879 degrees F).
1640. Just like Pluto, Charon takes 248 years to orbit the sun.
1641. An artificial satellite has two important parts - the antenna to send and receive information and a power source, like a battery or a solar panel.
1642. Parrots can copy sounds around them, including human words.
1643. As there is no gravity on the International Space Station, astronauts can grow about 3% taller within six months. When they return to Earth, it takes a few months to shrink back to their original height.
1644. The ancient Babylonians and Far East astronomers first observed Saturn.
1645. The northern pygmy owl has black feathers on the back of their head that looks like eyes. This helps them scare predators away.
1646. Our eardrums vibrate in the same way as the vibration source, which lets us hear different sounds.
1647. Penguins molt once a year. Until they grow back their feathers, which can take 2 -3 weeks, they cannot swim or catch food, so they eat lots of food before they shed their feathers to last them until they can swim again.

1648. The air that forms a tornado must be cold but not too cold. It should be a few degrees colder than the surrounding air.
1649. The Spanish telescope, Gran Telescopio Canarias is the largest reflecting telescope in the world.
1650. A person's nose and ear grow until the day they die.
1651. There were many flyby missions to Jupiter. One orbited the planet successfully from 1995 to 2002.
1652. At birth, a giant panda cub weighs about 5 oz (150 grams).
1653. The fifth brightest object in our solar system is Saturn.
1654. Our solar system consists of the sun, planets and dwarf planets, moons, asteroids and comets, and stars.
1655. Beavers move slowly on land, but they are good swimmers.
1656. When the gases and dust from a nebula become very big, it starts to collapse due to their strong gravity. This causes the material to heat up at the center of the nebula. The hot center is the beginning of a new star.
1657. Dogs have a better sense of smell than people, up to 10,000 or 1,000,000 times better! This is because they have 100 million receptors in their nose compared with our 6 million. The part of their brain devoted to analyzing smells is 40 times bigger than the same part in our brain.
1658. There are over 10,000 different domesticated sheep species in the world.
1659. One of Deimos' largest craters with a diameter of 1,609 km (1,000 mi) is named Swift. It was named after the author of the book Gulliver's Travels, Jonathan Swift. Jonathan wrote about Mars' two moons 151 years before they were discovered!
1660. The moon is 384 403 kilometers (238 857 miles) from Earth.

1661. A person would weigh the lightest on Pluto and heaviest on Jupiter.
1662. The Statue of Liberty is made up of more than 179,000 lb (81,000 kg) of copper.
1663. Scorpions belong to the Arachnida family, along with spiders, mites, and ticks.
1664. Perihelion is the closest point in a comet's orbit to the sun, while aphelion is the furthest point.
1665. As of 2013, there have been 38 expeditions to the ISS. An expedition may last a maximum of six months. Early expeditions had crews of 3 people. This was reduced to teams of 2 for safety. However, the crew numbers now regularly reach six people.
1666. Meerkats can see predators from 980 feet (300 m) away due to their strong eyesight.
1667. Sunflowers emit toxins that stop the growth of other plants nearby and can also kill them.
1668. There are several hypotheses about how Phobos and Deimos, Mars two moons, came about. Some scientists think that they came from the asteroid belt and Jupiter's gravity pushed them into orbit around Mars. A second hypothesis is that they were formed by dust and rock drew together by gravity as satellites around Mars.
1669. Sherlock Holmes used forensic science to investigate crimes.
1670. As of 2013, the tallest dam in the world is the Jinping-I dam in China. It is a concrete arch dam measuring 1,001 ft (305 m) high.
1671. The famous artist and scientist, Leonardo da Vinci, was ambidextrous. He could write and draw with both hands simultaneously, and he wrote words backward (from right to left), so you need a mirror to read them.
1672. The temperature of Earth's core is about 4,300 degrees C (7,772 degrees F).

1673. Galileo also invented the pendulum clock, a pump, the compass (sector), and the thermometer on top of his famous telescopes and space discoveries.
1674. Only female bees can sting - the workers and the queen bees.
1675. When Earth comes between the sun and the moon, a lunar eclipse occurs. The Earth's shadow covers all or part of the moon's surface.
1676. Different animals can see different lights; for example, many insects can see ultraviolet light.
1677. The ISS is arguably the single item most expensive ever built. As of 2010, the station's cost is estimated to be $150 billion.
1678. Neptune has thin wispy type clouds that cover the planet.
1679. Homer wrote about Orion, Bootes, and Ursa Major constellations in his poem Illiad and the Odyssey in the 8th century BC.
1680. A mother kangaroo can suckle two joeys that have been born at different times, and give them the different nutrients that they need to grow and develop.
1681. The largest dust storms in the solar system are on Mars.
1682. Most metals are solids and good conductors of electricity and heat.
1683. The titanic was powered by steam engines.
1684. The Messier 87 elliptical Galaxy is located in the constellation Virgo.
1685. Since the 1800s, guinea pigs have been used in scientific experiments. It is more common these days for research laboratories to use mice and rats in experiments.
1686. Bats live on all continents except Antarctica.
1687. Michael Faraday was a self-taught scientist. At the age of 14, he started an apprenticeship as a bookbinder, but he was very interested in chemistry. In 1812, he wrote to a

chemist, Sir Humphry Davy, and asked to be his assistant. Davy thought Faraday was very bold as he had never studied science or even been to university. Davy arranged for Faraday to work running the chemistry lab at the Royal Institution. This is where it all started.

1688. The international standard for measuring one kilogram or 2.2 lbs came from the weight of one chunk of platinum in the 1880s.

1689. It also rains on the other planets of our Solar System, but it may not rainwater! On Venus, it rains sulfuric acid, and the heat of the planet evaporates it before it hits the ground.

1690. An octopus squirts a black ink at its predators to try and getaway.

1691. Our teeth are covered by enamel, which protects them from tooth decay. Teeth enamel is the hardest mineral in our body, harder than bone.

1692. A baby duckling can fly by the age of 2 months.

1693. The most common type of primary cave is a lava tube, formed when hot lava continues to flow under lava on the surface that has cooled and hardened.

1694. Deimos (Mars moon) has an irregular shape and not round like the other moons.

1695. Calcium means lime, from the Latin word calx.

1696. The longest structure built by people is the Great Wall of China. It was built to protect against invasions from the north.

1697. The human ear comprises four main parts: the outer ear, eardrum, middle ear, and inner ear. The outer ear picks up sound waves (or vibrations), which travels down to the eardrum. The middle ear picks up the eardrum's vibrations and sends them to the cochlea in the inner ear. The inner ear changes the sound waves to electrical impulses that travel to the brain via the auditory nerve. The brain translates the impulses as sound.

1698. There are over 650 skeletal muscles in the body.
1699. Eagles can see five basic colors and ultraviolet light.
1700. A desert is an area that receives less than 16 in (40 cm) of rain in a year.
1701. Most of Antarctica is covered in ice that is more than 1 mile (1.6 km) thick.
1702. Some badger burrows or setts are hundreds of years old and used by generations of badgers.
1703. Gas giants used to refer to all giant planets.
1704. The surface of Europa, Jupiter's moon, is about 20 to 280 million years old, even though it is about 4.5 billion years old.
1705. There have been 56 uncrewed missions to Mars since 1960, of which only 26 have been successful.
1706. The electric power system on the ISS is connected by more than eight miles of wire.
1707. Fruit flies sent along with corn seeds were the first living things sent to space in 1947.
1708. A sonic boom is usually heard seconds after seeing the meteor, but only if the meteor is making a sound.
1709. A grasshopper's eardrum is located in their belly. It's protected by their wings and lets them hear the songs of other grasshoppers.
1710. Between 1984 and 2004, Olympic athletes were not allowed to drink large amounts of coffee (8 espressos in a few hours) as the caffeine in coffee was known to enhance performance.
1711. Zebras have strong eyesight and hearing, which helps them escape from predators.
1712. A toucan has a long tongue, up to 6 in (15 cm) to help it throw the food in its beak down its throat.
1713. You can tell the age of a tree by the number of rings in its

bark.

1714. Triton keeps the same face towards Neptune as it rotates on its axis and orbits the planet.
1715. Volcanoes can be found on the ocean floor and under ice caps!
1716. Flamingos generally don't migrate unless there are changes in their environment.
1717. Crocodiles can survive for months without eating.
1718. The Perseids is a large meteor shower that can be seen in the northern hemisphere about August every year. The Perseids contains rocks from the Swift Tuttle comet.
1719. Vostok Station in Antarctica holds the world record for the coldest temperature recorded at -128.6 deg F (-89.2 deg C) in 1983
1720. The temperature inside a hot air balloon is about 248 deg F (120 deg C). The balloon's envelope or top is made from a nylon material that melts at 446 deg F (230 deg C).
1721. Charles Darwin, Michael Faraday, Isaac Newton, and Stephen Hawking are all famous scientists from England.
1722. To find their way around the sky, astronomers use the constellations, such as Orion, the zodiac signs, and Ursa Major, to guide them.
1723. Deer shed their antlers every year and grow new ones.
1724. Kangaroos are social animals and live in groups called mobs, troops, or courts.
1725. The tentacle of a jellyfish contains thousands of cells called cnidoblasts, which hold the stingers.
1726. There are more than 3,500 mosquito species in the world.
1727. Massage used to be and still is a common treatment for muscle soreness. Newer technologies, such as hyperbaric chambers and ice baths, are often used now to improve healing and reduce inflammation.

1728. The compound uranium was named after the planet Uranus.
1729. A peacock's feathers look the best when it is 5 or 6 years old.
1730. Chameleon's can see ultraviolet light.
1731. Your stomach is lined with a thick layer of mucus to protect it from the acid produced to digest food and kill bacteria.
1732. Every day, many chemical reactions occur at homes such as cooking an egg or burning wood.
1733. The Local Group is a cluster of about 30 galaxies.
1734. Not every turtle can pull its head and feet into its shell. The sea turtle no longer has this ability.
1735. The orange is a hybrid of mandarin and pomelo.
1736. Gravity is the attraction of objects to each other. Objects with large mass have high amounts of gravity.
1737. Dogs can live up to 14 human years.
1738. A magnet creates a magnetic field around it that is invisible to the naked eye. Iron filings can be used to show magnetic fields.
1739. Ceres is considered not to have an atmosphere. However, a Herschel space telescope in 2014 showed that it might have water vapor in its atmosphere. This could be explained by sporadic ice being ejected by small impacts.
1740. An elliptical galaxy is a group of stars that bunch together to form an oval shape, a stretched out and elongated circle.
1741. The world's tallest twin towers, measuring 1,482 feet (451.8 m) is the Petronas Towers in Kuala Lumpur, Malaysia.
1742. Mercury has no moons or rings.
1743. About 20,000 species of bees exist in the world.
1744. The platypus is a mammal with a bill like a duck, a tail like a beaver, furs like an otter, and webbed feet.

1745. Cosmonaut means 'universe sailor' and refers to an astronaut from Russia.
1746. The word 'geyser' comes from an Icelandic word meaning to 'gush'.
1747. Volcanic eruptions can reflect radiation from the sun, resulting in the dropping of temperature by half a degree.
1748. Jupiter's magnetic field is 20,000 times stronger than Earth's magnetic field.
1749. Sunflowers have been used for food, medicine, oil, and dyes.
1750. Pluto has the same age as the solar system, i.e., 4.6 billion years.
1751. According to scientists, the moon was used as a calendar 6,000 years ago.
1752. The large intestine is the final stage of your digestive system. It absorbs water from the food that was not digested and passed the waste from your body.
1753. On the Mohs scale of mineral hardness, where 1 is the softest (talc), and ten is the hardest, diamond is 10.
1754. Mercury is named after the Roman messenger to the gods.
1755. Uranium has an atomic number of 92.
1756. A blizzard is a snowstorm with very strong winds.
1757. All turtles lay eggs to reproduce.
1758. Ganymede's (one of Jupiter's moons) temperature during the day ranges from -113 to -183 degrees C (-171 to -297degrees F).
1759. Alligators and crocodiles are relatives, but they are not the same reptile.
1760. Glaciology is the study of glaciers.
1761. Bald eagles build large nests to lay their eggs. The largest nest recorded measured 9.5 feet (2.9 meters) wide and20 feet (6.1 m) deep.
1762. Most owls are nocturnal creatures and hunt at night. The

northern hawk-owl and northern pygmy owl hunts during the day. Other owls such as the snowy owl may be active during the day, depending on the season and food availability.

1763. The Whirlpool Galaxy and its companion, M51b, are connected by a dust and gas bridge as they merge.

1764. The fifth most abundant element in the universe is neon, after hydrogen, helium, oxygen, and carbon. It only makes up 0.0018% of the Earth's atmosphere and is rare.

1765. On 31 October 2000, the first ISS crew mission called 'Expedition 1' was launched on a Russian Soyuz. On 2 November 2000, the 3 Russian cosmonauts docked in and entered the ISS. Since then, the space station has been occupied continuously, making it the most extended continuous human presence in space.

1766. You can tell if a giraffe is male or female by their horns. A female giraffe has smaller horns covered with hair at the top.

1767. Bald eagles are carnivores and only eat meat, mainly fish.

1768. Because of its ability to withstand very high temperatures, its resistance to oxidation and corrosion, nickel is the metal used to make 'superalloys.'

1769. Steam, diesel, and electricity can all power trains. Ropes, horses, and gravity pulled early trains.

1770. The Channel Tunnel is a rail tunnel 31.4 miles (50.5 km) long under the English Channel. It is 246 feet (75 m) deep at its lowest point under the sea and connects with France.

1771. Scientists have observed water trickling down Mars' crater walls and cliffs, which indicate that there may be water on Mars. As the water is not frozen, it is likely to be salty.

1772. NASA believes the astronauts on the first 1986 Challenger trip may have survived two minutes after it exploded. However, they would have then died when the spacecraft fell into the Atlantic Ocean at a speed of 321 kph (200 mph).

1773. A nebula is a giant cloud of dust and gas in space formed by the explosion of a dying star, such as a supernova, or where new stars are being created.
1774. Supernovas are one of the most violent naturally occurring phenomenons in outer space.
1775. A stingray defends itself with the venomous stingers on its tail.
1776. There are nearly 2,000 Scorpion species in the world. Only 30 - 40 have venom strong enough to kill a person.
1777. Elon Musk named the Tesla electric car after Nikola Tesla, the famous inventor.
1778. A beetle has two sets of wings. The elytra are the outer set of hard wings and protect the soft wings underneath, which are used for flying.
1779. There is no center of the universe!
1780. The Triangulum Galaxy is a spiral galaxy without a central bar. It has loosely wound arms that are attached to its galactic core.
1781. Stingrays have good eyesight, hearing, and touch. They also use their electrosenses for hunting for food.
1782. The wrinkles are seen on the surface of Mercury, ranging up to 1.6 km (1 mi) high and hundreds of kilometers or miles long, are called Lobate Scarps.
1783. More than half of the lead produced is used in lead-acid car batteries.
1784. Makemake travels through the Kuiper Belt like all the dwarf planets except for Ceres.
1785. Some lizards can live up to 50 years.
1786. Rain is a very important part of the water cycle. Moisture from oceans evaporates condenses in clouds, which then precipitates back to the ground as rain. The water on the

ground will run back into oceans and rivers, and the cycle starts again.

1787. Earth has enormous volcanoes. However, Mars has the largest known volcano in our solar system! It's called Olympus Mons and is 737 mi (600 km) wide and 13 mi (21 km) high.
1788. About 250 venomous snake species can kill a human with a single bite.
1789. Ceres is the smallest dwarf planet and the first to be discovered and visited by a spacecraft. It is found in the other Solar System and classified as an asteroid and a dwarf planet.
1790. An original British pound weighed a pound of silver.
1791. Magnesium is a light, strong silvery-white metal that tarnishes a bit when it comes into contact with air.
1792. Leonardo da Vinci created the first designs for a humanoid robot in 1495.
1793. Bees have two stomachs - one to digest their food and store honey for the colony.
1794. Meteoroids that fly into Earth's atmosphere and then bounce out again are called Earth grazing fireballs.
1795. Mount Rushmore is a sculpture carved into the side of a mountain by dynamite and over 400 workers. It took 14 years to carve 4 US presidents - George Washington, Thomas Jefferson, Theodore Roosevelt, and Abraham Lincoln.
1796. The largest crater on the moon that we can see from Earth, with a 294 km (183 mi) diameter, is the Bailly Crater.
1797. The large bill of a toucan helps it to stay cool and feed easily in one spot.
1798. Your tongue has eight muscles responsible for taste, chewing, swallowing, speaking, and clearing your mouth.

1799. There are more than 30,000 species of fish in the world. Scientists are discovering more and more.
1800. Based on a fossil, scientists believe octopi have been around for more than 296 million years!
1801. Titanium can be found in meterorites, our sun and the stars.
1802. Venus has no moons or rings.
1803. A male giraffe will "neck" with another male giraffe to fight over female giraffes.
1804. Lead has an atomic number of 82.
1805. Your heart beats about 100,000 times a day.
1806. Seals are now protected by international law. Their numbers were decreasing previously from being hunted for their meat, blubber, and fur.
1807. The four moons of Pluto are Nix (the Greek goddess of night and darkness), Charon (ferryman of Hades), Hydra (the nine-headed serpent who guards Hades) and S/2011 P 1 (named after the year it was found).
1808. Pluto is located on average 5,906,380,000 km (3,670,050,000 mi) from the Sun.
1809. You dream during the Rapid Eye Movement (REM) stage of your sleep.
1810. A crystal is formed when liquids cool and harden over time. Quartz is an example.
1811. There is strong evidence that Ganymede (one of Jupiter's moons) has an underground ocean covered by a very thick layer of ice (about 800 km or 497 miles thick) and a rock shell.
1812. Twice daily, Phobos, one of Mars' moons, rises in the west and sets in the east.
1813. Mosquitoes hatch from eggs. Like all other insects, they go through four lifecycles - egg, larva, pupa, and adult.
1814. The United States of America has the highest number of

scientists who have won the Nobel Prize. The United Kingdom and then Germany follow this.

1815. A wind storm is strong gusts of wind without rain.

1816. The distance from Saturn to the sun is 1,425,725,413 km (885,904,700 mi).

1817. The health of the atmosphere is significantly affected by humans. Damage to our atmosphere can occur due to the Greenhouse effect, global warming, destruction of the ozone belt, air contamination, and acid rain.

1818. The first synthetic diamond was made in the 1950's. Synthetic diamonds can be produced through high-pressure high-temperature synthesis, chemical vapor deposition, and detonation synthesis.

1819. You can stop a fire by removing the fuel source, the oxygen, or the heat. For example, if you remove the wood, a wood fire can be put out smother the fire with a blanket or throw water on it to cool it.

1820. Asteroids can be anywhere from 10 m (32 ft) to hundreds of km or miles in diameter.

1821. The Whirlpool Galaxy is a spiral galaxy. William Parsons discovered its helical structure in 1845, looking through his telescope in Ireland.

1822. As of 2013, Jerry L Ross and Franklin Chang-Diaz, both Americans, have each been to space seven times.

1823. Sally Ride, the first American woman to go to space in 1983, was also the youngest American to go to space.

1824. In 1969 NASA's Apollo 11 was the first human-crewed spacecraft to land on the moon.

1825. Oxygen is essential for human life.

1826. Chameleons are lizards and belong to the iguana family.

1827. Alexander Graham Bell was good friends with Helen Keller after introducing her to the school. She learned to write, read, and speak Braille.

1828. The right side of the brain controls the left side of the body, and vice versa.

1829. A weather vane is an instrument that indicates wind direction.

1830. Liquids form into spheres in space instead of flowing like on Earth.

1831. Seven of the eight planets are named after Roman gods or goddesses. This convention had continued since ancient times when Mercury, Venus, Mars, Jupiter, and Saturn were discovered.

1832. During World War II, people ate sugar beets and tulips when they didn't have food.

1833. Deimos (Mars moon) is named after the Greek god of war, who was a son of Ares (Mars) and Aphrodite (Venus).

1834. The Hubble Space Telescope took 50 years to be developed, built, and launched.

1835. Sheep can see behind themselves without turning their head because they have 300 degrees field of vision.

1836. There are more than 70 different stingray species on Earth.

1837. The Hubble Space Telescope completes 15 orbits around Earth every day—approximately one every 95 minutes.

1838. The fifth mass extinction on Earth could be due to the Ordovician-Silurian extinction events resulting from a supernova between 447 and 443 million years ago.

1839. Using forensic science, samples from a crime scene, like fingerprints, are analyzed in a laboratory.

1840. Earth's rotation slows down about 1.5 milliseconds every 100 years due to the moon's gravitational force. The same effect puts the moon into a higher orbit by about 3.8 cm or 1.5 every year.

1841. The month of March is called after the planet Mars.

1842. Four spacecraft have flown past Saturn - Pioneer 11, Voyagers 1 and 2, and Casini-Huygens.

1843. The symbol for platinum is Pt.
1844. Peafowls are related to pheasants.
1845. Crocodiles lay 1- to 60 eggs at a time.
1846. 97% of Earth's water is salted and found in oceans. This means 3% is freshwater, but more than 2% is frozen in our glaciers, leaving only 1% fresh water in lakes, rivers, and underground.
1847. Minerals are usually made up of more than one chemical element, although some are made of one. Diamond, for example, is made up of only carbon, while fluorite is made up of carbon and fluorine.
1848. Inner planets are denser than outer planets, so they rotate slower than the outer planets.
1849. Don Lind was selected to be an astronaut in 1966, but he didn't fly for 19 years until 1985 for various reasons such as canceled missions or he was back up or not needed.
1850. Helium means 'sun'.
1851. The Hubble and Spitzer Space telescopes have observed that most of the star formation in the Sombrero Galaxy occurs at the dust ring's outer tip.
1852. The cerebrum, cerebellum, hypothalamus, brain stem, and thalamus are important parts of our brains.
1853. When an asteroid collides with a planet, the result is called an impact event. An example of this is the extinction event 65 million years ago that made dinosaurs extinct.
1854. The tongue is a muscle that is attached to the floor of your mouth.
1855. Astronomy, which examines space objects' position, differs from astrology, which is a belief system for human behavior.
1856. Low gravity in space makes it hard for an astronaut to tell if they need to urinate, so they go to the toilet to empty their bladder every 2 hours.

1857. A tornado will usually travel a few miles or kilometers and then die out.
1858. The moon's surface temperature is extreme and varies from 107 degrees C (224.6 deg F) during the day to -153 deg C (-243.4 deg F) at night.
1859. The Chinese civilization built pyramids for some of their Chinese emperors.
1860. Dogs have earned themselves the nickname of "man's best friend."
1861. Magnesium is used in flashlight photography, flares, and fireworks because it is quick to light and produces a brightly burning flame.
1862. Hummingbirds have no sense of smell.
1863. A young male horse is known as a colt.
1864. Computers have different input and output devices such as the keyboard, mouse, and printer, which interact.
1865. When many meteors come together, a meteor shower occurs.
1866. A supernova exploding star produces silver and gold. A small supernova produces silver while a larger one produces gold.
1867. Cactus has no leaves like other plants. Instead, it has spines and thorns.
1868. Elliptical galaxies are typical in galaxy clusters.
1869. Due to their size, elephants don't have many natural predators. People are their main risk from poaching and the changes we make to their environment.
1870. Saliva must wet the food we place in our mouth before we can taste it.
1871. The space shuttle used oxygen and hydrogen as fuel.
1872. A peacock has bright, colorful feathers. A peahen has brown feathers.
1873. Mg is the symbol for the chemical element magnesium.
1874. The Olympic rings are five interlocking rings with the

colors blue, yellow, black, green, and red. They represent the five continents of Africa, Asia, Europe, Oceana, and the Americas linked together. Every national flag in the world has at least one of these colors.

1875. Neptune has no solid body (it's gas), so its equatorial clouds rotate around it in 16 hours.

1876. The study of birds is called ornithology.

1877. Koala fossils that are 20 million years old have been found.

1878. Carbon dioxide (CO_2) makes up 0.04% of the Earth's atmosphere and is important as plants use it during photosynthesis.

1879. Helium is the lightest noble gas followed by neon.

1880. Meerkats are very social animals and live in families of about 20 - 50 meerkats, and families will often live together in communities.

1881. In 1930, Pluto was named by an 11-year-old girl, Venetia Burney, who suggested the name as dark and like the god of the underworld. She was given a 5-pound note as a reward for choosing the name.

1882. Flamingos are very social and live in groups or thousands of birds.

1883. The ozone O_3, which combines three atoms of oxygen, is an air pollutant at ground level but filters out UV light in the upper atmosphere and protects us from harmful sun's rays.

1884. Eagles are at the top of their food chain.

1885. Gas giants have different nicknames, for example, Giant Neptunes, Hot Jupiters, and Super Jupiters.

1886. Life can only exist on Earth because of the atmosphere. If there were no atmosphere, the Earth would be too hot or cold, and Earth would become similar to the moon.

1887. One year after the Soviet satellite Sputnik 1 was launched, NASA was established.

1888. A hummingbird has fewer feathers than other birds so they can stay lightweight for flying.

1889. When magma cools and solidifies above or below the Earth's surface, it becomes igneous rock. Examples of igneous rock include granite, basalt, and obsidian.

1890. Voyager discovered the first 9 of Saturn's moons.

1891. Light takes 1,255 seconds to travel from Earth to the moon.

1892. A wild otter can live to the age of 16 years.

1893. Snails leave a layer of mucus behind them as they move.

1894. Glaciers cover about 10% of the Earth's surface.

1895. Modern technology with advanced computer modeling enables authorities to predict where flooding will occur and its severity.

1896. When two pieces of the same metal contact each other in space, they join together and are "cold-welded."

1897. 3. the square of the orbital period of a planet is directly proportional to the cube of its orbit's semi-major axis.

1898. The Taj Mahal in India, made from white marble, took about 20 years to build. It is 561 feet(171 m) tall and was built as the final resting place of the third wife of the emperor Shah Jahan.

1899. Diamonds are made of carbon atoms arranged in a strong tetrahedral structure, making it the hardest natural material in the world.

1900. The skin of a Polar Bear is black, but you can't see it because of the white fur that covers it.

1901. Some 'web' spiders have poor eyesight, so they use vibration to sense where their prey is in their web.

1902. Beavers have powerful teeth and jaws so they can fell wood to build dams and homes.

1903. Albert Einstein was not only famous for his theory of relativity. His other works include the photoelectric effect, which contributed to the development of solar power and Brownian motion, explaining capillary action. He also co-invented a refrigerator, Einstein-Slizard refrigerator, that worked on compressed gases.

1904. The bridge's design depends on what the bridge will be used for, the budget available to build the bridge, and the terrain over which it is constructed.

1905. Intense pressure and heat form are naturally occurring diamonds over billions of years. Deep volcanic eruptions often bring diamonds to the surface.

1906. Some bats migrate during the colder seasons to keep warm.

1907. The sun is the closest star to Earth.

1908. The ATP's fastest tennis serves 157.2 mph (253 kph) by John Isner in the 2016 Davis Cup. The fastest tennis serve, not recognized by the ATP, is 163.4 mph (263 kph) by Sam Groth at the Busan Open Challenger competition in 2012.

1909. The male giant panda leaves the female after mating, so the cubs are raised only by their mothers.

1910. The Venus Express was the first European spacecraft to orbit Venus. It was launched on 9 November 2005 and officially ended on 14 December 2014. The last signal received from the Venus Express was on 19 January 2015.

1911. Gold has been used in medicine to treat rheumatoid arthritis and some cancers. It is also used sometimes for diagnosis. Many surgical and life support devices have small amounts of gold in them.

1912. Ceres does not have a moon.

1913. Saturn's orbit around the sun is 29.4 Earth years.

1914. Copper has antibacterial properties, so brass (an alloy of copper and zinc) is used for doorknobs and handrails in many public buildings to reduce bacteria's spread.

1915. A baby shark (also called a pup) is ready to look after itself the minute it is born.

1916. Like horses, zebras sleep standing up.

1917. Dolphins breathe through a blowhole in the top of their head.

1918. Diamonds, graphite found in graphite lead pencils, and coal are all made from carbon, which comes in different forms.

1919. Seals only come out of the water to mate, give birth, or be young until their waterproof fur grows and run away from predators.

1920. An airship or a blimp is filled with helium lighter than air, so it lifts into the air.

1921. Jupiter's surface pressure and its high temperatures would make it impossible for any earth-life on the planet to exist.

1922. The 'envelope' or top of a hot air balloon is usually balloon-shaped. However, it can be designed to resemble an animal or cartoon character.

1923. William Lassel found Triton, one of Neptune's moons, 17 days after Johann Gottfried Galle found Neptune.

1924. There are more than 40,000 spider species in the world.

1925. The law of elasticity, also known as Hooke's law, states that the extension of a spring is proportional to the load applied to it.

1926. The Milky Way is a group of stars, gas, dust and other matter, about 100,000 to 120,000 light-years in diameter, brought and kept together by their mutual gravitational pull.

1927. In the 1980s, remote controls became a popular accessory to televisions.

1928. Waterfalls are an excellent source of energy, harnessed as hydroelectric power.

1929. The collagen found in horses' skin and hooves have good adhesive qualities, so these horse parts were used once to make glue. These days, horses are not killed any more to make glue.

1930. Recycling used materials for new products is important to our environment as it reduces waste, energy use, and pollution.

1931. Helicopters have one main rotor and a small rotor in the tail to counter the torque effect and stop it spinning in the other direction. Some have two horizontal rotors, such as a Chinook, which spin in opposite directions and lets the helicopter lift heavy objects.

1932. A female horse is known as a mare.

1933. The biggest artificial satellite that orbits Earth is the International Space Station.

1934. Olfaction is the technical term for the sense of smell.

1935. Our immune system is boosted with regular exercise.

1936. Male hippos are territorial in water and live in groups of up to 30 hippos. They are, however, solitary animals when they graze on the land.

1937. The Catholic Church persecuted Galileo for centuries. They thought he was blasphemous when he suggested the Earth orbited the sun. Pope John Paul II in 1992, 350 years after Galileo's discoveries, finally vindicated him in a statement apologizing for the Catholic Churches' treatment towards Galileo.

1938. The two species of beaver in the world are the European or Eurasian beaver and the North American beaver.

1939. Different metals have different properties; for example, gold doesn't corrode and is shiny, so it is often used to make jewelry. Copper is a great conductor of electricity, so used to make wire.

1940. Six spacecraft may be connected to the ISS at one time.

1941. Dolphins click and whistle to communicate with one another.

1942. 100% of copper can be recycled.

1943. There are over 500 million cats worldwide, and they have been one of the most popular pets throughout history.

1944. Cupronickel is a mixture of copper and nickel.

1945. Iron is the most common metal on Earth as it makes up much of the Earth's core, while aluminum is the most common metal found in the Earth's crust. Aluminum is often used to make cookware as it is a great conductor of heat.

1946. An electrocardiogram (ECG) measures the electrical impulses in your heart. Doctors can use an ECG to diagnose heart disorders.

1947. A shooting star is a meteor that burns up when it enters the Earth's atmosphere.

1948. Internet and the World Wide Web is accessible all over the world. As of 2019, 90% of adults in America use the Internet. China and India have the most people using the Internet for various activities such as shopping, business, social networking, news, and advertising.

1949. Kangaroos are herbivores and only eat plants.

1950. There are three main parts to a space shuttle - the orbiter, the external fuel tank, and the solid rocket boosters.

1951. Giant pandas like to live alone. They keep away from other pandas and mark their territory, usually about 1.9 square miles (5 square km).

1952. Submarines must be electrically heated for the crew as the ocean's temperature is very cold at about 39 deg F (4 deg C).

1953. Several thousand people live and work in scientific research facilities located in Antarctica.

1954. From 2010, the Akashi Kaikyo Bridge in Japan became the longest suspension bridge in the world, spanning 6,529 feet (1,991 m).

1955. Oceans cover 71% of the Earth's surface.

1956. Most of the modern telescopes are reflectors.

1957. A modern swimsuit is scientifically designed with fabric that makes the swimmer move faster in water than their natural skin.

1958. The highest quality protein of all foods is found in eggs.

1959. Butterflies are related to moths.

1960. The recording of data through observation with tools such as telescopes is called observational astronomy.

1961. Due to low oxygen levels, it is difficult for people to survive at altitudes over 26,000 feet (8,000 m), often called the 'Death Zone.'

1962. Audiology is the scientific study of hearing, balance, and hearing impairments.

1963. The airflow around an astronaut's head is maintained to avoid a bubble of carbon dioxide forming around their head.

1964. Mercury is slightly larger than our moon.

1965. A famous Isaac Newton quote: If I have seen further, it is only by standing on giants' shoulders.

1966. A lunar eclipse can be partial, full, or penumbral.

1967. Gold is a chemical element with an atomic number of 79.

1968. Uranus has two sets of rings around it. Nine inner rings are narrow and dark grey. It has two dusty rings, and two outer rings, one reddish in color, and the outermost one is blue. The rings contain dust-sized particles to large boulders.

1969. Charon has a northern region named Mordor after a region in the Lord of the Rings. It is darker than the rest of the moon from small particles of tar from Pluto's atmosphere.

1970. Contusion and hematoma are medical words that mean bruise. Fractures (broken bone) and abrasions are also common sports injuries.

1971. Hedgehog mothers sometimes eat their babies when their nest has been disturbed.

1972. All deer species have antlers except the Chinese water deer.
1973. Ladybirds, also known as ladybugs, are a type of beetle that helps control pests by feeding on aphids.
1974. Scientists believe that penguins formed their species 40 - 50 million years ago when Antarctica broke away from Gondwanaland. They used to live in warmer regions but had to adapt to colder environments.
1975. The chemical element Plutonium was named after Pluto in 1941.
1976. A female seal gives birth once a year.
1977. Venus is the only planet in our solar system that is named after a female.
1978. You can't find calcium in its natural state, only as calcium compounds such as calcium carbonate (limestone) and calcium sulfate (gypsum).
1979. Titanium is not magnetic.
1980. Snow is not white! It has no color. It looks white because of the sun's reflections, even when the sun is not out!
1981. You can tell the age of a male sheep or ram by the growth rings in his horns.
1982. Scientists give many nicknames to rocks on Mars, so they can easily remember them. Some of these names are Barnacle Bill, Shark, Moe, Pop Tart, and Cabbage Patch.
1983. Eclipse means 'downfall,'
1984. 7% of the weight of a human body is blood.
1985. The high acidic nature of lemon juice makes it a good cleaning product.
1986. Only queen ants and male drones have wings. The queen ant sheds its wings after it mates.
1987. It takes 100,000 years light to reach Earth from the sun's core but only 8 minutes 22 seconds from the sun's surface.
1988. Hummingbirds are most at risk when they enter a state

called torpor at night. They shut down some of their bodily functions to conserve energy, but it takes them up to 30 minutes to warm back up to take action.

1989. The world's largest flower can grow up to 3 feet (1 m) in diameter and weigh about 22 lb (10 kg). It is called the Rafflesia Arnoldii, also known as the Stinking Corpse Lily, and can be found in southeast Asia.

1990. Acid rain is rain, snow, or other precipitation with high levels of sulphuric and nitric acids. Acid rain mostly results from the burning of fossil fuels, vehicles, and industrial plants.

1991. Rhinoceroses are mammals.

1992. 2. a line joining a planet and the sun sweeps out equal areas during equal intervals of time

1993. A Deimos day (one of Mars' moons) is equivalent to 2.7 Earth days.

1994. Some jellyfish don't sting.

1995. Newer interactive devices such as guitars, microphones, and touch screens have added to the video game experience.

1996. The strongest winds in a hurricane are just around the hurricane's eye or center in the 'eyewall'.

1997. Most lakes have rivers and streams where water moves in and out of the lake. A lake that loses water by evaporation or underground seepage only is called an endorheic lake.

1998. Pluto is 456 times smaller than Earth.

1999. Anything that moves has kinetic energy, for example, a person riding a scooter.

2000. Lightning strikes last about 1 or 2 microseconds.

2001. Halley's Comet has been observed for thousands of years. Babylonian, Chinese, and European stargazers have all recorded observations of Halley's Comet.

2002. The first time that Halley's Comet was recorded was in a Chinese chronicle.

2003. No one has ever stepped on the far side of the moon.
2004. Scientists have been studying the behavior of ants for years to learn about their complex behavior.
2005. Frowning uses 43 muscles in your face.
2006. Eating pineapples can help boost your immune system and build strong bones because they are rich in vitamins, enzymes, and anti-oxidants.
2007. While all African elephants have tusks, only the male Asian elephant has them. Tusks are used to dig and find food.
2008. 88% of Earth's iron is in the core.
2009. A peacock sheds its train of tail feathers after they mate.
2010. A small star will live longer, up to hundreds of billions of years, than a giant star which will only live for a few million years. Our sun is medium-sized and will shine another 5 billion years.
2011. Lippershey was the first person to apply for a patent on a telescope in 1608. In 1609, Galileo made his telescope and was the first to look through it into space. He could see mountains and craters on the moon, as well as the Milky Way. He also discovered the rings of Saturn, sunspots, and four of Jupiter's moons.
2012. Siding Spring, an Oort Cloud comet that was observed close to Mars in January 2014, won't return to our Solar System for another 740,000 years.
2013. Machu Picchu was built with amazing engineering techniques for its time. It was built 7970 ft (2,430 m) above sea level on a mountain ridge without draft animals, iron tools, or a wheel. Archaeologists estimate that 60% of the construction was built underground. Mortar free walls, trapezoid-shaped walls, and inward and round corner doors and windows mean that many buildings didn't collapse from Peru's frequent earthquakes.

2014. An astronomical satellite is one used for observations planets and galaxies.
2015. Radio astronomy is the study of radiation with wavelengths of 1 mm or more.
2016. NASA has nicknamed two satellites that are chasing each other in space, Tom and Jerry.
2017. Spiders cannot chew or swallow their food. Their venom turns the inside of their prey to a liquid substance that they suck up.
2018. Chemical energy is stored in food, gasoline, batteries, coal, and natural gas. Food energy is measured in calories or joules.
2019. The first Kuiper Belt Object (KPO) was discovered in 1992 by Dave Jewitt and Jane Luu. It was a reddish colored speck further away than Pluto, and they wanted to call it Smiley! It has since been named 1992 QB1 (boring!).
2020. Ants are social insects that belong to the Formicidae family.
2021. For example, a dark nebula, the Horsehead Nebula, blocks all the light from interstellar grains of dust so you can't see anything behind it.
2022. Galileo Galilei discovered that a pendulum, a free-swinging weight hanging from a pivot, could be used to measure time.
2023. Compared to the Messier 87 with a diameter of 980,000 light-years and Hercules A with a diameter of 1.5 million light-years, the Milky Way is very small (100,000 light-years).
2024. There are more than 60 species of eagle.
2025. The tallest sunflower in the world is 30 ft 1 in (9.17 m) tall. It was grown in Germany in 2014.
2026. Spiders make silk to climb, build webs, build egg sacs, and wrap their prey.

2027. Mike Brown's team, who discovered Haumea, first saw it just after Christmas on 28 December 2004 and called it 'Santa.'
2028. In the 16th century, Nicolaus Copernicus presented the first heliocentric model of the universe, which explained how the sun was the center of the universe and planets revolved around it.
2029. Time is used to measure, and sequence or order events that happened in the past is happening now or will happen in the future.
2030. The tallest mountain in the solar system is on Mars.
2031. The biggest cat is the tiger, and it can grow as big as 11 feet (3.3 m) and weigh up to 660 lbs (300 kg).
2032. Nicolaus Copernicus, Polish astronomer, mathematician, and scientist, is famous for identifying that the sun and not Earth is at the center of our universe.
2033. A hedgehog has up to 6,500 spines.
2034. In geometry, pyramids have triangular sides that meet at the top or apex of the pyramid.
2035. Scientists believe that birds came from the group of carnivorous dinosaurs called therapods.
2036. Galileo had two daughters and a son, but he never married the mother of his children. His daughters were nuns who lived in a convent all their lives. His son studied medicine.
2037. The thickness of the central bulge of the Milky Way is 10,000 light-years.
2038. The scientific name for a jaguar is Panthera onca.
2039. Steel is an alloy of iron and a small amount of carbon to make it strong.
2040. Most volcanoes are found near tectonic boundaries. However, some form in the inside abnormal hot rock inside Earth—most of them are found in and around Hawaii.

2041. The best thermal conductor among all the naturally occurring substances is a diamond.
2042. A beaver can swim underwater for up to 15 minutes.
2043. Segmented waterfalls fall from many different streams of water, which are separated. They then converge in the pool of water at its base—how nice!
2044. The sun's mass occupies 99.86% of the mass of our solar system.
2045. The Sombrero Galaxy is also called Messier 104, M104 or NGC 4594.
2046. The largest lizard, growing up to 10 feet (3 m) long, is the Komodo dragon.
2047. Rhodium is mainly used by automobile manufacturers in catalytic converters to clean car emissions.
2048. Ducks have three eyelids.
2049. Chameleons can survive in different habitats from deserts to rainforests.
2050. Zinc is also called 'spelter.'
2051. Beavers use their tails for swimming and alert other beavers to danger by slapping their tails on the water.
2052. The sun is white, not yellow. The Earth's atmosphere makes it look yellow.
2053. On average, a person will walk the distance of 5 times around the world (at the equator) by the time they turn80 years old.
2054. The string tension of a tennis racquet determines the amount of control or power a tennis player has. The higher the tension, the more control and less power. Most tennis racquets are strong at about 50 - 70 pounds (220 - 310 newtons).
2055. Most insects have six legs.
2056. The female spider monkey has the longest tail of all primates. Its tail can measure up to 3 feet (90 cm) when its body is only 2 feet (60 cm) long.

2057. Parrots and cockatoos belong to the Psittaciformes family.
2058. People and animals have muscles to maintain posture, move, and keep their internal organs functioning properly. For example, your heart is a muscle that pumps to circulate blood.
2059. You can sit inside some very large reflecting telescopes.
2060. Alessandro Volta, physicist, and chemist, invented the electric battery and was the first person to isolate methane gas.
2061. Slow and fast-twitch muscles have different functions. Slow twitch (type I) carries oxygen more efficiently using fats, proteins, and carbs as energy. It works well for aerobic sports such as cycling. Fast twitch (type II) muscle has low oxygen-carrying proteins, so they are good for anaerobic exercises like sprinting. They contract quickly, but fatigue easily.
2062. Jupiter is the fastest rotating planet in our solar system. Its days are only ten hours long.
2063. Scientific studies have shown that concussion injuries in sports, which are often considered temporary, can have long term medical problems.
2064. People have 9,000 taste buds compared with pigs that have 15,000.
2065. The scientific name for a bat is Chiroptera. This comes from a Greek word meaning 'hand wing'. They have four long fingers and a thumb on each wing.
2066. The lifespan of a platypus is about 12 years.
2067. Every year, approximately 500 meteorites hit Earth. However, only a handful ever make it to scientists to study as most of them fall into the ocean.
2068. The word 'panther' is used to describe three big cats - the jaguar, the leopard, and the cougar.
2069. Halley's Comet has an elliptical orbit around the sun.

2070. Mars and Earth have similar seasons as they have similar tilts.
2071. Betelguese is the largest type of star in our universe, bigger than the sun! It is near the end of its life, and when it explodes into a Supernova, it will light up the sky for nearly two months.
2072. The largest bird on Earth is the ostrich, which also lays the largest eggs in the world.
2073. Mice and rats are often used in scientific experiments due to their similarities with people. They're also small, take up less space and reproduce quickly, giving scientists more specimens. They're also easily modified genetically.
2074. No two people see the same rainbow.
2075. Silicon is a very important part of high technology devices. Silicon Valley in California is named for having a high number of technology-related companies in one area.
2076. A drone is an uncrewed aircraft that is remotely controlled.
2077. The Iron Age was a period following the Stone and Bronze Ages when tools were made from iron and steel. The Iron Age started about 1200 BC and ended around 550 BC.
2078. Video games have positives and negatives; while they improve eye-hand coordination and problem-solving at an early age, young people are also exposed to violence.
2079. Camels can rehydrate faster than any other mammal. In less than 15 minutes, it can drink up to 30 gallons (113 l) of water.
2080. The scientist Charles Darwin and Abraham Lincoln, American President, were born on the same day 12 February 1809.
2081. A snake's ears are internal, not external.
2082. Uranus rotates in a backward direction, similar to Venus,

but different to all the other planets, including Earth.

2083. Cattle regurgitate and rechew their food.

2084. Oil refineries convert crude oil into gasoline or petrol, diesel, kerosene, jet fuel, and liquefied petroleum gas (LPG).

2085. The famous physicist Albert Einstein only started speaking from the age of three.

2086. Our nervous system is our body's electrical wiring. It includes our nerves and neurons which carry messages to and from our organs.

2087. Charon, Pluto's largest moon, has no atmosphere.

2088. A famous Isaac Newton quote: "Truth is ever to be found in simplicity, and not in the multiplicity and confusion of things."

2089. Monkeys can count and do basic maths!

2090. Neither Venus nor Mercury has an orbiting moon. All other planets do.

2091. As the smallest bird on Earth, hummingbirds lay the smallest eggs of all birds.

2092. Oxygen has no color, taste, or odor under normal conditions.

2093. Capuchin monkeys are very intelligent and can use tools and learn new skills.

2094. The planet with the most craters in the solar system is Mercury.

2095. The dwarf planet Sedna, discovered in 2003, is believed to be located in the inner Oort Cloud.

2096. Silicon is a good semiconductor because it is a metalloid.

2097. A burner in a hot air balloon burns a mixture of liquid propane and air to make an open flame. The flame heats the air trapped in the top of the balloon, also known at the 'envelope' of the hot air balloon. The hot air inside the envelope is less dense than the surrounding air, so the balloon rises.

2098. Scientists have been studying squirrels to find stroke treatment.
2099. Guinea pigs are social animals and like human affection.
2100. A koala has two thumbs on each hand.
2101. The Messier 87 Galaxy is not a spiral galaxy like the Milky Way. Instead, it is elliptical, and it is one of the most massive galaxies in our universe. Messier 87 is expanding as it continues to absorb smaller galaxies and matter.
2102. Uranus' inner moons consist of half water ice and half rock. Scientists don't know the composition of the outer moons, but they believe them to be captured asteroids.
2103. Gravity is the force by which a planet or other body pulls objects towards its center. That's how planets orbit the sun.
2104. Mercury has extreme temperatures. The side that faces the sun can have a temperature of up to 427 deg C (800 deg F) while the opposite side away from the sun can be as cold as -173 deg C (-279 deg F). The reason for this is that Mercury doesn't have an atmosphere to regulate its temperatures.
2105. Penguins spend half their lives on land and the other half in the sea.
2106. Jupiter's surface temperature is -108 degrees celsius (-162.4 deg F).
2107. Pluto was reclassified as a dwarf planet when Eris was discovered.
2108. Scientists believe that eyes evolved over 500 million years ago, giving an advantage to animals who could see. Those who couldn't see didn't survive.
2109. Modern clocks are very accurate due to the invention of sundials, water clocks, mechanical clocks, digital displays, and atomic clocks.
2110. The giraffe's spots help camouflage them from predators.

2111. Some dolphins are nearly extinct as we continue to fish, pollute their waters, and change the environment they live in.
2112. Ducks can see color.
2113. Muscles can be skeletal, cardiac, or smooth. Skeletal muscles control our movements. Cardiac muscles pump oxygen. Smooth muscles are involuntary and move substances through bodily organs such as the esophagus and stomach.
2114. You can use a fire extinguisher to put out a fire. Fire extinguishers contain different materials for different types of fires. For example, water fire extinguishers can put out wood fires. However, only a dry powder fire extinguisher will put out a fire from flammable gases or metals.
2115. If you have no sense of smell, you have 'anosmia.'
2116. Plongeur, launched in 1863, was the first submarine not propelled by human power. Compressed air was used for propulsion.
2117. A herbivore is an animal that only eats plants.
2118. The average temperature of a candle flame is 1,800 deg F (1,000 deg C).
2119. Chameleons can change color as they have special pigment cells called chromatophores under their skin.
2120. Total solar eclipses cannot be observed at the north or the south poles.
2121. On the Periodic table, hydrogen is the first element with an atomic number of 1. Hydrogen is very flammable and is the most common element in our Universe.
2122. Guinea pigs are herbivores, and their favorite foods are grass and fruit and vegetables.
2123. Many species of otter are vulnerable to extinction. The giant otter, hairy-nosed otter, marine otter, South

American river otter, and sea otter are the most endangered.

2124. About 400 active satellites orbit above Earth are greater than 35,786 km (22,236 mi) above the Earth's surface. These are known as High Earth Orbit satellites.

2125. At the age of 17, Aristotle went to study philosophy and logical thinking at Pluto's Academy.

2126. There is much natural copper on Earth, enough to last us over five million years.

2127. There are three types of ants in a colony - queen ant, female workers, and male ants called drones.

2128. NASA's Voyager 2 spacecraft, launched on 20 August 1977, flew past Uranus in 1986, about 81,500 km (50,641 mi) from the planet.

2129. The inner Oort Cloud starts about 2,000 Astronomical Units from the sun.

2130. The stripes on every zebra have a different pattern.

2131. Snakes evolved from lizards.

2132. The inner planets don't have any rings around them.

2133. The highest mountain on Venus is the Maxwell Montes, about 8.8 km (5.4 mi) high, similar to Mt Everest, the highest mountain on Earth.

2134. The north pole of a magnet will generally point towards the north pole of Earth.

2135. After tigers, lions are the next biggest cat species. They can run at great speeds of up to 50 mph (81 kph) for short periods as they don't have much stamina.

2136. A turtle's shell is made up of approximately 60 bones covered by scutes or hard plates.

2137. The Dutch astronomer Christiaan Huygens discovered Titan, a Saturn moon, in 1655.

2138. In 2004, astronomers believed a meteorite that fell to Earth in Yemen in 1980, may have come from Phobos, a Mars moon.

2139. We know that our universe is expanding because of the astronomer Edwin Hubble. Hubble's law, which explained that the redshift level in the light coming from a galaxy increased in proportion to the distance as the galaxy moves further away, proves that the universe is expanding. This helped Albert Einstein with his work on his theory of relativity.

2140. A famous Galileo quote: "See now the power of truth; the same experiment which at first glance seemed to show one thing, when more carefully examined, assures us of the contrary."

2141. Keo is the name of a spacetime capsule designed to carry messages from the present Earth to humans in 50,000 years. It was supposed to have launched in 2003 and still hasn't been launched in 2019.

2142. Blood not only delivers all the nutrients and oxygen around our body, but it also removes our unwanted waste.

2143. Peacocks fight other peacocks with the spurs on their feet.

2144. Pb is the chemical symbol for lead.

2145. There are over 250 different species of owl in the world.

2146. A sunflower's stem can grow to 10 feet (3 m) tall and the flower head up to 11.8 in (30 cm) wide.

2147. A galaxy that is very small with about 10 million stars is called a dwarf galaxy.

2148. Hydra is the largest constellation and covers 3.1% of the night sky.

2149. The sex of an alligator is determined by the nest's temperature in which they hatch from their egg. An alligator becomes female if the nest is below 82.4 degrees F (28 degrees C). If the nest is above 91.4 F (33 C), the alligator becomes male. If the nest temperature is 87.8 F (31 C), it will produce an even number of male and female alligators.

2150. Meteorites that have crashed on Earth have contained small traces of Martian material in them. This has enabled our scientists to study Mars in greater detail.
2151. A weather satellite monitors the weather.
2152. Based on the size of our moon, 49 of them could fit into Earth.
2153. The Universe in a Nutshell,' 'A Briefer History of Time,' and 'George's Secret Key to the Universe,' a children's book with a strong focus on science, are also written, Stephen Hawking.
2154. Zoology' comes from two Greek words that mean 'animal' and 'knowledge.'
2155. Rabbits are famous for reproducing quickly. They have three to eight babies, three to four times a year.
2156. Alexander Graham Bell not only invented the telephone in 1876, but he also invented the wireless telephone, called the photophone, in 1880. He thought this was a greater invention than his telephone and could be used by sailors to communicate with the land when telegraph wires were down.
2157. Without a spacesuit, a person can only survive for 15 to 30 seconds in space if they breathe out during this time. The lack of oxygen in space would kill them.
2158. Helium is used faster than it is being replenished. Gas companies are looking at new technologies for obtaining or recycling helium.
2159. No spacecraft has landed on Europa, although many have visited it. The Galileo spacecraft that was launched in 1989 traveled to Jupiter and its moons.
2160. A food allergy happens when the body's immune system thinks the food item is harmful and attacks it. About 8% of children and 2% of adults are allergic to food, including peanuts, gluten, and prawns.
2161. The word for a group of owls is a 'parliament.'

2162. Scientists think that people started to use fire to cook their food in a controlled way about a million years ago.

2163. Hydrogen becomes a liquid under high pressure and extremely low temperatures (20.28 kelvin or –252.87°C/ –423.17 °F). It is often stored as a liquid as it takes up less room than the gas form.

2164. A mouse can squeeze its body to get into holes as small as 0.2 in (6 mm).

2165. Many people are allergic when their skin touches nickel.

2166. Copper is used in many industries. 60% is used in electrical wires, 20% in roofing and plumbing, and 15% in industrial machines. Copper or copper alloys are also used by some countries to make their coins.

2167. A full lunar eclipse happens when Earth passes directly in front of the moon. Halfway through the eclipse, the moon may appear blood red in color.

2168. Protect the environment and remember the 3 R's - reduce, reuse, and recycle.

2169. Earth has a molten metal core, which results in a magnetic field; Mars doesn't have one, so it doesn't have a magnetic field today, but evidence exists that it may once have a magnetic field. Not only did it have one, but it also reversed just like how Earth's magnetic field changes every few thousand years.

2170. Meteor showers happen regularly or yearly when the Earth passes through the dusty debris left by a comet or an asteroid. For example, the Eta Aquariids meteor shower that falls in May and the Orionids meteor shower that falls in October come from Halley's Comet.

2171. If you weighed 100 kg (220 lb) on Earth, you would weigh 38 kg (83.6 lb).

2172. A vegetarian is a person who doesn't eat meat or fish. A vegan is one who doesn't eat any animal products, including eggs and honey.

2173. Most horses live for 25 - 30 years. The oldest horse on record was Billy, who lived till he was 62 during the 19th century.
2174. The only planet to be less dense than water is Saturn.
2175. Grasshoppers have been around for 250 million years.
2176. Callisto, one of Jupiter's moons, may have a subsurface ocean where life could exist.
2177. The gall bladders store the bile that is secreted by the liver and breaks down fat.
2178. Nuclear fission or fusion can be used to build nuclear weapons that can cause enormous destruction. The United States dropped atomic bombs on Hiroshima and Nagasaki at the end of World War II, killing about 200,000 people.
2179. Lightning strikes our planet more than 8.6 million times a day. Each bolt of lightning contains about 1 billion volts of electricity.
2180. Uranus is the coldest planet with an average temperature of -197 to -224 degrees C (-322 to -371 degrees F).
2181. The kakapo parrot is endangered, with only 210 left in the world (as at 2020). Every kakapo is tagged, and they all live in New Zealand on islands where predators have been removed.
2182. Inner planets have volcanoes, canyons, craters, and mountains on their surface. Earth is the only planet known to have water on its surface. Other planets have underground or subsurface oceans.
2183. The largest crater on Deimos, one of Mars' moons, is Voltaire, with a 3,057 km (1,900 mi). Voltaire was named after Francois-Marie Arouet, a French writer who had a pen name, Voltaire.
2184. Many stories have been told about 'the man in the moon' who was reportedly placed there for stealing. What he took has been a topic of debate for years!

2185. Approximately 20% of the air freezes on Mars during winter.
2186. Lightning is electric current through our atmosphere. Ice in a thundercloud collide with one another and create an electrical charge. When the cloud is full of electricity, it discharges it as lightning.
2187. There are over 170 chameleon species in the world.
2188. By volume, the world's largest pyramid is the Great Pyramid of Cholula in Puebla, Mexico.
2189. In 2006, Ceres, Pluto, Eris, Makemake, and Haumea were all given the status dwarf planet.
2190. The sun appears half the size it does on Earth when you are on Mars.
2191. Whales can have teeth or no teeth. The Baleen whale uses a plate that is shaped like a comb to filter their prey.
2192. An electric circuit is a path through which an electric current flows. It can be a closed-loop allowing the electric current to flow or open because the path is broken.
2193. We can only see an object in space if the light is reflected off it. That's why space is so dark.
2194. All the pagers in the world stopped working when a satellite failed in 1998.
2195. An asteroid about the size of a car hits Earth's atmosphere every year but burns up before it hits land.
2196. A lizard is a reptile. They have a skeleton, breathe air, and are covered in scales.
2197. There is debate about whether life existed on Mars from a Martian meteor that hit Earth 13,000 years ago in Antarctica. Scientists believe the meteor had microscopic fossils of bacteria indicating there may have been life once on Mars.
2198. Jupiter is the fifth planet from our sun and the largest planet in the solar system with a radius of nearly 11 times its size.

2199. The Earth has its magnetic field due to its iron core.
2200. A chameleon is one of the few animals that can change its color.
2201. Smiling uses 17 muscles in your face.
2202. An F1 tornado on the Enhanced Fujita Scale means the tornado's winds are traveling at 73 - 112 mph (117 - 180 kph). It can move tiles on a roof, damage mobile homes, and flip a motorbike and its rider over.
2203. Aztec pyramids in central Mexico were built about 600 years ago, while Mayan pyramids were built about 3,000 years ago. They mostly stepped pyramids.
2204. Wasps use their venom to protect themselves from predators.
2205. Most snails are herbivores and only eat plants, but some species are carnivores (eat meat) and omnivores (eat meat and plants).
2206. Pigs communicate with each other by grunting and squealing.
2207. Lead is easily extracted from rocks and is rarely found in its pure metallic form.
2208. Many automated systems discover asteroids near Earth, but it is rare for them to cross paths with Earth.
2209. There are more than 100,000 species of wasp in the world.
2210. On 16 June 1963, Valentina Tereshkova became the first woman in space on Vostok 6. She was from the Soviet Union.
2211. Basalt metamorphizes into granulite when subjected to extreme heat and pressure over time.
2212. Stingrays are related to sharks.
2213. Deimos' orbit is moving away from Mars while Phobos is getting closer and will collide with Mars in about 50 to 100 million years. In the future, Deimos will move out of Mars' gravity and will no longer orbit the planet.

2214. When hydrogen burns to make helium, nuclear fusion occurs in a star's core and creates a star's energy.
2215. Phobos (one of Mars moons) has no atmosphere.
2216. Buzz Aldrin hit a man in the face in 2002 when the man claimed the moon landings were fake.
2217. Nuclear plants produce radioactive waste that is very dangerous, so it needs to be safely and carefully disposed of.
2218. Big supergiant and hypergiant stars burn up faster than smaller stars and explode into bright supernovae when they die.
2219. Crocodiles don't sweat and cool down by opening their mouths.
2220. People have receptors on their tongue to taste our food, but some animals have receptors in strange places. For example, flies and butterflies have taste organs on their feet to taste an object by landing on it.
2221. Scientists believe seals evolved from land-based animals that walked on feet before they developed fins.
2222. Most reptiles have four legs and a skeleton, except for snakes that descended from a four-legged animal.
2223. In Rome, Italy, the Colosseum was built between 72 AD and 8on AD from stone and concrete. It is the largest amphitheater in the world.
2224. On Io, one of Jupiter's moons, there are over 400 active volcanoes.
2225. 80% of the world's magnesium supply comes from China.
2226. Deimos is one of Mars' moons. It means to dread or terror. The other moon is named Phobos, which means fear.
2227. Plato nicknamed Aristotle' The Mind'.
2228. A funicular or vehicular railway moves a vehicle up and down a steep slope using cables that counterbalance each other.

2229. Peacocks can fly short distances, usually up into trees, when they are in danger.
2230. The gray squirrel can also be white, black, or brown. They forget where they bury their acorns!
2231. The Oort Cloud is shaped like a sphere and has an outer spherical shape and an inner disk shape.
2232. The Black mamba is the fastest and the most deadly snake in the world. It can move up to 15 mph (24 kph).
2233. It's easier to see meteors at night.
2234. A bicycle is a two-wheeled machine that uses momentum, force, and friction to turn kinetic energy into movement, getting you from A to B.
2235. Arctic seals dig 'breathing' holes in the ice where polar bears wait for them to come out to catch them.
2236. Rain provides much of the water that plants need to survive.
2237. When a moon is first discovered, it is given a provisional designation until the IAU approves an official name and confirms the moon's discovery.
2238. A centrifuge can be used to separate blood cells from plasma.
2239. The glass retains its color when recycled, so its color often separates it.
2240. A layer of mucus on the clownfish's skin makes them immune from sea anemone's venomous tentacles.
2241. Special cells in our nose help us smell.
2242. Nickel is used to making magnets, guitar strings, and a green tint in glass.
2243. Light is electromagnetic radiation in physics. The light that you see is the visible part of the electromagnetic spectrum.
2244. The World Meteorological Organisation (WMO) gives hurricanes their names. The names cannot be used again for six years.

2245. Water that drives turbines connected to generators can create electricity. This is called hydropower.
2246. Silicon is a solid at room temperature. It has a melting point of 2,577 °F (1,414 °C) and a boiling point of 5,909 °F (3,265 °C).
2247. A famous Stephen Hawking quote: "The human race is so puny compared to the universe that being disabled is not of much cosmic significance."
2248. Mice have poor eyesight but good senses of smell and hearing.
2249. The top two causes of death in the world are Ischaemic heart disease and stroke.
2250. The lifecycle of a beetle is very much similar to the lifecycle of a butterfly. They hatch from an egg into a short caterpillar, then turns into a pupa. When they come out of their 'sleeping bag' pupa, they are a beetle with three body parts and six legs.
2251. Jellyfish are usually see-through or semi-translucent.
2252. It took 199 years to build the Leaning Tower of Pisa from 1173 to 1372. Wars stopped construction twice during this period.
2253. Relative to its planet, our moon is the largest in the solar system.
2254. Without gravity in space, nothing pushes the bubbles up in fizzy drinks in space. You won't be able to burp out the gas from Coca Cola!
2255. An ant has superhuman strength and can carry 10 to 50 times its weight.
2256. The driest continent on Earth is Antarctica.
2257. The fuselage of an airplane is the body of the airplane. It is hollow to reduce the plane's weight and can come in different shapes for different purposes. For example, a supersonic fighter has a long slender fuselage to reduce

drag and increase speed compared with an airliner, which is wider to carry more passengers.

2258. Scientists are studying the banana's genetic material to engineer a more resistant variety to disease.
2259. NASA's Mariner 9 was the first spacecraft to orbit Mars in 1971 successfully. It returned pictures of huge volcanoes and canyons, frozen underground ice and dried up rivers.
2260. The queen bee only has one job, and that is to lay eggs.
2261. Gravity and electric fields work the same way. The difference is that gravity only attracts, but electric fields can also repulse.
2262. A kangaroo can hop as fast as 30 mph (48 kph).
2263. A spider has eight legs.
2264. Al' Aziziyah in Libya holds the world record for the hottest temperature recorded at 136 deg F (57.8 deg C) in 1922
2265. A chameleon's eyesight is so strong that small insects are 16 - 32 feet (5 - 10 m) away.
2266. A tetrahedron has a triangular base and three triangular sides that meet at the top.
2267. An astronaut's footprint will last on the moon for millions of years as there is no weather or atmosphere on the moon.
2268. The ancient Babylonians were the first ones to record their Jupiter sightings.
2269. Butterflies can only see red, green, and yellow colors.
2270. Hares are herbivores and only eat plants.
2271. Our moon is tilted 20 - 30 degrees as it orbits Earth. The moons from other planets orbit the equator of the planet.
2272. Ultraviolet astronomy is the observation of ultraviolet wavelengths from space or the Earth's upper atmosphere.
2273. 1. the orbit of every planet is an ellipse around the sun
2274. All mammals, including humans, have hair or fur.

2275. The titanic was a luxury passenger liner that was intended to carry people from Southampton England to New York City. It was 882 feet (269 metres) long and 175 feet (53 metres) high. It left Southampton on 10 April 1912 and sank 5 days later when it hit an iceberg.
2276. Leopards are night animals, coming out to hunt at night.
2277. A mushroom or toadstool is a fungus and doesn't need sunlight to make energy for themselves.
2278. Penguins can stay underwater for up to 20 minutes because they have special adaptations in their muscles and blood to increase their oxygen levels.
2279. Giant pandas love bamboo and can eat 12 hours a day, up to 28 lb (12.5 kg).
2280. Mars' environment resembles the Antarctic deserts on Earth.
2281. Carbon comes from the Latin word carbo, which means coal.
2282. When the clouds' temperature is very cold, water vapor freezes before it becomes water and forms snowflakes. Snowflakes are ice crystals that form around particles of dirt in clouds.
2283. An insect has antennae, but a spider doesn't.
2284. Galileo was most famous for creating telescopes with 3x and 30x magnification that let him discover Jupiter's four largest moons, Io, Callisto, Europa, and Ganymede. These moons are now called the Galilean satellites. He also discovered craters and mountains on the moon, the phases of Venus, and the Milky Way stars.
2285. Pluto is symbolized by a P interlocked with L. These happen to be the first two letters of Pluto and also Percival Lovell's initials. Percival was the astronomer at the Lowell Observatory, named after him, who started to search for planets beyond Neptune.
2286. A star explodes in the universe every second.

2287. Neil Armstrong, the first man to step on the moon, was late in submitting his NASA application by a week. His friend had to slip the form into the pile so that it was accepted.

2288. Ernest Rutherford discovered and named the atomic nucleus, the proton, and the alpha and beta particles.

2289. Chlorine combines with almost all other elements to create compounds called chlorides.

2290. Hummingbirds are the only birds that can hover for a few minutes.

2291. Before the 1970s, many sports equipment was made of wood and steel. In modern times, more lightweight, strong materials like aluminum are used for improved performance.

2292. Buzz Aldrin once quoted 'Mars is there, waiting to be reached.'

2293. A dwarf planet that orbits outside of Neptune is known as a plutoid. Pluto, Haumea, Eris, and Makemake are all plutoids. Ceres is not.

2294. Lionesses (female lions) are the main hunters of a pride of lions.

2295. Asteroid means 'star-like' and was given its name in 1802 by William Hershel.

2296. A tropical storm near the United States is called a hurricane. Near Japan, they are called typhoons, and in the South Pacific or Indian oceans, they're called cyclones.

2297. Glacier comes from a French word meaning 'ice'.

2298. Albert Einstein, the great physicist, married the only female physics student in his class, Mileva Marić. She gave up her studies when she married Einstein.

2299. Jaguars are lone animals and only come together with another jaguar to mate.

2300. Like the cobra, some snakes bite their prey with their fangs, injecting venom to kill it before eating it.

2301. The New Horizons spacecraft that was launched in 2006 finally flew past Pluto on 14 July 2015, making the first close observation of a Kuiper Belt object.

2302. There are many hamster species, but only five of them are usually kept as pets. These are the Syrian, Campbell's Russian Dwarf, Winter White Russian Dwarf, Chinese and Roborovski hamsters.

2303. Haumea has two moons, Namaka and Hi'iaka, who were named after the goddess of childbirth.

2304. The second-largest planet in our solar system is Saturn. The largest is Jupiter.

2305. Electric eels can give electric shocks up to 500 volts when hunting or if they need to protect themselves.

2306. Over 40,000 artifacts have been excavated from Machu Picchu, which was voted as one of the new Seven Wonders of the World in 1983.

2307. Cu is the symbol for copper.

2308. Radio waves, which can travel through space, are used by astronauts that are in space to communicate to Earth.

2309. Henry Moseley was an English physicist who is most well known for discovering the atomic number of chemical elements and arranging the atomic numbers' Periodic table. He also created the world's first atomic battery. Atomic batteries have long lives and are now used in spacecraft and pacemakers.

2310. A reflection nebula formed during a star's rapid evolution between the asymptotic giant branch phase and the subsequent planetary nebula phase is called a protoplanetary nebula. The Red Rectangle Nebula is an example of a protoplanetary nebula.

2311. The entrance to a beaver's home is underwater, so it's very difficult for other animals to enter their homes.

2312. Some fish, such as the flatfish, can use camouflage to hide on the ocean's bottom.
2313. The Bowhead whale is the longest living mammal and can live up to 211 years.
2314. Ceres is round, unlike many asteroids in the Asteroid Belt, which are irregularly shaped. It is large enough for gravity to shape it into a sphere.
2315. Pure uranium quickly oxidizes in air.
2316. The Milky Way has a long bar in the center from where the spiral arms spin out.
2317. Camels can run for long periods at 25 mph (40 kph).
2318. Solar energy comes from the movement of light. The Mojave Desert in California, USA, has the largest solar power plant in the world.
2319. The Great Wall of China is 3,915 miles (6,300 km) long from one end to the other. However, all the different sections' total length would add up to about 13,670 miles (22,000 km).
2320. Callisto has been considered the most suitable place for a human base of further exploration. It is not geologically active, and life may be possible in its underwater ocean.
2321. The largest hot air balloon that can carry passengers carried 32 passengers in 2014.
2322. Mammal skin, including humans, have three layers - the epidermis (outer layer), dermis, and subcutis (deepest layer).
2323. Hamsters have poor eyesight and rely on the ascent to find their way around. They rub their back on objects to leave their scent, which they can follow when returning home.
2324. Conduction is the movement of heat from one object to another when they are touching.
2325. Some scientists believe that in the future, the sun will move and join the Andromeda Galaxy.

2326. A spider that gets its prey by hunting instead of making webs usually has excellent eyesight and can sharp fangs. The trapdoor spider is an example.
2327. Electricity is made from the steam coming from burning coal in a furnace with a boiler. The steam spins turbines and generators to create electricity.
2328. According to scientists, the universe is expanding out at exponential rates.
2329. Japan is the snowiest place on Earth.
2330. Iron and steel can be painted, coated or galvanized (coated with zinc) to prevent rusting.
2331. The inner ear is located inside the hardest bone in the body, the temporal bone.
2332. Gravitational interactions with two companion galaxies called M32 and M110 are distorting the spiral arms of Andromeda Galaxy.
2333. Cats have very flexible bodies—great for chasing mice and rats.
2334. Three rhinoceros species, Black, Sumatran, and Javan, are nearly extinct due to loss of habitat and being hunted for their horns.
2335. Owls have large eyes that they can't move around, so they must turn their heads around.
2336. Tulips belong to the lily family.
2337. More than a third of the world's uranium is produced in Kazakhstan.
2338. In 2019, a pair of mated male penguins in a Dutch zoo 'stole' a penguin egg as their egg, but the egg wasn't fertilized, so it didn't hatch!
2339. Most meteorites have been found in Antarctica than anywhere else on Earth.
2340. Although the Magellanic Clouds are irregular galaxies, they are often referred to as spiral galaxies. They have a bar in the center of the galaxy.

2341. In ancient times, philosophers thought that thunder was caused when clouds collided with each other.
2342. The radius of a rainbow depends on the refractive index of the water droplets in the air. A droplet of water with a high refractive index, such as saltwater spray, will produce a smaller rainbow and vice versa. Rainwater rainbows are larger as their refractive index is low.
2343. Ag is the chemical symbol of silver.
2344. Parrots eat both meat and plants. Their favorite food is seeds.
2345. The first person to observe Mars through a telescope was Galileo Galilee in 1609.
2346. Otters are nocturnal mammals, actively hunting at night.
2347. Dogs were domesticated over 15,000 years ago.
2348. Long-period comets come from the Oort Cloud caused when something happens to one of the icy objects in the Oort Cloud, resulting in it falling towards the sun. Comets C/2012 S1 (ISON) and C/2013 A1 Siding Spring are two examples of Oort Cloud comets.
2349. The largest monkey species, the Mandrill monkeys, have fangs larger than a lion's fangs. They also have multi-colored bottoms.
2350. The Pinwheel Galaxy doesn't have a massive black hole at its center like most other galaxies. Instead, it has several smaller black holes.
2351. There's a rocky core at Jupiter's center, slightly bigger than Earth, but weighing about 20 times as much.
2352. The strongest Martian winds happen when Mars is closest to the sun.
2353. Louis Pasteur developed the first vaccine for rabies, which led to the development of other vaccines.
2354. Prime numbers can only be divided by itself and one. The prime numbers under 30 are 2, 3, 5, 7, 11, 13, 17, 19, 23, 29.

2355. A cognitive psychologist is also called a brain scientist. They study how the brain works and treat issues relating to cognitive impairment.
2356. A group of monkeys is called a tribe, mission, or troop.
2357. Zinc's melting point is 787.1 °F (419.5 °C), and its boiling point is 1,664.6 °F (907 °C).
2358. Petrol and diesel continue to be the main fuel used for internal combustion engines in cars. Hybrid and electric vehicles are becoming more popular.
2359. Submarines use gyroscopes to navigate underwater. They use GPS when they're on the surface.
2360. Radon can be found naturally in some hot springs.
2361. Jellyfish are not fish.
2362. An adult jellyfish is called a medusa.
2363. The lightweight body of a cheetah with strong legs makes it the fastest animal on land. It can run as fast as 70 mph (113 kph).
2364. The largest office building globally is the Pentagon, with about 6,500,000 square feet (604,000 sq meter) of the floor used as offices.
2365. Mosquitoes have good senses to help them find people to bite. They like people with O-type blood and high body heat. They also prefer to sweaty people and pregnant women.
2366. You have to trim a domesticated horse's hooves every five to eight weeks as they keep growing and can get too long.
2367. Paper, plastic, glass, metal, textiles, and electronics are all materials that can be recycled.
2368. A red supergiant star, for example, Betelgeuse, is larger than a yellow dwarf star. A red hypergiant is even bigger than a supergiant.
2369. The study of insects is called entomology.
2370. Thirteen otter species exist in the world.
2371. Objects sucked into black holes are torn apart due to the

strong gravitational pull.

2372. Horses don't get fleas, but they get lice.
2373. The Celsius and Centigrades temperature scales are the same.
2374. An astronomical unit is a distance from Earth to the sun.
2375. The closest planet to the Sun is Mercury.
2376. Once, an astronaut was almost turned down to become an astronaut as he suffered from hay fever. NASA then realized that there's no pollen in space!
2377. A reflection nebula can't emit its light and therefore reflects the colors of other nearby stars. It often looks blue. Usually, an emission nebula is nearby if a reflection nebula exists.
2378. In 1972, more color televisions were sold than black and white televisions.
2379. Silver and copper are the best conductors of electricity. Copper is cheap, so used more commonly than silver.
2380. The ISS (International Space Station) weighs approximately 1 million pounds (453 tonnes).
2381. Venus' atmosphere contains mostly carbon dioxide.
2382. The Leaning Tower of Pisa in Italy leans because when it was built, the soil under it could not support the tower (14,500 tons).
2383. A horse can stand up or lie down to sleep.
2384. Jupiter has a strong magnetic field! You would weigh 2.5 times more than you would on Earth.
2385. Technologies such as the computer and television have reduced the amount of physical activity in people. A person's health can be affected if they don't get enough exercise.
2386. There has only been one spacecraft that has flown past Uranus.
2387. Uranium is required to make nuclear power.
2388. A rainbow produced by fog droplets is called a 'fogbow.'

They are usually very big and white, although you might be able to see some faint colors. A fogbow seen in a cloud is a cloud bow.

2389. Hummingbirds are given their name for the humming sound their wings make beating very fast.
2390. Every day, hundreds of tons of material from asteroids and comets fall toward Earth, but they do not reach Earth. They are destroyed as they pass through our atmosphere. They are then called a meteorite when reaching Earth.
2391. Nikola Tesla, engineer, scientist, and inventor, is most famous for inventing the Alternating Current (AC) electric system, the rotating magnetic field, and the Tesla coil.
2392. Plants need water, sunlight, and carbon dioxide to live.
2393. Stephen Hawking was such a well-known physicist and scientist that he appeared on TV shows like Star Trek, The Simpsons, The Big Bang Theory, and Last Week Tonight with John Oliver.
2394. Pluto's atmosphere is made up of nitrogen with a little bit of carbon monoxide and methane.
2395. Before its launch, the Spitzer Space Telescope was named the Space Infrared Telescope Facility.
2396. Trees are all perennial plants and live for more than two years. They can live for thousands of years.
2397. Magnesium makes up 2% of the Earth's crust. It occurs naturally only in combination with other elements in minerals such as dolomite.
2398. The world record for the highest hot air balloon flight is 68,900 feet (21,000 m). Oxygen was needed at the higher altitudes.
2399. There are over 2,900 snake species in the world.
2400. A spider is not an insect.
2401. When your airways become constricted or narrow, you

may get asthma.

2402. Every year, a piece of asteroid (meteoroid) falls into our atmosphere, resulting in a fireball. Before reaching the ground, the meteoroid usually burns up.

2403. Scientists believe that climate change, pollution, and overfishing have led to an increasing number of jellyfish globally.

2404. The long legs of a camel keep it high away from the hot desert ground. It has a pad of thick tissue called a pedestal when it sits. It keeps its body off the ground.

2405. The IAU demoted Pluto from being a planet to a dwarf planet in 2006.

2406. The word platinum means 'little silver' in Spanish.

2407. The Outer Event Horizon, the Inner Event Horizon, and the Singularity are the three main parts of a black hole.

2408. Lightning is always white, but it appears in different colors depending on the atmosphere it travels through.

2409. A crab communicates by drumming and waving its pincers.

2410. The 'decibel' was named after Alexander Graham Bell to honor his work in acoustical science. A decibel, the unit that measures the magnitude of noise, is one-tenth of a 'bel'.

2411. When an astronaut is selected to be a NASA trainee, they train for 20 months. They often train underwater in swimming pools to test equipment and simulate spacewalks.

2412. Lead is bluish-white, which turns to grey when it comes into contact with air.

2413. The far side of the moon is thicker than the near side.

2414. There are no large mountains or volcanoes on Callisto, Jupiter's second-largest moon, only impact craters and multi-ring structures. The impact craters' size can range from 0.1 km (0.06 miles) to over 100 km (60 miles).

2415. Three types of bats solely drink blood and nothing else. They are the common vampire bat, the hairy-legged vampire bat, and the white-winged vampire bat.
2416. The ability of minerals to scratch each other is measured on the Mohs scale of hardness.
2417. Iron, aluminium and nickel are bonded with titanium to produce strong lightweight alloys.
2418. The fastest horse breed in the world is the thoroughbred horse. It is often bred for racing.
2419. Aristotle, a famous Greek philosopher, lived from 384 BC to 322 BC.
2420. Occasionally there is no full moon in February.
2421. Wasps have a chemical signal between themselves, so if you attack their nest, they communicate with other wasps to come and help them defend their nest.
2422. The simple experiment of sprinkling magnetized iron shavings on a piece of paper covering a bar magnet (resulting in the shavings arranging themselves in semicircular arcs at both ends of the magnet) shows the outline of a magnetic field. Michael Faraday was the scientist who first performed this experiment in the 1800s. It's still a popular science experiment carried out today.
2423. The sun takes longer to heat the air above the sea than land. This causes a difference in the air pressure creating a sea breeze.
2424. Edwin Hubble never won a Nobel Prize for physics because astronomers were not eligible at the time. Hubble worked hard towards the end of his life to change this, which it did after he died. Unfortunately, you can't backdate or award the Nobel Prize after a person has passed.
2425. About 30% of a hummingbird's weight is in its chest muscles for flying.

2426. Seals have a short term memory for about 18 seconds.
2427. The universe is so big that we can only see about 5% of the universe.
2428. Because Earth is flattened at the poles and bulges at the equator, it is not round. It is the geoid, an elliptical spheroid shape.
2429. You're looking back in time when you look at the stars as their light takes millions of years to reach Earth.
2430. A hurricane is also called a cyclone, typhoon, or tropical storm.
2431. Oils are liquid fats at room temperature. Fats usually refer to the solid form at room temperature. Liquid and solid fats can be grouped into lipids.
2432. Al Tarif, Beta Cancri, is the brightest star in the Cancer constellation.
2433. Triton (one of Neptune's moons) is the largest moon in our solar system. With a diameter of 2,706 km (1,681 mi), it is the 16th largest object and bigger than Pluto or Eris.
2434. Europa, Jupiter's moon, is about 780 million km (485 million mi) from the sun.
2435. A protein is made up of hundreds and thousands of small amino acids.
2436. Venus' diameter is about 12,104 km (7,521 mi), nearly the same size as Earth's.
2437. The Messier 87 Galaxy is made up of gas and dust, surrounded by hot gas.
2438. Diving ducks tend to be quite heavy so they can dive further underwater.
2439. Arachnology is the study of spiders.
2440. Jupiter weighs double the total weight of all the other planets put together.
2441. The Andromeda Galaxy has a double nucleus with a massive star cluster at its center and a hidden supermassive black hole at its core.

2442. Silicon is found in oxides and silicates in many minerals. More than 90% of the Earth's crust is composed of silicate materials, which means silicon is the second most common Earth element. Oxygen is the most common.
2443. Gorillas are divided into two species. The scientific name for the western gorilla is Gorilla gorilla.
2444. Modern cell phones have infrared, Bluetooth, and other wireless capabilities.
2445. In 2016, there were over 1.32 billion cars, trucks, and buses in the world.
2446. The clear part in front of your eye is called the cornea. It refracts or bends light that enters the eye.
2447. A horse is more intelligent than a cow but less intelligent than monkeys, whales, and dogs.
2448. Liquid hydrogen is used as rocket fuel.
2449. Hedgehogs grunt, squeal and snuffle when they communicate with each other.
2450. One of Saturn's moons, Titan, has a liquid gas (methane and ethane). Kraken Mare is 150,000 square miles (388,500 square km).
2451. A group of hares is called a 'drove'.
2452. Charles Messier first found the Whirlpool Galaxy in 1773.
2453. Nikola Tesla, Michael Faraday and Thomas Edison are all known as the Father of Electricity.
2454. Only one probe has successfully landed on Titan - many have been very close.
2455. The Spitzer Space Telescope is orbiting at around 26 million miles from Earth.
2456. The material used to make sports equipment has changed over the years, thanks to scientific developments. For example, carbon fibers are now used to build bicycles as they are light and strong. Graphite fibers, used for skis, tennis racquets and golf clubs, help with absorbing shock.

2457. Plastic is harder to recycle than other materials.
2458. Volcanoes can send ash into the air up to 17 mi (30 km) high.
2459. Albert Einstein's second son, Eduard, had schizophrenia and lived for most of his life in a psychiatric institution.
2460. Some astronomers would classify Pluto as a comet if it were closer to the sun.
2461. A koala is not a bear.
2462. Digital television transmissions store information on a computer and are more reliable than analog broadcasts.
2463. A cheetah can survive without water for up to four days.
2464. Former US presidents appear on the US currency, such as George Washington on the $1 note, Thomas Jefferson on the $2 note, Abraham Lincoln on the $5 note.
2465. An adult male giant panda can weigh up to 330 lb (150 kg).
2466. In the wild, a mallard duck can live up to 10 years.
2467. Copper has different colors. Pure copper is red-orange. It turns brown when it comes into contact with air and blue-green if exposed to air and water.
2468. A hedgehog replaces its baby spines with new ones when it grows into an adult. The spines are not poisonous and do not come out easily like a porcupine's.
2469. The Andromeda Galaxy is the closest galaxy to the Milky Way and is about 80,000 light-years away.
2470. Snails that live in water breathe through gills. Snails that live on land breathe through lungs.
2471. Earth's density varies in different parts; for example, the crust is less dense than its metallic core. Earth's density averages 5.5 grams per cubic centimeter.
2472. Writing the number googol is easy - 1 followed by 100 zeros, but writing the number googolplex (1 followed by googol zeros) is almost impossible!

2473. Kangaroos regurgitate to re-chew their food like cows to help digestion.
2474. Very little light reaches Venus due to its thick clouds. From space, it looks white.
2475. A hummingbird's heart beats at 1,200 beats per minute. A person's heart beats 60 - 100 beats per minute.
2476. Good bacteria can help you digest food and can be found in yogurt. Bad bacteria can make you sick.
2477. As of 2013, the ISS's construction and maintenance were supported by 174 spacewalks outside of the modules, which is nearly 1,100 hours (46 days).
2478. The Eurocopter X3 is the fastest helicopter globally and can fly up to 293 mph (473 kph).
2479. The World Wide Web is not the same as the Internet. The WWW is a collection of linked pages accessed using the Internet and a browser. In contrast, the Internet is a network that links computers all over the world.
2480. The main diet of sloths is the buds, shoots, fruit, and leaves from the Cecropia tree. Some sloths also like insects, reptiles, and small birds.
2481. Nitrogen becomes liquid at low temperatures. The boiling point of liquid nitrogen is 77 kelvin (−196 °C, −321 °F). Liquid nitrogen has many applications, including food storage at cold temperatures, cryogenics, as a computer coolant, and the removal of warts.
2482. The Milky Way will collide with the Andromeda galaxy in about 4.5 billion years.
2483. There is no evidence of strong radio or x-ray emissions from the Pinwheel Galaxy center, which indicates it doesn't have a black hole.
2484. The world record for the longest submerged submarine is 111 days.
2485. A decade is 10 years, a century is 100 years, and a millennium is 1,000 years.

2486. The tip of a pig's snout is connected to the muscle, making it flexible for them to root around in the ground for food.
2487. The Hubble Space Telescope orbits Earth about 560 km (350 mi) above the planet.
2488. Platinum can bond easily with other elements on the periodic table.
2489. A vertebrate's nervous system has two parts, the Central Nervous System (CNS) and the peripheral nervous system (PNS). Your brain, spinal cord, and retina (of your eye) are all part of the CNS. All other nervous system structures belong to the PNS.
2490. Our taste buds, which you can't see, sit on top of the bumps on our tongue, called papillae. They allow you to taste salty, sour, bitter, sweet, and umami (savory).
2491. The size of Kuiper Belt Objects (KPO) is challenging to measure as they are so far away. Their reflectiveness determines them - the infrared observations are measured by the Spitzer Space telescope, which estimates the size.
2492. Four European ATV cargo spacecraft, four Japanese HTV cargo spacecraft, three SpaceX Dragons, 37 Space Shuttle missions, and 89 Russian spacecraft have used the ISS as a spaceport.
2493. The motor car or the automobile came soon after the invention of the internal combustion engine in 1807.
2494. A white tiger carries a rare gene that only occurs 1 in every 10,000.
2495. Psychologists and psychiatrists are different. A psychologist provides counseling while a psychiatrist is a medical doctor who can prescribe medication as part of their treatment.
2496. Pioneer 10 was the first spacecraft to get up close to Ganymede on a mission to Jupiter. In 1979 Voyager 1 and Voyager 2 found that Ganymede was larger than

Titan, Saturn's moon, which at the time was considered to be more significant. In 1996 the Galileo spacecraft flew by Ganymede and discovered its magnetic field.

2497. Boats and ships float due to the principle of buoyancy. Buoyancy is an invisible upward force when an object is placed in water. If the object is dense, it will sink as the force can't keep it up. If the object is less dense than water, the object floats.

2498. When a baby 'calf' whale is born, groups of female or male whales will come together to look after it.

2499. Bees use their touch to precisely measure the dimensions of their cells as they build them from wax.

2500. Blood plasma is 90% water with nutrients, electrolytes, proteins, glucose, and hormones.

2501. A gas giant is a large planet made mostly of hydrogen and helium. Jupiter and Saturn are two gas giants in our solar system. Uranus and Neptune are also considered to be gas giants as they are made of heavy unstable substances.

2502. Nicholas Copernicus thought that Mars moved backward as Earth overcook Mars in its orbit around the sun.

2503. Pigs and human organs are similar, so pigs have been used in medical research for many years.

2504. The fastest duck recorded is Red-breasted merganser. It flew just over 100 mph (161 kph) when it was chased by a plane!

2505. After observing comets to be 'stars with hair,' the Greek philosopher Aristotle gave the name comet, which means 'hair of the head' in Greek.

2506. If a tornado is rated as F5 on the Fujita Scale, it means it can cause enormous damage. F0 means it will cause a small amount of damage.

2507. Clownfish are born male and change to females when the dominant female of their group dies.

2508. A metamorphic rock started as one type of rock, and over time, it changed into another type of rock by extreme pressure and heat. Examples of metamorphic rocks include marble, slate, and quartzite.
2509. Depending on the star's temperature, it can be brown, red, orange, yellow, white, or blue in color.
2510. Eris is three times further away from the sun than Pluto at 96.4 astronomical units (more than 14 billion km). It takes sunlight more than 9 hours to travel to Eris.
2511. The most recent monkey to be discovered is the lesula monkey. It was found in the Congo in Africa in 2007.
2512. Metamorphic rocks from beneath the Earth's surface are brought up to the surface by uplift and erosion.
2513. Charon's astrological symbol is a floating circle on top of a crescent, resembling the name's mythical meaning of a boatman going across the River Styx.
2514. About 1.9% of seawater mass is chloride ions, making chlorine the third most abundant element in our oceans.
2515. There are more than 330 marsupial species in the world. Two-thirds live in Australia and the other third in South America.
2516. Diamonds are valued based on their four Cs - cut, color, carat, and clarity.
2517. Digestion can be mechanical (chewing the food) or chemical (enzymes breaking down the food).
2518. An otter has thick fur which traps air, making them very buoyant (easy to float on water).
2519. A seal's lifespan is about 25 to 30 years.
2520. The peacock spreads its tail feathers to attract female peahens or to scare predators off.
2521. Earth is the largest inner planet, then Venus, Mars, and Mercury.
2522. Locusts are short-horned grasshoppers.
2523. Methane (CH_4) is the simplest hydrocarbon compound.

2524. Pigs roll in mud to help cool their bodies down.
2525. An electric eel has enough electricity to kill a horse.
2526. It is not easy to send spacecraft to Mercury due to its closeness to the sun, so only three have been launched since 1973.
2527. About 20 different types of amino acids make up a protein. Our body cannot make nine, so we must eat foods rich in these essential amino acids such as meat, eggs, fish, nuts, and grains.
2528. A strawberry is not a berry but a short part of the stem or plant that holds the seeds.
2529. The human eye can't see infrared light due to its long wavelength.
2530. Helium is lighter than air. Balloons, airships, and blimps are usually filled with helium. It is preferred over hydrogen, which is 7% lighter because it doesn't react with other chemicals, so it has a lower fire risk.
2531. The largest jellyfish, Stygiomedusa gigantea, has an umbrella-shaped bell up to one meter wide and four long tentacles up to 10 meters long. It has only been sighted about 115 times in the last 110 years.
2532. The pull of Earth's gravity is stronger at the poles, so a person standing at the equator will be lighter and weigh 68 kg (150 lb) instead of 68.4 kg (150.8 lb) at the North Pole.
2533. Your senses send information to your brain, which interprets the information and sends back an appropriate response.
2534. Wilhelm Röntgen, a German physicist and mechanical engineer, received the first Nobel Prize in Physics in 1901 to discover x-rays.
2535. Music is the science of putting sounds together in a pleasing or meaningful way.
2536. Chameleons are loners because they have no friends!

2537. True seals live in the Arctic and Antarctic regions. Fur seals and sea lions live in the northern Pacific Ocean.
2538. The shape of the Pinwheel Galaxy is distorted from its interactions with its satellite galaxies.
2539. The hollow bones in birds help them to fly.
2540. Hares live above the ground while most rabbits live in burrows or tunnels underground.
2541. The Voyager 1 space probe launched in 1977 will reach the Oort Cloud in about 300 years, taking another 30,000 years to travel through it.
2542. Uranus has 27 moons in orbit.
2543. NASA is working on proving warp drives and travel faster than the speed of light. The space around a spacecraft would need to move, not the spacecraft itself.
2544. Ganymede is the third of the Galilean satellites. It orbits Jupiter every seven days and 3 hours, at a distance of 1,070,400 km (665,000 mi) from the planet.
2545. Scorpions have eight legs, two pincers and a tail with a venomous stinger at the tip.
2546. Meteoroids can travel through space at speeds of up to 42 km per sec (26 miles per sec).
2547. You need at least a 4-inch telescope to see the Pinwheel Galaxy. However, to see its amazing spiral structure, you need an 8-inch telescope.
2548. Ducks live in fresh and seawater, on every continent except Antarctica.
2549. An otter spends many hours grooming itself every day to keep clean.
2550. Even though Uranus is four times bigger than Earth, you need a telescope to see it.
2551. Punchbowl waterfalls descend in a tight stream and spread out into a wide pool at its base.
2552. Scientists are unable to agree on why a bicycle stays upright.

2553. Climate change is increasing the risk of floods worldwide due to the extreme weather changes associated with climate change.

2554. All eagles are carnivorous and eat meat and fish.

2555. An emission nebula, such as the Omega Nebula, is made up of ionized gases that emit light of various wavelengths and colors. The cause of an emission nebula is usually by a nearby hot star.

2556. A comet's nucleus is made of ice and can range from a few meters (feet) to a few kilometers (miles) wide.

2557. It is safe to watch a lunar eclipse as the moon isn't giving off its light.

2558. Bats have a unique mating behavior where the male and female meets at a hibernation site, called hibernacula, to mate.

2559. The largest black hole that has been found in the center of a galaxy is in the Sombrero Galaxy.

2560. Jellyfish move around by taking water into its bell and then squirting it out behind them to propel themselves forward.

2561. The Sombrero Galaxy is smaller than the Milky Way and has a diameter of 49,000 light-years.

2562. Platinum is a shiny grey-white transition metal that can be thinned (malleable) and stretched into a thin wire (ductile).

2563. An emission nebula that is formed by glowing and expanding ionized gases is called a planetary nebula. The Cat's Eye Nebula is an example of a planetary nebula.

2564. When you look at the Milky Way at night, you only see about 0.0000025% of the billions of stars in the galaxy.

2565. Mark Twain was born on 30 November 1835 during an appearance of Halley's Comet, and he predicted he would die during the next one, which he did!

2566. Snakes have three chambers in their heart compared with people who have four.
2567. An F0 tornado on the Enhanced Fujita Scale means the tornado's winds are traveling at 40-72 mph (64-116 kph). It can cause damage to trees, signposts, and traffic lights.
2568. All moons have two things in common - they both orbit a planet and reflect light from the sun.
2569. Polar bears have a strong sense of smell so they can find seals up to a mile (1.6 km) away.
2570. A polar bear is the largest land carnivore. Their favorite food is a seal.
2571. Due to its proximity to the sun, the sun's rays are seven times stronger on Mercury than on Earth.
2572. Yuri Gagarin, a Russian, was the first person in space. In 1961 he orbited Earth in 108 minutes on the spaceship Vostok 1.
2573. In 1610, Galileo Galilei discovered the four largest moons of Jupiter with a telescope.
2574. Ursus maritimus' is the scientific name for a polar bear. It means 'sea bear.'
2575. The lightest, simplest, and most common chemical element in the Universe is hydrogen.
2576. There are six faint rings around Neptune.
2577. A shark has two rows of teeth. The front teeth fall out and are replaced with the second row of teeth.
2578. Magnesium is a third lighter than aluminum, so it is preferred in alloys that make airplanes and missiles.
2579. Uranus is four times bigger than Earth and the third largest planet in our solar system.
2580. In 1922, the celestial sphere was divided into 88 constellations by The International Astronomical Union and an American astronomer Henry Norris Russell.
2581. A computer scientist applies the knowledge of information theory and computation to computer

systems. They focus on theory while computer engineers focus on the hardware.

2582. The Eiffel Tower was designed to resist wind; however, as it is made of iron, which expands as it heats up, the top of the tower can move up to 7 inches (18 cm) away from the sun on sunny days.

2583. An octopus can drop one of its arms when trying to escape a predator. A new arm can then grow back.

2584. Five Argentinians have won the Nobel prize - two for physiology or medicine, one for chemistry and two for Peace.

2585. The Hubble Space Telescope has the same storage capacity as 20 car batteries.

2586. The Mississippi River is 2,320 miles (3,730 km) long and stretches over 7 miles (11 km) wide. It flows through 10 states.

2587. Crews aboard the ISS have eaten more than 25,000 meals since 2000.

2588. Iron is used to build machines, buildings, and cars, usually in the form of steel.

2589. The densest planet and the third most massive is Neptune.

2590. The comet's fuzzy outline (also called a coma) is created when it gets close to the sun.

2591. Dutch tulips are one of the tallest flowers in the world.

2592. A black hole is a very dense object in space where no light can escape.

2593. Charles Darwin and Galileo Galilei both dropped out of medical school.

2594. Galaxies are classified into four main types by their shape - elliptical, spiral, lenticular, and irregular.

2595. Natural gas mainly contains methane.

2596. Ants don't have lungs. They breathe in and out through tiny holes in their body.

2597. Lightning strikes somewhere on Earth every second.
2598. When you put two positive or two negative charges together, they repel each other. If you put a positive with a negative charge, i.e., opposite charges, they will attract each other.
2599. Muscle' comes from the Latin word musculus, which means 'little mouse.' The term describes the shape of some muscles and the shape of a contracting muscle, which can resemble a mouse moving under a rug.
2600. A snake smells its prey with its forked tongue.
2601. Impact craters, created by the collision of space objects, exist on all the inner planets.
2602. Pi is the circumference of a circle divided by its diameter. It is an irrational number and starts with 3.14, but it never repeats or ends. To 30 decimal places: 3.141592653589793238462643383279
2603. Wild mice are herbivores and only eat plants and fruit. Domestic mice are omnivores and eat almost anything they find.
2604. A stroke is often caused by a blood clot in the brain, resulting in damage to the nearby brain tissues.
2605. Obesity is a high-risk factor of type 2 diabetes and heart disease.
2606. The Spanish Gran Telescopio Canarias telescope contains a mirror with a diameter of over 9 meters (30 ft).
2607. Coal begins as a plant matter. Over time it changes form through a process of metamorphosis.
2608. Venus' surface has been described as similar to molten lead.
2609. A female elephant (cow) have babies from the age of 12. They are pregnant for 22 months.
2610. Astronauts from the USA need to learn Russian so they can run the ISS in Russian.
2611. Scientists disagree with philosophers over what time

really is. Scientists believe it is a real part of the universe, but philosophers think it's just the way we put events into an order.

2612. An elephant's trunk can sense the size, shape, and temperature of an object it holds. It uses its trunk to lift food and water.

2613. When a total solar eclipse happens, the air temperature will drop suddenly by about 20 degrees, and the immediate area turns dark.

2614. People worldwide spend much time on social media websites such as Twitter and Facebook. Social media is one of the best ways for people to connect all over the world.

2615. Cattle are the most common ungulate (mammal with hooves).

2616. Peacocks don't like snakes.

2617. The water vapor plumes detected on Europa, Jupiter's moon, in 2019 are similar to those observed on Enceladus, Saturn's moon.

2618. A cyclone is a powerful storm where winds and rain circle around a quiet, calm 'eye.' The warm moist area rises, creating clouds and wind, and when the wind is stronger than 74 mph (119 kph), it creates a cyclone. A cyclone is also called a hurricane or typhoon.

2619. Ducks eat stones, sand, and gravel to help them digest food in their stomach.

2620. Owls aren't fussy who built their nest - they use nests or holes in trees that have been built by other animals.

2621. A solar eclipse occurs when the moon completely covers the sun.

2622. The retina is the part of your eye behind your eyeball that picks up light and sends electrical signals to the brain via the optic nerve.

2623. Lava is magma that has been forced to the Earth's surface.

2624. There is no sound in space.
2625. We can successfully detect Jupiter's radiation from Earth.
2626. Wind turbines in windmills transform the energy from the wind into electricity.
2627. Stephen Hawking developed the scientific theory known as 'Hawking radiation,' which states that black holes emit thermal radiation due to the black hole's quantum effects. He proved black holes shrink and die.
2628. When scuba divers depressurize too quickly, nitrogen bubbles form in the bloodstream causing decompression sickness or the bends. This can happen to astronauts as well.
2629. The Whirlpool Galaxy has a massive black hole at the center of its spiral.
2630. Mercury is one of the five planets you can see without a telescope. The others are Mars, Jupiter, Saturn, and Venus.
2631. Cactus grows in dry, rocky places, often in a desert.
2632. When supernovas explode, elements such as gold and uranium are formed due to the high temperatures.
2633. Octopus, squid, and cuttlefish are all cephalopods. They have limbs attached to their head.
2634. The advantages of an underwater tunnel over building a bridge are that it usually needs less land. The weather has no impact, and it doesn't impact the scenery above. It is, however, usually more expensive than building a bridge.
2635. Clyde W Tombaugh discovered Pluto on 18 February 1930. It was the ninth planet from the sun.
2636. The fifth-largest moon in the solar system belongs to Earth.
2637. Hippopotamus means 'river horse'.
2638. Mars' atmosphere mainly contains carbon dioxide.
2639. Many scientists believe that Saturn's moon Titan has

similar conditions to Earth's early years, except temperature due to its distance from the sun.

2640. Ernest Rutherford read his first science book at the age of 10.
2641. Venus has a perfectly circular sphere.
2642. Saturn is known best for its rings, made up of ice and small amounts of dust. Saturn's rings are thought to be made of comets or asteroids torn apart from its strong gravitational pull.
2643. When helium cools to nearly absolute zero (-460 deg F or -273 deg C), it becomes a liquid that will flow against gravity and over a container's sides!
2644. A flyby mission is estimated to take about 16 years to Makemake with assistance from Jupiter's gravity.
2645. Scientists believe that approximately three-quarters of the universe is made up of dark matter or energy.
2646. Turtles are cold-blooded.
2647. The steam locomotive was invented in 1797 in England.
2648. Lightning occurs more frequently on Venus than on Earth.
2649. There are two types of daddy-longlegs. The animal daddy-longlegs belong to Opiliones, live under rocks, and do not spin silk or make webs. They are not spiders that belong to the order Araneae. Both these orders belong to the broader family of Arachnids. There is also a daddy-longlegs spider, which is the more common spider that we see.
2650. Some of the most densely populated globulars are among the 450 globular clusters around the Andromeda Galaxy.
2651. Johannes Kepler's three laws of planetary motion are:
2652. Many submarines can make 10,000 to 40,000 gallons (38,000 - 150,000 liters) per day of fresh water by distilling the seawater.

2653. There is a six-sided jet stream coming out of Saturn's north pole.

2654. Albert Einstein was a German mathematician and physicist known for his theory of relativity and the famous equation $E = mc^2$ (energy equals mass multiplied by the speed of light squared). In the simplest terms, this means that energy and mass or matter are interchangeable i.e., different forms of the same thing.

2655. There are more than 4,500 species of crabs.

2656. Some sea snakes can stay underwater for longer periods by breathing through their skin.

2657. An octopus has blue blood containing copper-based cytoglobin. It does the same thing as a person's red blood, which contains iron iron-based hemoglobin and carries oxygen.

2658. The black ink that octopus squirts at its enemy can sting their eyes. If the octopus doesn't then swim away, the ink can hurt their own eyes, and they could die.

2659. Jellyfish are not fish.

2660. Astronauts and cosmonauts coming from 15 different nations have visited the ISS. There have been 352 flights to the ISS, including 211 individuals, 31 of whom were women, and 7 were 'space tourists.'

2661. The melting point of nickel is 2,651 °F (1,455 °C), and its boiling point is 5,275.4 °F (2,913 °C).

2662. Brakes on a bicycle use friction to stop the bike. When you press the brakes, rubber pushes on the wheels' rims, turning kinetic energy into heat, which slows you down.

2663. Tigers are fast and can run up to 40 mph (65 kph).

2664. About 100 million pieces of junk orbit Earth at about 27,000 km/hr (17,000 mph).

2665. Orville and Wilbur Wright, known as the Wright brothers, created the first successful controlled airplane in 1903.

2666. No spacecraft has landed on Ganymede, one of Jupiter's moons.
2667. Robotics is the design, construction, and use of robots with the aim that robots will help humans in their day to day lives.
2668. The labrador is the most popular breed of dog in the world. They are gentle, obedient, and intelligent.
2669. A network of computers enables users to share data stored in different locations.
2670. Internet gaming enables people all over the world to play against and interact with each other.
2671. Jupiter turns on its axis every 9 hours and 55 minutes. This rotation flattens the plan and gives it an oblate shape.
2672. Astrophysics is a specialized branch of astronomy that focuses on the physics of the Universe.
2673. Charon, Pluto's moon, can be pronounced "SHAR-on" or "CARE-on." Both pronunciations are correct.
2674. From 1989 to 1994, one of the largest storms ever, known as the Great Dark Spot, was observed on Neptune.
2675. Martian dust storms can last for months and continuously change its surface.
2676. A meteorologist studies the atmosphere and forecasts weather.
2677. Computer space' and 'Pong' were among the first coin-operated video games played in the 1970s.
2678. Spiders have four openings or glands called spinnerets in their abdomen, which makes silk.
2679. Elephants swim by using their trunk as a snorkel.
2680. The first remote control for television was called "Lazy Bones." It was developed in 1950 and was connected to the television by a wire.
2681. Owls belong to two families - one with heart-shaped faces (barn owls) and round-shaped faces.

2682. A bat is the only mammal that can fly. Other mammals can only glide.
2683. The wind is moving air.
2684. A grasshopper has six legs, two pairs of wings, two antennae, and small pincers to tear off food.
2685. The moons of Jupiter are sometimes called the Jovian satellites, the biggest of which are Ganymede, Callisto Io, and Europa. Ganymede measures 5,268 km across, making it bigger than Mercury.
2686. We have two sets of teeth during our life - 20 baby teeth and 32 adult teeth. Adult teeth replace baby teeth from the ages of six to twelve. Other animals, like sharks, grow new teeth every few weeks.
2687. A famous Albert Einstein quote: "Whether you can observe a thing or not depends on the theory which you use. It is the theory which decides what can be observed."
2688. Rust is formed when the iron is in contact with oxygen and water. Another word for rust is corrosion.
2689. Leonardo da Vinci is best known for being the Mona Lisa, the Vitruvian Man, and the Last Supper painter. He was born on 15 April 1452 and died on 2 May 1519.
2690. Saltwater crocodiles have large heads with their eyes, ears, and nostrils at the top of their head. This lets them see, hear, and breathe when they are nearly totally underwater.
2691. Hummingbirds are 97% efficient in converting the sugar from the nectar they drink into energy.
2692. It was only in 1833 that scientists believed that meteors came from our solar system.
2693. The coldest world in the solar system is Triton, one of Neptune's 14 moons.
2694. The clouds of Mercury, ferric chloride hydrocarbons, and sulphuric acid surrounding Venus create the most corrosive acid rain of all planets.

2695. A hummingbird's tongue is as long as its bill.
2696. A grasshopper can leap up to 10 inches (25 cm) high and 3.2 feet (1 m) long.
2697. The common garden snail is considered a pest to farmers.
2698. Scientists believe octopuses are very intelligent, with short and long term memory.
2699. Fan waterfalls descend horizontally and are quite wide like a fan.
2700. A total solar eclipse can only last for 7.5 minutes.
2701. Dark matter is the matter that holds stars and dust together in a spiral galaxy. It makes up most of the mass.
2702. Due to its rapid rotation, Haumea is one of the densest dwarf planets.
2703. Iron, nickel, cobalt, and gadolinium are the only elements producing a magnetic field at room temperature.
2704. The moon will be about 23,500 km (14,600 mi) further away from Earth in about 500 million years.
2705. The Cancer Constellation used to be named 'the crayfish' 3,000 years ago in Babylonian times.
2706. Blood plasma is a yellow liquid that contains our blood cells.
2707. Ear wax, made by skin glands in your ear canal, lubricates and protects your ear from dirt and dust.
2708. Charon has more craters in its northern hemisphere than in its southern hemisphere. This means the north hemisphere is older than the southern hemisphere. The south side has undergone some resurfacing that may have buried old craters.
2709. An elliptical galaxy is very bright, so there would be light all day and night if Earth were situated in one.
2710. Mars came closest to Earth on 27 August 2003. The next time it will happen, this close will be in the year 2287.
2711. Peafowls are social birds and travel in groups of up to ten. They are very territorial.

2712. Owls have a reversible toe that can point forwards or backward.

2713. Amphibians can survive on land and in water. When on land, they live near swamps and water as they need to keep their skin moist to survive.

2714. Astronauts don't have much taste in space as we rely on gravity for food to hit our taste buds. Our sense of smell also contributes to our taste. In space, fluids build up in the sinuses without gravity, another reason why food tastes bland in space.

2715. The word telescope means "far" and "to look and see" in Greek.

2716. Dark matter or dark energy are the parts of the universe that scientists can't see or detect.

2717. Venus has no seasons as it doesn't tilt on its axis.

2718. Lung cancer was common in uranium miners in the 1940s and 1950s due to radon exposure, leading to improved mining ventilation systems worldwide.

2719. Quadrillion, quintillion, sextillion, octillion, and nonillion follow million, billion and trillion.

2720. The epiglottis is a flap of tissue at the back of our throat or pharynx. It closes when you swallow such food doesn't go down your windpipe or trachea.

2721. Driving at 96 kph (60 mph), you would reach Mars in 271 years and 221 days.

2722. The moon surface has been bombarded by micrometeorites over time, covering it in a layer of crushed powdered rocks and dust.

2723. Jupiter is the largest planet in our Solar system and is so big that it could fit 1,300 Earths inside it.

2724. Magnesium burns in hydrogen, nitrogen, and carbon dioxide, so it's difficult to extinguish a magnesium fire. Covering it with sand or a dry chemical fire extinguisher is the most effective way to fire magnesium.

2725. Elliptical galaxies are listed as type E, followed by a number representing the degree of their ellipticity.
2726. The chances of a rocket or spacecraft colliding with an asteroid are about one in a billion.
2727. Millions of volts of electricity are present in lightning.
2728. Most deer have white spots when they're born, but they lose them by age.
2729. Panthera pardus is the scientific name for a leopard. It belongs to the Felidae group of cats.
2730. An earthquake is caused by the rapid release of energy, which creates seismic waves that move rocks in the Earth's crust.
2731. The center of an atom is called a nucleus, and it has a positive charge.
2732. The female black widow spider is the most poisonous in North America. It is known to produce the strongest silk of all spiders.
2733. Triton (one of Neptune's moons) has the coldest temperature of all the objects in our solar system. The average temperature on Triton is -235 degrees C (-391 degrees F).
2734. Distillation equipment in submarines can turn seawater into freshwater for drinking.
2735. Alexander Graham Bell invented the telephone in 1876. Ten years later, over 150,000 people in the United States owned a telephone.
2736. A lightning rod on top of the Empire State Building is hit by lightning about 23 times a year.
2737. Smoking is bad for your health and can cause lung cancer and other lung-related disorders.
2738. Ancient civilizations didn't discover Uranus as it was not bright enough (and they hadn't invented telescopes yet).
2739. The red dwarfs are the most common stars. They live

longer and shine less than any other type of star. Our sun, in comparison, is a yellow dwarf star.

2740. Anthracite is a shiny metamorphic rock and a type of coal with a high carbon count and not many impurities.

2741. Nickel is used as a catalyst to make margarine, shorten, and some soaps to help change some substances from liquid to solid.

2742. When you study zoology, you also study biology, physics, chemistry, English, algebra, and statistics. A Bachelor's degree in Zoology is usually required to work as a Zoologist.

2743. Albert Einstein's theory of relativity improved on Newton's law of universal gravitation.

2744. Zebras zigzag when running away from predators.

2745. A submarine uses special filters and burners to remove unwanted dust and particles from the air inside.

2746. The second-largest species of penguin is the King Penguin. Four layers of feathers help them stay warm in Antarctica, where they live.

2747. Diamond is a different form of carbon.

2748. The solar wind is a stream of energized charged particles coming from the sun. The magnetic field around Earth shields these particles from reaching Earth to protect it from radiation damage.

2749. A mineral is a naturally occurring substance that has been formed by geological processes. Minerals have specific physical and chemical properties and are usually solid.

2750. The Triangulum Galaxy is considered as an isolated galaxy because it has not interacted with other galaxies recently.

2751. Scientists believe that Andromeda was created when small galaxies collided about five to nine million years ago.

2752. The deep orange color in fireworks is made using calcium salts.
2753. A peacock is technically a male peafowl. The female peafowl is called a peahen, but people often refer to both of them as peacocks.
2754. The inner planets are known as rocky planets, while the outer ones are known as gas giants.
2755. Shiny dust particles left behind by comets are shooting stars.
2756. The Local Group is a group of galaxies, including the three largest, Andromeda, the Milky Way, and the Triangulum Galaxy. It is about 10 million light-years in diameter. In addition to the three mentioned, it contains about another 30 smaller galaxies.
2757. Alligators are social reptiles - a group of them is called a congregation.
2758. There are 13 species of crocodile.
2759. Apart from Earth, Venus was the first planet to be seen from space.
2760. Rh is the chemical symbol for rhodium. Its atomic number is 45.
2761. Hummingbirds mostly drink nectar from flowers, but they also eat insects and fruit.
2762. Tungsten has the second-highest melting point of all the elements.
2763. Other animals lived with dinosaurs but were not dinosaurs. These included Pterodactyls, which were flying reptiles and Plesiosaurs, water reptiles.
2764. Titanium has an atomic number of 22.
2765. The kakapo from New Zealand is the only parrot that can't fly.
2766. Food must be prepared and stored carefully to reduce bacteria, which can result in food poisoning.

2767. There are rumors that you can see the Great Wall of China from the moon. These are not true.
2768. Different countries have different cuisines all over the world, depending on their culture, social and religious beliefs, economy, and what foods are available.
2769. Many science subfields have come out of astrology, including planetary science, stellar astronomy, galactic and extragalactic astronomy, cosmology, and solar astronomy.
2770. The Hubble Space Telescope is the first telescope that was designed to be repaired in space. Astronauts have fixed it in space five times. The last repair mission was in 2009.
2771. A crocodile's ears have a flap that closes when they go underwater.
2772. Nikola Tesla, famous for his design of the alternating current electric system, was born during a lightning storm.
2773. You need iron in your body to be healthy. If you don't have enough, you can feel weak. Foods high in iron include red meat, beans, and lentils.
2774. To recognize his contributions to science, Queen Victoria's husband, Prince Albert, gave Michael Faraday a comfortable home at Hampton Court. He lived with his family for the rest of his life.
2775. When a supernova occurs, it shoots billions of atoms in every direction, forming nebulae made up of clouds of dust, gases, hydrogen, and helium.
2776. A horse has a nearly full field of vision and can see 360 degrees because their eyes are on the side of their head.
2777. To convert degrees Celsius to degrees Fahrenheit, follow this equation: (Temperature in deg C x 1.8) + 32.
2778. Stephen Hawking died on 14 March 2018. 14 March is known as Pi day, named after the first three numbers of

the mathematical symbol pi (3.14). By coincidence, Albert Einstein was also born on the pi day in 1879.

2779. Jaguars are carnivores and only eat meat.

2780. Charles Messier discovered the Triangulum Galaxy in 1764 and named it as object 33 or M33.

2781. Some snakes, like the python, wrap themselves around their prey to kill it before swallowing it. This is known as constriction.

2782. Sea otters can use tools, such as empty shells and rocks, to break the shells of crabs, mussels and sea snails to eat their meat.

2783. Snails live in freshwater, saltwater, and on land.

2784. Although Europa is only one-fourth of Earth's diameter, its subsurface ocean may contain twice as much water as all of our oceans combined. This makes it a widely considered place to look for life outside of Earth.

2785. An adult female sheep is called a ewe.

2786. Earth's gravity is about 9.8 meters per second square.

2787. A meerkat survives longer in captivity, living up to 14 years compared with ten years in the wild.

2788. You will always see lightning before hearing thunder as light travels faster than sound.

2789. The universe is approximately 13.7 billion years old.

2790. The Apollo 11 astronauts couldn't get insured from their trip, so they signed photos of themselves and left them for their families to auction - in case they didn't return.

2791. Of the five dwarf planets, only two have been visited by space probes. In 2015 NASA's Dawn and New Horizons reached Ceres and Pluto.

2792. The spiral arms of the Milky Way contain the new stars, whereas its center has mainly old stars.

2793. The International Space Station (ISS) has two bathrooms, a gym, and is bigger than a six-bedroom house.

2794. Kangaroos are marsupials, which are mammals.
2795. Fifty-two computers control ISS.
2796. Cats love to play. By play fighting, kittens are practicing and learning hunting and fighting skills.
2797. No plans have been announced from India or Japan for a human trip to Mars.
2798. Geckos are good climbers because their toes are covered in fine hairs that 'sticks' to walls.
2799. Animal intestines are used for tennis racquets' strings as they are soft, resilient, and provide the most energy return.
2800. A supersonic plane can break the sound barrier and fly faster than the speed of sound of 768 mph (1,235 kph). It is used almost exclusively for research and military purposes.
2801. Snake charming still occurs in some parts of the world where a person plays the flute to 'charm' a snake out of its basket. Snakes do not respond to music. Instead, they move to the movement of the flute.
2802. Tulipmania' was three years from 1634 to 1637 when tulips were so valued in Holland that they were used for currency. Today, the Netherlands is still the largest producer of tulips in the world.
2803. The Bell Boeing V22 Osprey is a hybrid helicopter that can change from an airplane into a helicopter in 12 seconds. It could travel up to 351 mph (565 kph) as a plane, but it is not technically a helicopter even though it takes off and lands like a helicopter.
2804. The Hubble Space Telescope has observed a neutron star at the center of the Crab Nebula.
2805. Sunflowers were planted in the Chernobyl and Fukushima disasters areas to absorb toxic metals and radiation from the soil.
2806. The sun moves at 136 mi per sec (220 km per sec).

2807. Earth's life cannot exist on Mars due to the low atmospheric pressure (amongst many other things like very little water).
2808. The Atacama Desert in Chile is the driest place in the world. It rains less than 0.05 mm every year.
2809. Hummingbirds have great maneuverability.
2810. Flying squirrels can only glide, not fly.
2811. An astronomer is a scientist who studies objects in space.
2812. There are six different sloth species, either with two or three toes.
2813. Light travels at different speeds through different mediums, measured by the refractive index. The higher the refractive index, the slower the speed that light travels through. For example, the refractive air index is 1.0003, which means light travels faster through the air than glass, which has a refractive index of 1.5.
2814. We can see Halley's Comet every 75 to 76 years as it nears Earth. The last time we saw Halley's Comet was in 1986 and the next time is expected to be in the year 2061.
2815. A geyser is a water and steam that is ejected forcefully into the air. Geysers are mainly formed near active volcanic areas.
2816. The ISS supports over 100,000 people working in 16 countries and 37 states across the US.
2817. Scientists believe Ceres, dwarf planet, has a rocky core with an icy inner mantle 100 km (62 mi) thick. The ice mantle may contain as much as 200 cubic km of water, which is more fresh water than Earth.
2818. Drones or male bees come from unfertilized queen bee eggs while workers and queen bees come from fertilized eggs.
2819. Scientists are unsure why flamingos stand on one leg.
2820. Wild camels are one of the most endangered large

mammals. There are less than 1,000 wild camels in the world.

2821. Most jellyfish are carnivores and eat plankton.

2822. Giant pandas are vulnerable to extinction - there are less than 1,900 giant pandas left on Earth.

2823. Zebras, horses, and donkeys all belong to the same Equidae family.

2824. Moose is the largest deer.

2825. A geologist is a scientist who studies what Earth is made of. They also study the history of Earth and the processes that formed our planet.

2826. An astronaut has to use about 70 to 110 tools to complete their spacecraft tasks when they perform an extra-vehicular activity or moonwalk.

2827. Hungary has famous mathematicians, including Farkas Bolyai (geometry), Paul Erdos (Erdos numbers), and John von Neumann (Quantum mechanics and digital computing).

2828. A snake sheds its skin to get rid of parasites and ticks, and to get a new one!

2829. Beavers can see underwater as their eyelids are transparent.

2830. The Spitzer Space Telescope is around the size of a car.

2831. The scientific name for tomato is Lycopersicon.

2832. Ants are as old as dinosaurs, but they survived the extinction event that killed all dinosaurs.

2833. An international research team led by NASA in November 2019 detected water vapor for the first time above Europa's surface using a spectrograph at the Keck Observatory in Hawaii. Suppose scientists could study the composition of these plumes. In that case, it will help them to determine if life is possible on Europa.

2834. Gorillas are endangered, mainly because humans destroy their environment and poachers who hunt them and other animals.

2835. Owls have asymmetrical ears so they can precisely locate their prey.

2836. In some countries, water quality is poor and drinking; it results in diseases and bacteria like E. coli.

2837. On 20 August 1909, The Yerkes Observatory took the first pictures of Pluto. However, at the time, astronomers didn't know it was Pluto.

2838. Penguins live at the South Pole, but there are none at the North Pole.

2839. Owls can't see objects close up, but their far vision is excellent.

2840. Hair grows from follicles under our skin. The hair in follicles is alive. The hair above your skin is dead.

2841. One galactic year is the time it takes for the sun to orbit the Milky Way.

2842. Dung beetles feed on animal droppings, which speeds up the circulation of nutrients back into the food chain.

2843. In 1921, Albert Einstein won the Nobel prize for his work on the photoelectric effect, not for his work on relativity.

2844. Bicycles have evolved over the past 200 years since the velocipede's invention in 1817 by Baron Karl von Drais. The velocipede was a two-wheeled machine that you had to run beside to move it. Pedals were introduced to velocipedes in the late 1800's.

2845. The amount of melanin decides the color of your skin. If you have light-colored skin, you have small amounts of melanin.

2846. A penumbral lunar eclipse happens when part of the outer surface of Earth's shadow falls on the moon. It is harder to observe a penumbral lunar eclipse than a partial or total eclipse.

2847. The Niagara Falls in the USA has the highest flow rate of all waterfalls on Earth. It comprises three waterfalls - the American Falls, the Bridal Veil Falls, and the Horseshoe Falls.

2848. About 95% of all animals have eyes. The small copepod is the only animal species that has only one eye. Brittlestars and sea urchins can see without eyes.

2849. A rock is a naturally occurring solid made of minerals. The Earth's crust is made up of rock.

2850. The naked eye can sometimes see the Triangulum Galaxy. However, it can usually be found with a pair of binoculars or a telescope.

2851. Air quality must be maintained in a submarine for its occupants to survive. People breathe in oxygen and breathe out carbon dioxide. In a closed ship like a submarine, oxygen must be replenished. The carbon dioxide must be removed as too much makes the air toxic.

2852. Hydrogen comes from the Greek words' hydro' and 'genes' meaning 'water creator'.

2853. Johannes Kepler was a German astronomer and mathematician who was most famous for his three planetary motion laws.

2854. A famous Isaac Newton quote: "Plato is my friend - Aristotle is my friend - but my greatest friend is truth."

2855. The fastest fish globally is the sailfish, which can swim up to 70 mph (112 kph).

2856. An astronaut lost his wedding ring on a mission to the moon, but he found it again during a later spacewalk!

2857. Boats and ships are designed to float on water. Boats have been around for over 8,000 years.

2858. Hedgehogs like to live alone and only get together with another hedgehog to mate.

2859. The platypus has sensors in its duck-bill that picks up electrical signals made by other animals to find food.

2860. Reptiles have smaller brains than mammals.
2861. The sun makes up 99.86% of the Solar System while Jupiter and Saturn make up most rest.
2862. The Oort Cloud is named after a Dutch astronomer Jan Oort.
2863. Four of Jupiter's moons are larger than Pluto!
2864. CO2 levels in our atmosphere are increasing at accelerating rates, increasing the global temperature on Earth. About 3/4 of the increase is from fossil fuels' burning - coal, oil, natural gas - and the remaining quarter from deforestation.
2865. The jaguar has the strongest bite of any big cat, relative to its size, and twice that of the tiger.
2866. The fourth most common element in the Earth's crust is iron. It makes up about 5%.
2867. There are seven species of honeybee, which is the everyday bee that you see.
2868. The most violent weather in our solar system happens on Neptune.
2869. Makemake is essential in the history of the solar system. Along with Eris, it was one of the objects that led the International Astronomical Union to create a new classification group of dwarf planets.
2870. The Hubble Space Telescope can observe many things but not the Sun or Mercury.
2871. The outside layer of a tree is the bark that protects the tree. Bark has an outer dead layer and an inner living layer that carries sap full of sugar from the leaves to the rest of the tree.
2872. The five space shuttles were named Enterprise, Columbia, Challenger, Discovery, and Atlantis.
2873. Our salivary glands make approximately 1.5 liters of saliva every day.
2874. Paleontology is a branch of biology.

2875. The first person to determine the law of gravity and explain planets' motion was Sir Isaac Newton.
2876. Lead has many uses. In construction, it is used for roofs and gutters. Ballast keels of sailboats and scuba diving belts are made from lead, as are bullets. X-ray equipment also uses lead.
2877. Different time zones exist all over the world. When it is 4 o'clock in the afternoon in Sydney, it is 2 o'clock in the morning in New York.
2878. Radon was discovered by Friedrich Ernst Dorn in1900.
2879. The freezing point of seawater will decrease depending on the amount of salt in the water. Seawater freezes at 28.4 deg F (-2 deg C) compared with water (no salt) that freezes at 32 deg F (0 deg C).
2880. The melting point of titanium is 3,034 °F (1,668 °C) and its boiling point is 5,949 °F (3,287 °C).
2881. Crude oil or petroleum is a thick black liquid that comes from underground fossilized plants and animals.
2882. Zebras will try and scare predators away if one of their group or family is wounded.
2883. Eris, dwarf planet, was nicknamed Xena for a short period, after the television warrior.
2884. Blood with oxygen leaves the heart through arteries. Blood in your arteries looks red. The aorta is the main artery leaving the left ventricle.
2885. The smallest unit of time is called Planck time.
2886. People have been recycling for thousands of years.
2887. Galileo Galilei (commonly just called Galileo) was an Italian astronomer, physicist, mathematician, philosopher, and inventor. He was often called the 'Master of Modern Physics,' born on 15 February 1564, and died on 8 January 1642.
2888. The most common type of flood is river flooding. If the

water flow rate goes above the river's capacity, then the surrounding area will be flooded.

2889. Asteroids used to be common in the past, but not so much anymore.

2890. A shark can smell a drop of blood up to 0.25 mile (0.4 km) away.

2891. Peachicks (baby peafowl) always play moving in a clockwise direction.

2892. Ants don't have ears, so they 'hear' by sensing vibrations in the ground through their feet.

2893. Archaeology involves art history, classics, physics, chemistry, and geography.

2894. A meteoroid in space becomes a meteor when it enters Earth's atmosphere, becoming a meteorite when it hits Earth's surface.

2895. Our sun is believed to be an average-sized star, but it is so big that you could fit 1,000,000 planet Earth inside it.

2896. Hares need to run fast to survive. The Brown Hare can run up to 48 mph (77 kph), the same speed as their predator, the red fox.

2897. The fur of a polar bear is transparent, not white. It looks white because it reflects sunlight.

2898. Multiplayer role-playing games, such as World of Warcraft (WOW), have enabled many players to interact in the same virtual world, creating fictional characters and experiencing challenges and quests that the video game offers.

2899. The Hubble Space Telescope was scheduled to last until 2014, but it has continued to work today.

2900. The diameter of the Pinwheel Galaxy is approximately 170,000 light-years.

2901. Mariner 9 was the first spacecraft to orbit Mars in 1971. Although many photographs were taken of Deimos, it didn't land on the moon.

2902. The horn of a rhinoceros is made of keratin, which our hair and fingernails are made of.
2903. Horses have good hearing.
2904. Chute waterfalls force large amounts of water through narrow passages—they create high-pressure streams and are quite dangerous.
2905. Chlorine has a chemical symbol of Cl and an atomic number of 17.
2906. Many jellyfish stings through their tentacles. Most are mild and not dangerous to people.
2907. The same person who discovered Haumea discovered its two moons.
2908. Magnetic levitation will increase the speed of trains in the future. Powerful electromagnets will propel trains over and enable them to glide over guideways with little or no friction between the train and the track.
2909. A male horse is known as a stallion.
2910. The Cancer constellation can be seen in the southern hemisphere from summer to autumn.
2911. Jupiter's volcanic moon Io has colorful areas made by the sulfur.
2912. Haumea has an equatorial diameter (from one side to the other side passing through the center) of 1,960 to 1,518 km (1,217 to 943 mi). It has a polar diameter of 996 km (618 miles).
2913. Palm Islands in Dubai holds the record for the largest artificial human-made island in the world.
2914. Hedgehogs, echidnas, and porcupines are all different animals from different families.
2915. Mosquitoes belong to the Culicidae family.
2916. A physicist is a scientist who researches physics. They study everything from tiny atoms to the whole universe.
2917. The fastest train globally is the Shanghai Maglev, which travels at speeds up to 267 mph (429.7 kph).

2918. A rainbow produced at night from moonlight is called a 'moonbow.' These are rare, and we only see it as white.
2919. Draculin, an anticoagulant found in Vampire bats' saliva, is being used in medicines as a blood thinner.
2920. Most coal forms are sedimentary rock i.e.; sediments cover it over time. Anthracite, a hard, shiny black coal, is a metamorphic rock.
2921. Ernest Rutherford discovered two types of radiation, the alpha and beta particles. He coined alpha, beta, and gamma for the three most common types of nuclear radiation.
2922. Only three planets spin anticlockwise - Pluto, Venus, and Uranus.
2923. Hippology is the study of horses.
2924. Titan, the largest Saturn moon, is made up mostly of water ice and rock, with a frozen surface of liquid methane and landscapes covered in nitrogen.
2925. When Galileo's remains were moved from the initial burial place to a burial place of honor 100 years after his death, three fingers, a vertebra, and a tooth were removed from his corpse. Over time they were lost, but in 2009, two fingers and the tooth turned up at an auction. The third finger, Galileo's middle finger of his right hand, has been on display in many museums since the 1800s.
2926. Neon has a melting point of -433.46 °F (-258.59 °C) and a boiling point of -410.94 °F (-246.08 °C).
2927. Insects have no internal skeleton, but they have an external shell that protects their soft organs.
2928. Earth's atmosphere comprises 78% nitrogen, 21% oxygen, and smaller amounts of other gases, including argon, carbon dioxide, helium, and neon.
2929. Scientists have identified over 1,000 objects in the Kuiper Belt with many hundreds of thousands more to discover.

2930. The study of the relationship between triangle angles and sides is called trigonometry.
2931. Temperature is measured on the Celsius, Fahrenheit, or Kelvin scales.
2932. Full moons vary in size, depending on whether it's far away or closer to Earth.
2933. In 2018, a 46,000-year-old bird was discovered in Siberia. The bird, a female horned lark, lived during the last Ice Age while mammoths and woolly rhinos lived.
2934. When lightning strikes the ground, its heat fuses dirt and clays into silica, creating a glassy looking rock called a fulgurite. Fulgurites are rare to find.
2935. A shark has no bones. Their skeleton is made of cartilage, similar to human ears and noses.
2936. Insects are cold-blooded.
2937. Bacteria are made up of a single cell.
2938. A tornado is a very fast tube of air that spins between the ground and a cloud.
2939. Platinum's melting point is, and its boiling point is 6,917 °F (3,825 °C).
2940. A hummingbird can only perch or move sideways with its legs. It can't walk or hop like other birds.
2941. Scientifically speaking, a pumpkin is a fruit as it has seeds.
2942. The Milky Way rotates at a very fast speed of 270 km per sec (168 miles per sec). So where you were an hour ago is 965,606 km (600,000 mi) away.
2943. Due to its thick atmosphere, Venus is the hottest planet even though Mercury is closer to the sun. The dense toxic environment traps the heat on Venus.
2944. Charon, Pluto's largest moon, is covered with mountains, canyons, and landslides. It has a unique large mountain called 'Mountain in a Moat' coming out of a depression.
2945. The sixth planet from the sun is Saturn.

2946. An otter is a mammal that belongs to the Lutrinae family, with weasels and badgers.
2947. Many comets are formed in two of our solar system's outermost regions, the Oort Cloud and Kuiper Belts.
2948. Eris is about the same size as Pluto, with a diameter of about 2,325 km (1,445 mi).
2949. A meteoroid is also known as a 'space rock,' i.e., only in space. When it enters the Earth's atmosphere, it is called a meteor.
2950. There are more than 2,000, naturally occurring organic chlorine compounds.
2951. There are about 400 million dogs globally, and they have been one of our most popular companions throughout history.
2952. In the video game Destiny, Ceres was colonized by an alien race called the Fallen and destroyed by a civilization of post-humans who inhabit the Asteroid Belt.
2953. Stingrays are carnivores. Their favorite foods are clams and shrimps.
2954. Albert Einstein hated playing the violin when he was young but grew to love it and played it until he died.
2955. Antarctica is considered a desert because of its low rainfall.
2956. Cooking changes the chemical composition of food and changes its texture, flavor, and nutrition.
2957. Earth's moon stabilizes our climate, creating seasons. Without the moon, we would not be able to live on Earth.
2958. Nearly all massive galaxies have a black hole at its center.
2959. When lightning hits the ground, it looks for the shortest route to something with a positive charge, like a tree or a tall building, even a person.
2960. An ant colony can have millions of ants in it.

2961. Astronomers believe the center of all galaxies has a black hole.

2962. The higher an object is, the bigger its gravitational potential energy. For example, when you ride a bike uphill, gravitational potential energy increases and is converted to kinetic energy when you ride the bike downhill.

2963. Helium is mostly found as a gas, but it can also be a liquid or solid at near absolute zero temperature.

2964. Comet orbits tend to be elliptical.

2965. NASA launched a Unity module aboard the Space Shuttle Endeavour, which was successfully attached to the Zarya module. The Unity module was fitted with all of the long-term human living requirements.

2966. About 70% of Earth is covered in water.

2967. Squirrels live on every continent except Antarctica and Australia.

2968. Applications are available in cell phones for different functions - word processing, playing games, web surfing, and calendars.

2969. Bees sense their surroundings by smelling, tasting, touching, seeing, dancing, and using electrical and magnetic fields.

2970. Explorer 1, USA's first artificial satellite, was launched three months after Sputnik 1.

2971. Amateurs can easily find the Sombrero Galaxy with a good set of binoculars or a good telescope halfway between Virgo and Corvus.

2972. Lead is a soft, malleable heavy metal. It is also ductile and can be drawn out into a thin wire.

2973. Johannes Kepler observed a supernova and named it Kepler's Star in 1604, which faded after one year.

2974. Computers are found not just in laptops and desktops

but also in everyday devices such as mobile phones, toys, and microwaves.

2975. Baboons communicate with more than 30 sounds.

2976. The first building to have over 100 floors was the Empire State Building. It was also the tallest building from 1931 until 1972 when the World Trade Center was built.

2977. The pilot of a hot air balloon controls the speed of ascent and descent by releasing air through a vent at the balloon's top.

2978. Venus is also called the Morning and Evening Stars as it is bright at both times.

2979. The animal with the largest tongue is the blue whale. It weighs up to 425 stone (2.7 tons).

2980. An octopus has a parrot shaped beak for breaking crab shells when eating them.

2981. There are over 350,000 beetles in the world, which makes them the largest group of animals on Earth.

2982. There are only two types or species of alligator. The American alligator is larger and can grow up to 11.2 feet (3.4 meters) long and weigh up to half a ton (1,000 lbs. or 454 kilograms). The Chinese alligator is smaller, growing up to 4.6 to 4.9 feet (1.4 to 1.5 m) long and usually weighs about 50 lbs. (22.7 kg).

2983. Zinc is used in sunscreen and insect repellents to protect our skin.

2984. The Gotthard base tunnel in Switzerland is the longest railway tunnel globally, measuring 35.47 mi (57.09 km) long. The Delaware Aqueduct in New York holds the longest tunnel of 85 mi (137 km). It was drilled through solid rock and is New York's main water supply tunnel.

2985. Approximately 75% of our entire freshwater supply comes from glacier ice.

2986. Ants have two stomachs - one to store their food and store food to share with other ants.

2987. The three parts to your small intestine are duodenum, jejunum, and ileum.
2988. Hippos are closely related to whales, dolphins, and porpoises.
2989. A major acute injury in sports medicine is described as a severe head, spine, or brain injury.
2990. Some seals make caves in the snow to live in while others never leave the water and make holes in the ice to breathe air.
2991. A frog's eyes help them to swallow food. When they blink, their eyeballs push down, resulting in a bulge in its mouth roof. The bulge squeezes the food inside the mouth down the back of its throat.
2992. Ecology is a branch of biology that studies living organisms and how they interact with each other in the environment.
2993. Yerkes Observatory in Wisconsin has the largest refracting telescope. It was built in 1897.
2994. Mosquitoes are attracted to clothing with strong contrasting backgrounds.
2995. Peggy Whitson set a record on 2 September 2017, 665 days spent aboard the ISS.
2996. The bicycle's handlebar acts like a lever. The longer the handlebar, the easier it is to turn the bike.
2997. Hamsters, like guinea pigs, are small rodents that are kept as pets.
2998. Shin guards protect players' shins from injury in sports such as hockey, cricket, and soccer. The ancient Greeks and Romans wore shin guards made of bronze for protection.
2999. All parrots have curved beaks and two toes on each foot facing forwards and two toes facing backward.
3000. Persephone, Pluto's wife, was one of the names considered for Eris, the dwarf planet.

3001. It is not very easy to tell the difference between a meteorite and merely a rock. Dark meteorites can be seen easily in sandy deserts and equally in icy regions like Antarctica.

3002. There are seven different types of bridges based on their structure - beam, truss, cantilever, arched, tied arch, suspension, and cable-stayed bridges. The most expensive type of bridge to build is the suspension bridge.

3003. The Carpenter bee, Mason bee, and Mining bee are examples of solitary bees that live alone.

3004. Crocodiles have a transparent (see-through) third eyelid, which protects their eyes when they're underwater.

3005. More than 25% of natural medicines were discovered in rainforests.

3006. Mt Chimborazo, a mountain in the Andes with a height of over 6,096 meters (20,000 feet), sits higher on Earth's bulge and is, therefore, the closest point to space, not Mt Everest which is only the tallest mountain from sea level.

3007. Eris is about one fifth the size of the Earth's radius with a radius of 1,163 km (722 mi).

3008. The center of the black hole is the Singularity, which has the strongest gravitational pull.

3009. A magnet has a north and a south pole. The north pole attracts the south pole of another magnet and vice versa. Like poles repel, unlike poles attract.

3010. Guinea pigs are not pigs and do not come from Guinea. Instead, they were originally from South America. Nobody knows for sure where their name came from.

3011. Submarines can go faster underwater as they don't have resistance from waves on the ocean's surface.

3012. Saturn has the most moons in the solar system. Some are awaiting confirmation. Jupiter is next.

3013. If you combine all of the asteroids in the Asteroid Belt, it would be about our moon's size.

3014. Venus has no liquid water.

3015. It's very expensive to build a dam - the Itaipu Dam between Brazil and Paraguay cost 20 billion dollars in 1984.

3016. 20% of Earth's bird species live in the Amazon rainforest in South America.

3017. Stephen Hawking was such a wild wheelchair driver that he once crashed his wheelchair and broke his hip.

3018. Ganymede, Titan, Io, Callisto, Triton, Europa, Mercury, and our moon are larger than Pluto.

3019. Diamond means 'unbreakable'.

3020. After Saturn, Uranus is the next least dense planet.

3021. NASA mapping satellites discovered Mayan ruins, which were overgrown by jungle and may never have been found.

3022. Stephen Hawking, the British theoretical physicist, is famous for his work in cosmology, the origin of the universe, and quantum gravity.

3023. Badgers live in dry open grasslands, but as they are adaptable animals, they can also live in woods, quarries, seacliffs, and moorlands.

3024. Ants are social insects and live in large groups or colonies.

3025. The most common duck is the Mallard or wild duck.

3026. More than 230 people from 18 countries have already visited the ISS.

3027. The largest turtle can grow up to 5.25 feet (160 cm) while the smallest turtle can grow to 3.1 (7.9 cm).

3028. Over 10,000 species of birds exist on Earth.

3029. A bicycle converts the energy we use in our body into kinetic energy or movement of the bike.

3030. Aristotle was the first scientist to classify animals into different groups.

3031. In the human body, electricity makes your heartbeat and can be measured using an electrocardiogram or ECG.

3032. Two spacecraft have traveled to Mercury and a third on its way. Mariner 10 was a flyby mission that was launched in 1973 to Venus and Mercury. NASA's messenger was launched in 2004 and landed on Mercury in 2015. The last spacecraft, Bepi/Colombo, was launched in 2018 by ESA/JAXA and arrived on Mercury in December 2025.

3033. Like lions, Cheetahs have low stamina and can only run at fast speeds for a few minutes before they get tired.

3034. Hummingbirds are very small birds, with most species growing between 3 - 5 in (7.5 - 13 cm) long.

3035. M51b, the Whirlpool Galaxy's companion, is a dwarf galaxy.

3036. NASA admitted in 2006 that they had taped over the original tapes of the moon landing, hence speculating that the arrival was not real.

3037. The lowest and saltiest lake in the world is the Dead Sea, between Israel and Jordan.

3038. Male hummingbirds use their beak to fight off and stab other male hummingbirds when mating.

3039. Asteroids often collide, which ends up throwing them out of orbit or hitting other planets.

3040. The moon's gravity is about 1/5 of Earth's.

3041. Because 'A Brief History of Time,' written in 1988, was still very hard to understand for non-scientists, Stephen Hawking wrote 'A Briefer History in Time' in 2005 to make it easier to understand.

3042. A sea turtle can remove the salt from the seawater that they drink by using a special gland.

3043. You can use thunder to tell how far away a storm is. Count the number of seconds between when you see the lightning and hear the thunder. Divide this by five, and this gives you the number of miles away the storm is.

3044. Crabs are decapods i.e.; they have ten legs. Their claws are the first pair of legs.
3045. You can see things under ultraviolet or black light that you can't see with your naked eye. For example, police can detect blood with UV light.
3046. Penguin chicks don't go into the water as they don't have waterproof feathers.
3047. The strength of a tornado and the damage it causes is measured on the Fujita Scale or Enhanced Fujita Scale.
3048. As hydrogen is lighter than air, Zeppelin airships were filled with hydrogen from 1852 to 1937. In 1937 the Hindenburg airship was destroyed in a midair fire over New Jersey.
3049. NASA's Mariner 4 was the first spacecraft to successfully fly by Mars in 1965, taking 228 days to reach the planet. The images it sent back didn't show any oceans or vegetations which scientists had hoped to find. In 2008 scientists obtained evidence that suggested liquid water and maybe life once existed on Mars.
3050. Komodo dragons are lizards that only eat meat.
3051. Objects can leave and escape the Outer Event Horizon section of a black hole.
3052. Life on Earth requires water.
3053. A refracting telescope uses a concave and a convex lens.
3054. ROY G.BIV is a good way to remember a rainbow's colors - red, orange, yellow, green, blue, indigo, and violet.
3055. It takes about one minute for your heart to pump blood around your body.
3056. Some boats are propelled by motor engines e.g., powerboat, some by people e.g., kayak and some by sails.
3057. Cane toads were first brought to Australia in 1935 to control sugar beetles on sugar cane farms. They have since become a pest.

3058. Charon's surface, covered in ice, differs from Pluto's, covered in frozen nitrogen, methane, and CO2.
3059. A horse's skeleton has about 205 bones in it.
3060. Uranus receives direct sunlight for about 42 years and dark for the next 42 years during half of its orbit.
3061. Smoke, toxic gasses, dust, volcanic ash, and salt are all contaminants in Earth's atmosphere.
3062. A forest with more than 80 in (2,000 mm) of rainfall is called a rainforest.
3063. Benjamin Franklin invented the lightning rod, which transmits the electricity from lightning strikes through a grounded wire. This protects the building where the lightning rod is installed.
3064. Compared to other planets, of which it is not, Pluto has a very slow rotation and takes six days, 9 hours, and 17 minutes to rotate once. Jupiter rotates the fastest in less than 10 hours.
3065. Urine is not an effective treatment to relieve jellyfish stings.
3066. Cacti have special adaptations that help them to survive in the desert. Due to their thorns, many animals can't get close enough to drink from them. Small thin roots grow near the surface to collect as much rainwater as possible. A deep taproot can reach underground water when it hasn't rained for a long time.
3067. Only a handful of mammals have no hair, including the elephant, hippo, rhinoceros, walrus, pig, and whale.
3068. Clownfish communicate by making popping and clicking noises.
3069. Scientists estimated that in 3.6 billion years, Neptune's largest moon Triton would be torn apart.
3070. Crocodiles' jaws have little opening strength - you could hold their jaws shut using a rubber band.
3071. A baby marsupial is born without eyes or hind legs. It

continues to grow and develop through the milk they receive when suckling on their mother's nipples.

3072. As of 2018, approximately 8,378 satellites have been launched into space since the first one in 1957. Less than 40% are operational, i.e., only 1,957 of the 8,378.

3073. Only female mosquitoes bite.

3074. If you cut a bar magnet in half, you will end up with two bar magnets, each with its north and south pole.

3075. According to scientists, horses evolved from smaller 'dawn horses' about 50 million years ago.

3076. Money is used for paying for goods and services and for reflecting on their value.

3077. A hummingbird's lifespan is about 3 - 5 years, but some have lived to 12 years.

3078. Zebras are black animals with white stripes, not white animals with black stripes.

3079. The only dwarf planet with an atmosphere is Pluto. It is too thin and poisonous for humans. When Pluto is closest to the sun (at its perihelion), its atmosphere is gas. When it's furthest from the sun (at its aphelion), the atmosphere turns into ice.

3080. Neptune's surface temperature is freezing at -201 deg C (-329.8 deg F).

3081. Seals are very intelligent creatures.

3082. As of February 2020, you cannot buy a fully autonomous car or 'self driving car'. Self-driving cars rely on artificial intelligence, and engineers have been working on it for years to make it safe and reliable.

3083. Nearly four billion years ago, asteroids crashed into Mars, creating a large plain the Caribbean Sea (2,092 km or 1,300 mi). Hellas is the name of this plain.

3084. Oceans cover about 70% of the Earth's surface. They contain enough water to fill a cube 621 miles x 621 miles (1,000km x 1,000km).

3085. The heaviest lemon on record in the Guinness Book of Records was grown in Israel in 2003. It weighed 11 lb 9.7 oz (5.265 kg), had a circumference of 29 in (74 cm), and was 13.7 in (35 cm) high.
3086. Some well-known nebulae are Eagle Nebula, Barnard's Loop, Boomerang Nebula, Pelican Nebula, and Tarantula Nebula.
3087. The average distance between stars in the Milky Way is about five light-years or 48 trillion km (30 trillion miles).
3088. You can hear a lion's roar up to 5 miles (8 km) away.
3089. Uranus has 27 moons, all named after William Shakespeare and Alexander Pope's characters.
3090. A 5,300-year-old corpse, Otzi the Iceman, had tattoos that were inked from carbon (charcoal).
3091. Angels Fall in Venezuela is the tallest waterfall globally—its waterfalls 3,212 ft (979 m) before crashing down at its base.
3092. Earth's magnetic field deflects solar wind, which are charged particles from the sun.
3093. Penguins can drink saltwater. They have a special gland that filters salt out of their body.
3094. An F5 tornado on the Enhanced Fujita Scale means the tornado's winds are traveling at 261 - 318 mph (419 - 512 kph). This is strong enough to lift a car into the air and rip a house up off its building foundations.
3095. The British anthropologist Jane Goodall did very similar work to the American zoologist, Dian Fossey. Jane mainly studied chimpanzees in Tanzania, and Dian studied Gorillas in Rwanda.
3096. Most tornadoes last for less than 10 minutes—some last up to 30 minutes.
3097. Regular exercise increases your lung capacity.
3098. Waterfalls contribute to erosion and can create large cave-like shelters at its base.

3099. Charon's (one of Pluto's moons) crust looks like it has been split open as it resembles a chasm four times as long as the Grand Canyon and twice as deep in some places.
3100. Owls have 14 vertebrae in their neck, which lets them turn their head 270 degrees.
3101. Speleology is the scientific study of caves.
3102. The Titanic was the largest ship of its time at 882 feet (269 m) long. The largest cruise ship, Royal Caribbean's Oasis of the Seas, is five times the Titanic size.
3103. In ancient times during a solar eclipse, the Chinese believed that an enormous dragon swallowed the sun. They made as much noise as possible to try and scare the dragon away.
3104. Memory is stored on a computer as ROM (read-only memory) or RAM (random access memory).
3105. Pluto was the first object to be discovered in the Kuiper Belt.
3106. Cats have great hearing and sense of smell.
3107. The masseter or jaw muscle is the strongest muscle in your body.
3108. A glacier is a large mass of densely packed ice that has been formed over many years. Glaciers constantly move due to the slope of their surface, the pressure, and gravity forces.
3109. 99% of the mass of our solar system is made up of the sun.
3110. There are many different energy types, including kinetic, chemical, solar, gravitational, nuclear, and thermal energy.
3111. Charon remains permanently in one place in Pluto's sky ('tidal locking'), never rising or setting as it takes to the same time to orbit Pluto as Pluto does to orbit the sun. The same surfaces always face each other.
3112. Astronomers have strong maths and physics skills.
3113. Lycopene is a phytonutrient that has been linked with

good heart and bone health and the prevention of some cancers. Watermelon, tomatoes, red grapefruits, and guava all contain good amounts of lycopene.

3114. Spiders live on all continents except Antarctica.

3115. Baby otters can swim when they are about two months old.

3116. The Cancer constellation can be seen in the Northern hemisphere from late autumn to spring.

3117. Mosquitoes like to hovers around people, other mammals, and birds. They can sense carbon dioxide and lactic acid from 100 feet (36 m) away.

3118. On top of his work with pasteurization, germ theory, and vaccinations, Louis Pasteur also developed a technique to eradicate a disease in silkworms, which was a big relief for the silk farmers.

3119. The venom of the Australian Jack Jumper ant can cause anaphylactic shock in people who are allergic to their venom. Death from their stings, however, are very rare.

3120. The leaves of a tree are the food factories of the tree. They contain green chlorophyll, which uses the sun's energy to convert carbon dioxide from the air and water from the soil into sugar and oxygen. The sugar is food for the tree, and oxygen is released back into the air. This process is called photosynthesis.

3121. Fe is the chemical symbol for iron.

3122. When a mosquito first becomes an adult, it mates and feeds. A male mosquito will feed on plant nectar while a female mosquito looks for animals or people to bite as it feeds on blood.

3123. Toads hibernate in winter.

3124. When charged with electricity, neon gives off a brilliant red-orange color. Neon tubes were used as advertising signs and accounted only for the reddish-orange color. All the other colors in neon tubes are made from other noble gases or fluorescent lighting. Despite containing different gases, they are still called 'neon tubes.'

3125. The most famous Comet is named Halley's Comet.

3126. Steel is 1,000 times stronger than pure iron.

3127. Mars has six spacecraft in orbit, and two robots are roving its surface. NASA and ESA have plans to send further robots to Mars.

3128. High tides, also known as spring tides, occur at full and new moon when the moon and sun line up with Earth. Neap tides occur when the sun and moon are at right angles to Earth.

3129. Charon's craters were named after Star Wars and Star Trek characters, Darth Vader, James T Kirk, Spock, and Uhura.

3130. In 2007, when testing a missile, China shot down one of their satellites.

3131. All insects have three body parts - thorax, abdomen, and head.

3132. A glacier cave is formed by melting ice within a glacier.

3133. Our solar system lies about 27,000 light-years from the Galactic Centre of the galaxy, within the disk of the Milky Way Galaxy.

3134. The Tropic of Cancer is named after the Cancer Constellation. It is the most northern latitude reached by the sun.

3135. Mike Brown, the person who first discovered Eris, the dwarf planet, wanted to name Lilah after his new baby. In the end, he didn't call it this, as it would have been controversial for the rest of his family.

3136. As a result of the Earth's gravitational pull, moonquakes occur (like Earthquakes but on the moon).

3137. A torpedo is an underwater guided missile. It is self-propelled and self-guided and contains explosives.

3138. According to the Big Bang theory, the universe started as a small hot ball that cooled as it expanded.

3139. Magnetic compasses can navigate north, south, east, or west by using the Earth's magnetic field.

3140. A wolf pup is born deaf and blind and won't hunt with the pack until about eight months old.

3141. Wild pigs are important in our ecosystem. They dig or 'root' and encourage new plants to grow and spread seeds of fruit plants.

3142. You can watch DVD's and Blu-ray discs and play games through television sets.

3143. An octopus can change its color to camouflage itself when predators are near and to warn other octopi of danger.

3144. Saturn's thin rings, about 20 m (65.5 ft) thick, extend more than 282,000 km (175,000 mi) from the planet.

3145. Carbon is an amazing element. Arrange its atoms one way, and it becomes a soft black substance called graphite. Arrange them a different way, and it becomes a transparent hard diamond.

3146. Shinkansen trains in Japan can travel fast due to their streamlined aerodynamic body, which reduces wind resistance. They are also designed to minimize vibration and operate a different type of speed control system. Wide gauge tracks were also built to carry lots of goods and people.

3147. Nitrogen is an important part of all living things.

3148. Mice like to travel along walls and edges of rooms.

3149. The largest organ in our body is our skin.

3150. In 1668, Sir Isaac Newton invented the reflecting telescope, but it became a popular tool in Astronomy around 100 years later.

3151. The chemical symbol for copernicium is Cn, and it has an atomic number of 112. It was named after the famous astronomer and scientist Nicolaus Copernicus.

3152. Beavers have a good sense of smell, touch, and hearing, but their eyesight is poor.
3153. Strong winds blow on Saturn at speeds of over 800 kph (500 mph).
3154. Fertilizer is a chemical that helps plants grow. Nitrogen, phosphorus, and potassium are usually found in fertilizers. Manure is also added to soil as a fertilizer.
3155. The European badger is the largest type of badger, followed by the American badger. The smallest badger is the Honeybadger.
3156. In 1978, Charon, Pluto's largest moon, was discovered by James Christy, a US Naval Observatory scientist, when he observed a very slight bulge on Pluto. He suggested Charon after his wife's nickname, "Char" for Charlene.
3157. Poison ivy produces a sap called urushiol, which can cause an itchy rash if you touch it.
3158. NASA and ESA are working together to plan a human trip to Mars by 2035.
3159. Insects were the first group of animals that could fly.
3160. A scorpion must have soil to survive.
3161. The circumference of Neptune at its equator is 155,600 km (96,685 mi).
3162. The largest land dinosaur in the world, Argentinosaurus, was a reptile.
3163. In ancient times, philosophers used to think that the gods were angry at them and made the moon disappear during an eclipse.
3164. A Dutch astronomer Christiaan Huygens was the first person to identify Saturn's rings, but he only saw one.
3165. Eris, a dwarf planet, is so far away from the sun that its atmosphere continually freezes and collapses. Scientists believe that the sun will begin to thaw Eris' icy surface as it moves closer to the sun. They believe there is a rocky surface under the ice.

3166. Copper is known as 'man's eternal metal' because of its versatility and durability.
3167. Sand is a silicon compound called silicon dioxide or silica. Additionally, glass is made by heating sand to very high temperatures.
3168. Pigs are very intelligent and social mammals.
3169. A molecule of water consists of two hydrogen atoms and one oxygen atom.
3170. Meerkats are omnivores. Their favorite foods are beetles, caterpillars, spiders, and scorpions. They also eat eggs, small reptiles, fruit, and plants.
3171. An anagram of Albert Einstein is "ten elite brains."
3172. A black hole is about the size of a massive star.
3173. The Statue of Liberty was built in France and sent to the US as a gift. It has the date of the American Declaration of Independence, 4 July 1776, inscribed into the tablet. It is 151 feet (46 m) high and 305 ft (93 m) from the torch's ground.
3174. A male platypus has an ankle spur on its back feet that is venomous, not strong enough to kill a person, but can cause pain and swelling.
3175. The Andromeda Galaxy is getting closer to the Milky way at about 100 to 140 km/s (62 to 67 m/s).
3176. A nerve is a fiber (axon) that sends electrical impulses through your body. Each fiber is covered by myelin that makes the messages go fast through your nerve cells (neurons).
3177. The ear trumpet is a primitive funnel-shaped hearing aid that was invented in the late 17th century. It was used by people who were partially deaf.
3178. Starfish is not a fish.
3179. There are over 350 parrot species in the world.
3180. A solitary bee doesn't make honey. Instead, they pollinate flowers, trees, and crops.

3181. Over 30 species of mice have been identified.
3182. Louis Pasteur, the French chemist, and microbiologist invented Pasteurization. This process reduces bacteria in food without changing the taste of food. Milk is an example of a food that has been pasteurized.
3183. A diesel submarine charges batteries, which powers the propellers and allows the submarine to go underwater. As the battery power is limited, diesel submarines cannot stay underwater as long as nuclear submarines.
3184. A female kangaroo is only pregnant for 21 - 38 days before the baby kangaroo is born.
3185. A rabbit is a small mammal with a short fluffy tail, whiskers, and long ears.
3186. Jupiter has four moons - Europa, lo, Ganymede, and Callisto.
3187. One Portabella mushroom has more potassium than a banana.
3188. There are approximately 42 different species of toucan.
3189. Along with ancient pyramids, some modern building uses the pyramid shape. The famous art gallery, the Louvre in Paris, has a large glass pyramid. The 30 story Luxor Hotel in Las Vegas is a large pyramid that has about 4,000 rooms.
3190. URL, which stands for Uniform Resource Locator, is the same as the website address.
3191. Camels are very social animals and like to move around in herds. They blow on each other's faces when greeting each other.
3192. The five officially recognized dwarf planets are Ceres, Pluto, Haumea, Makemake, and Eris, in order from their distance from the sun.
3193. Compression sportswear are often worn by modern-day athletes to reduce the risk of injury and accelerate muscle recovery.

3194. Owls live on every continent except Antarctica.
3195. Flying fish can glide because of the large fins they have, which act as wings.
3196. A cat lives about 12 - 15 years.
3197. Europa orbits Jupiter at a distance of 670,900 km (414,000 mi) from the planet. It takes 3.5 years to complete one orbit, and as it is tidally locked, the same sides always face Jupiter.
3198. Wild cacti are becoming endangered from building developments, animal grazing, and collectors. Some species can only be exported with special permits.
3199. Collisions and impacts from the material may have impacted the orbits of Titan and Saturn's other moons intro their current positions.
3200. The inner planets may have no or a couple of moons. Mercury and Venus have no moons while Mars has two, and Earth has one.
3201. The British anthropologist Jane Goodall has been given many awards for her work with chimpanzees and conservation. These include the J. Paul Getty Wildlife Conservations Prize, the Living Legacy Award, the Rainforest Alliance Champion Award, Disney's Eco-Hero Award, the Kyoto Prize, and the Benjamin Franklin Medal in Life Science. In 2002, she was also named a United Nations Messenger of Peace.
3202. Galileo used a refracting telescope that was shorter than 5 cm (2 in).
3203. Many people think volcanoes are only large cone-shaped mountains. However, they can also be wide plateaus, fissure vents, and building domes.
3204. Sound travels at 767 mph (1,230 kph), whereas light travels at 670 million mph (approx 300 million meters per second).
3205. Our solar system makes up less than one-trillionth of our

universe.

3206. Horsetail waterfalls remain in contact with the ground beneath them.
3207. Hippos sleep underwater and come up every 3 - 5 minutes to breathe without waking up.
3208. The typical length of a platypus is about 20 in (50 cm) from head to tail.
3209. More than 700 types of igneous rocks exist on Earth.
3210. Water erosion on Mars may have created its channels and canyons.
3211. Cattle are red/green color blind.
3212. Oxygen reacts easily with other elements to form oxide compounds.
3213. Neptune is the only planet that you can't see without a telescope.
3214. The life cycle of a star begins in a cloud of dust called a nebula.
3215. There are 12 zodiac constellations: Aries, Taurus, Gemini, Cancer, Leo, Virgo, Libra, Scorpius, Sagittarius, Capricornus, Aquarius, and Pisces.
3216. Acid rain is rain with high acid levels in it, from sulfur dioxide and nitrogen oxides in the air released from factories and power stations.
3217. While only seven astronauts can fit on a space shuttle at any one time, it has flown over 600 astronauts into space.
3218. A bee has two pairs of wings, making the buzzing sound that we hear as they flap their wings.
3219. Platinum can be natural (pure) or extracted as by-products of nickel and copper.
3220. Pigs can run up to 7 mph (11.2 kph).
3221. The Big Bang Theory, the Lambda-CDM model, and dark matter are all theories of theoretical astronomy.
3222. Dolphins are very playful. They like to jump out of the water, ride waves, and often interact with people.

3223. If a rocket could travel at the speed of light, it would take it 100,000 years to travel across the Milky Way from one side to the other.
3224. Some rhinos have two horns, and some have one.
3225. The Outer Space Treaty rules that the moon can be used for peaceful purposes by everyone. It prohibits the use of weapons of mass destruction or military bases to be built on the moon. So there will never be a war on the moon!
3226. If a rhino horn breaks off, it can grow back.
3227. Leonardo da Vinci was way ahead of his time and one of the first to postulate why the sky is blue, writing in one of his notebooks that people perceive the sky to be blue due to the sun's illumination particles of moisture in the atmosphere.
3228. The metamorphic rock granulite is formed from the igneous rock basalt.
3229. Some grasshoppers can change color to camouflage itself and to avoid being detected by predators. For example, the hooded leaf grasshopper mimics a leaf, and the stick grasshopper can mimic a stick.
3230. Quasars, the furthest known objects in our universe, are a matter which breaks apart as it goes into a black hole. The nearest Quasar is billions of light-years away.
3231. The first planet to be discovered through a telescope is Uranus.
3232. Bald eagles are monogamous and only have one mate for their entire life.
3233. The design of the Eiffel Tower is so popular that there are similar buildings built all over the world. A half-scale replica was built in the Paris Las Vegas Hotel in the USA and a full scale one in Tokyo, Japan.
3234. The energy that you get from food is measured in joules or calories.
3235. Many scientists believe that dinosaurs became extinct

about 65 million years ago when an asteroid hit Earth.

3236. When an owl finishes hunting for the day or night, they return to their 'roost' to rest.

3237. Microbiologists, physiologists, geneticists, zoologists, and ecologists all work in the scientific field of biology.

3238. Titanium is orbiting Earth right now! Parts of the International Space Station is built from titanium.

3239. The study of snow, snow science, how and where it forms and changes, helps scientists understand how snow affects our planet. It helps them forecast storms and the effect on climate, glaciers, water supplies, people, and plant and animal life.

3240. The odor of household bleach is the chlorine.

3241. Between 3 to 4 million years ago, meteorites bombarded the moon, a phenomenon known as 'lunar cataclysm.'

3242. 4% of our body mass is bone marrow.

3243. The volume of the Earth's moon is equivalent to the size of the Pacific Ocean on Earth.

3244. A fireball is a meteor that burns brighter than usual.

3245. Flamingos are pink because the plankton and algae they eat are full of beta carotene. Beta carotene is the pigment that makes carrots orange.

3246. Nickel was discovered in 1751 when Baron Axel Fredrick Cronstedt tried to extract copper from the ore pumpernickel.

3247. When you practice an action over and over again, you create muscle memory. This is important when learning a new sport.

3248. The first space shuttle flew out on 12 April 1981.

3249. Isaac Newton and Galileo Galilei were both musicians. Newton played the violin, and Galileo played the lute. Galileo never knew Newton as he lived from 1564 to 1642, and Isaac Newton was born in 1643, the year after Galileo died.

3250. NASA's Hubble Space Telescope is the first astronomical observatory placed into orbit around Earth.
3251. Jupiter's circumference is 439,264 km (272,946 mi), and its diameter is 11 times the size of Earth's.
3252. Research has found that the antibacterial, anti-inflammatory, and anti-oxidant properties of mushrooms are useful in reducing blood pressure, moderating blood sugar, and reducing cholesterol. They also enhance the immune system and can help in fighting different cancers.
3253. Hedgehogs are nocturnal - they sleep all day and come out at night to eat.
3254. Butterflies and moths belong to the group of insects called Lepidoptera, which means they have wings covered with scales.
3255. The Chinese first used paper money about 1400 years ago during the Tang Dynasty.
3256. Polar bear cubs stay with their mothers for about 2.5 to 3 years to learn how to hunt, swim, and survive.
3257. Nickel has an atomic number of 28.
3258. The golden ratio is approximately 1.618. The golden ratio is often used in art, geometry, and architecture. The Parthenon in Greece and the Taj Mahal in India have been designed in the golden ratio.
3259. There is no friction or gravity in outer space so that planets can orbit the sun.
3260. A mutation occurs when the DNA of an organism changes, and a new characteristic is formed.
3261. Ice is solid water, and steam is the gas state of water.
3262. Scientists have found that many meteorites consist of a nickel-iron alloy.
3263. The staples bone, also known as the stirrup bone, in our ear, is the smallest in our body.
3264. An ostrich can run up to 60 mph (97 kph).

3265. The first reusable space equipment was the space shuttle.

3266. Pneumonia, emphysema, tuberculosis, and bronchitis are all lung disorders.

3267. The original Celsius scale had a freezing point at 100 degrees and the boiling point at 0 deg.

3268. Convection is a way in which heat travels. For example, when water is heated, the heated molecules rise to the top, and the cooler ones go to the bottom. The cooler molecules then become heated and rise to the top, and this cycle, called the convection current, continues.

3269. Many of Michael Faraday's inventions, such as his first electric motor, are on show at the Faraday Museum at the Royal Institution in Westminster, England. A copy of his magnetic laboratory is also displayed in the museum.

3270. Helium is part of the noble gas group of chemical elements. The other five are neon, argon, krypton, xenon, and radon. The outer shell of electrons is full, so they are unlikely to participate in chemical reactions. Neon is the least reactive element, followed by helium.

3271. Some chameleons give live births while others lay eggs.

3272. Your pancreas makes the enzymes in your small intestine.

3273. Earth has a tilt of about 66 degrees.

3274. Hamsters have short lifespans. Some species only live 1 -2 years while others live up to 4 years as pets.

3275. Crabs belong to the crustacea family, along with lobsters, krill, shrimp, and barnacles.

3276. The stonefish is the most poisonest fish in the world.

3277. A frog's tongue is attached to the front of their mouth to stick it out further than humans. A human tongue is attached to the back of the mouth.

3278. The number of platypus in the world has decreased due to climate changes and the clearing of land and the natural environment where they live.

3279. Scientists have disputed for years how many senses a

person has. They agree that we have five main senses - touch, sight, hearing, taste, and smell. Other senses include your ability to detect temperature or pain, your balance, and kinesthetic sense.

3280. The Hubble Space Telescope is about the size of a school bus.
3281. Humans make an artificial satellite.
3282. There is no twilight before nightfall as there's no atmosphere on the moon.
3283. Mars is the fourth planet from the sun.
3284. Aristotle thought the heart was the center of intelligence, not the brain.
3285. Haumea orbits the sun in 285 Earth years.
3286. An engineer applies scientific and mathematical knowledge to create solutions for technical problems.
3287. You have five main sense organs - eyes, ears, nose, tongue, and skin.
3288. Carbon monoxide (CO), an odorless gas made by the burning of fossil fuels, is toxic to people and animals.
3289. Hippos spend most of their time in the water as it helps keep their body temperature down.
3290. Bats are nocturnal mammals i.e.; they are active at night.
3291. Uranus has also known as the 'most boring planet in our solar system.'
3292. If you were on Pluto, you could see stars during the day as the sky is dark.
3293. Ceres takes 4.6 Earth years to orbit the sun, traveling about 413,700,000 km (257,061,262 mi). It takes 9 hours and 4 minutes to rotate around its axis.
3294. Because there is no wind or rain on the moon, the astronaut's footprints from Apollo 11 will last for over 100 million years or more.
3295. Hares and rabbits are different species of the Leporidae family, just like goats are different from sheep.

3296. Crocodiles, alligators, turtles, tortoises, lizards, and snakes are all reptiles.
3297. A carbohydrate is a chemical mixture or compound of oxygen, hydrogen, and carbon.
3298. The same energy is required to ride a bicycle at a low or medium speed and walk.
3299. The Helix Nebula is the closest to Earth, approximately 700 light-years away! This means it would take you 700 light-years to travel there if you could travel in the light!
3300. Salt is the most common chlorine compound.
3301. The world's largest steel structure is the National Stadium in Beijing, China. It is also known as the 'Bird's Nest' and contains 26 miles (41.8 km) of unwrapped steel. This engineering marvel was built for the 2008 Olympic games and is known as the most energy-efficient and environmentally-friendly stadium globally.
3302. Astronomy means 'law of the stars' in Greek.
3303. A scientist who studies insects is called an entomologist.
3304. Dolphins have exceptional vision and hearing. They can locate objects through their echolocation sense.
3305. The Cancer constellation is very difficult to see as it is one of the dimmest constellations.
3306. When rolled up into a ball, a hedgehog must stay still. It cannot roll along.
3307. Forensic scientists use ultraviolet light to see things that they can't see with the naked eye.
3308. The branch of physics that studies atomic nuclei and their interactions is called nuclear physics.
3309. A comet is a small solar system object that orbits the sun.
3310. Helicopters use the same science as airplanes to fly. Planes make a lift in the airfoils in the wings, and helicopters generate lift with airfoils built into their rotors, and not in a straight wing.
3311. It remains a mystery what happened before Big Bang.

3312. Limnology is the study of inland water bodies and ecosystems.
3313. Isaac Newton was not just interested in physics; he was also very interested in alchemy and wanted to find the 'philosopher's stone' that would turn metals into gold.
3314. Guion "Guy" Bluford Junior was the first African American in space on the space shuttle Challenger in 1983.
3315. Most food comes from plants and animals, but fermented foods and fungus that we eat, such as miso and truffles.
3316. The record for the highest outdoor elevator in the world belongs to the Bailong Elevator in China. Also known as the Hundred Dragons Elevator, it is built on the side of a cliff and is 1,070 feet (326.1 m) high, carrying up to 50 people in one trip.
3317. The diameter of a professional basketball is half the diameter of a basketball hoop.
3318. Beetles make up about 30% of all animals.
3319. Alexander Graham Bell also invented a hydrofoil boat with wings that broke a world water speed record at the time, traveling at over 70 miles per hour (112 kph).
3320. On rare occasions, sunlight is reflected 3 or 4 times within a water droplet in the sky, producing very faint third and fourth rainbows.
3321. Uranium-235 is the only naturally occurring isotope that can sustain a nuclear fission reaction.
3322. A lunar eclipse is easier to see than a solar eclipse.
3323. The sun's inner core is about the same temperature as Earth's inner core.
3324. Just like you can count how old a tree is by counting the rings in its trunk, you can count how many layers the wax plug is in a whale to tell its age.
3325. In a refracting telescope, the closer the lenses are, the blurrier the image.

3326. Makemake is a dwarf planet and the third-largest after Pluto and Eris.
3327. The moon orbits Earth in an anticlockwise direction.
3328. A spiral galaxy eventually burns through its gases. As their dust start formation slows down, they lose their spiral shape and become an elliptical galaxy.
3329. The femur is the longest bone in our body.
3330. Galaxies that form a lot of new stars at a fast rate is called a starburst.
3331. As there is no magnetic field on the moon, a compass wouldn't work.
3332. In 1952, Albert Einstein was asked if he would be the second president of Israel. He was 73 years old at the time. Einstein turned it down, saying he didn't have the "natural aptitude and the experience to deal properly with people."
3333. The four forces of flight are lift, drag, thrust, and weight. Flying a kite demonstrates the four forces of flight.
3334. A fracture cave is formed when more soluble mineral rocks dissolve between layers of less soluble rock.
3335. Most butterflies are active during the day, and most moths are active at night.
3336. A quote by Stephen Hawking on James Clerk Maxwell: "Maxwell is the physicist's physicist."
3337. Lime, or calcium oxide, makes a brilliant light when exposed to an oxyhydrogen flame. Before electricity was invented, this was used to light up theaters to perform 'in the limelight'.
3338. All planets are named after a God except Earth.
3339. About 80% of what we taste comes from the smell. You will find it hard to taste the flavor of food if you hold your nose and can't smell it.
3340. The Cancer constellation, a medium-size constellation with 506 square degrees, is the 31st largest.

3341. A comet experiences heat when it nears the sun, causing its ices to sublimate or sizzle. It may cause a small jet of material shooting out of the comet-like a mini geyser if the ice is close to its surface.
3342. Jupiter is the solar system's fourth brightest object.
3343. Cheetahs hunt for food during the day when lions and leopards hunt at night.
3344. The difference between the warm and cool air temperatures as they push against each other in the atmosphere determines the wind's speed. The bigger the difference in temperature, the faster wind blows.
3345. Taipans, Australian brown snakes, sea snakes, coral snakes, vipers, and cobras are very venomous snakes.
3346. Solar eclipses happen more frequently than lunar eclipses.
3347. Edwin Hubble, one of the most important astronomers of the 20th century, discovered the shape and size of the Milky Way. He also proved other galaxies besides the Milky Way in a universe much bigger than our galaxy.
3348. Edwin Hubble, the famous American astronomer, fought in World War I and II. In 1917 he served in France for a year, and in 1942, he helped the Army develop weapons technology.
3349. Our body uses carbohydrates as its main energy source. Carbohydrates are broken down into glucose for energy. In contrast, the body breaks down fats and protein to build tissues and cells. Most food has carbohydrates, some more than others.
3350. A platypus has no stomach.
3351. The roof of your mouth is the floor of your nasal cavity.
3352. One of the most difficult engineering projects was the construction of the Panama Canal. Approximately 25,000 people died during the project from disease and landslides.

3353. The moon represents a person's emotion and subconscious state in astrology. The sun is associated with fatherhood, while the moon is associated with motherhood.

3354. One of the world's longest known animals is the Lion's Mane jellyfish with tentacles longer than a blue whale. The longest tentacles measured 120 ft (36.6 m) long.

3355. Television is a popular technology that lets us watch entertainment, advertising, sports, and news.

3356. Although it is further away from the sun, Pluto's orbit took it closer than Neptune to the sun in 1979.

3357. The wild jaguar only lives in North and South America.

3358. The International Space Station (ISS) is the largest artificial body in orbit. It is 109 m (357 ft) in length, which makes the area of the space station span about an American football field.

3359. Wolves in the Arctic often have to go for days without eating as they cannot find food.

3360. A hummingbird group is called a flock, bouquet, glittering, hover, shimmer, or tune.

3361. James Clerk Maxwell, the Scottish scientist, and physicist is most well known for 'Maxwell's Equations', explaining the properties of electromagnetic fields.

3362. Halley's Comet's nucleus is small and measures about 15 km (9.3 miles) long, 8 km (5 miles) wide, and 8 km (5 miles) thick. In comparison, the coma can stretch up to 100,000 km (62,137 mi).

3363. Jupiter orbits the sun once every 11.8 Earth years.

3364. A tunnel boring machine can dig through sand, clay, and hard rocks and is commonly used to excavate big tunnels. The biggest tunnel-boring machine has a diameter of over 46 feet (14 m).

3365. A volt is a basic unit that measured voltage or electric potential energy.

3366. The heat will not flow from a colder body to a hotter body. This is the second law of thermodynamics by Lord Kelvin.
3367. The space shuttle launches vertically like a rocket and lands horizontally like an airplane.
3368. When a submarine is underwater but close to the surface, the crew can use a periscope to look outside. The periscope allows them to see 360 degrees.
3369. The main function of the heart is to pump blood around the body.
3370. Saturn has the second shortest day of all the planets, lasting 10 hours and 34 minutes. Jupiter has the shortest.
3371. Earth was called the Blue Planet when astronauts first went into space and saw it covered in oceans.
3372. Ceres, with a diameter of 950 km, is now a dwarf planet. However, it was first known as an asteroid in 1801 when Giuseppe Piazzi found it.
3373. A frog is an amphibian. It lays eggs that hatch into tadpoles and later metamorphoses into a frog.
3374. The compound nitroglycerin is a liquid used to create explosives.
3375. Most animals with spines have two lungs.
3376. Your sense of smell is about 10,000 times more sensitive than your taste.
3377. A rounder ball played in rugby. It contained an inner tube made of a pig's bladder, hence the nickname "pigskins" for American footballs. The ball's evolution to a more oval shape has also evolved the game with more forward passes in American football.
3378. A golf ball has dimples to reduce drag and let it go further than a ball with no dimples on it.
3379. The metamorphic rock slate starts as the sedimentary rock mudstone.
3380. Extreme sports athletes are often considered brave due to

the high risks of the sport. The become famous by performing new 'tricks', such as Tony Hawk's 900 in skateboarding and Heath Frisby's first snowmobile front flip.

3381. The Kuiper Belt is named after the astronomer who predicted its existence, Gerard Kuiper.
3382. The chemical symbol for Zinc is Zn.
3383. The Royal Family paid William Herschel (the person who discovered Uranus) 200 pounds to look through his telescopes.
3384. Some pigs can swim.
3385. Haumea rotates very quickly on its axis, which means a day on Haumea lasts about 3.9 hours.
3386. A sloth can turn its head about 270 degrees because it has extra vertebrae in its neck.
3387. As Pluto is about the same size as one of Neptune's moons, Triton, some scientists think it may have orbited Neptune and was pulled out of its orbit to go into Plut's.
3388. The Empire State Building was built in 410 days, much faster than expected. It was the tallest building for 41 years from 1931 to 1972. There are 73 elevators in the Empire State Building.
3389. Pyramid shapes have been used for thousands of years to build structures. The most famous are the Pyramids of Giza in Egypt, built as tombs for Pharaohs and their families.
3390. Many asteroids and comets have collided with the moon in the past, creating many impact craters. As the moon has no atmosphere, it has no weather to erode these craters.
3391. Before Ceres was classified as a dwarf planet in 2006, it was considered a planet and then an asteroid.
3392. Some meteoroids travel at speeds of 42 km/sec (26 mi/sec) through our solar system.

3393. Nerve cells work by a combination of chemical and electrical actions.
3394. Due to expanding or contracting steel at different temperatures, the Sydney Harbour Bridge can rise or fall up to 7.1 inches (18 cm). The bridge is made from 6 million rivets and weighs 39,006 tonnes.
3395. A honey badger is also called a 'ratel' because it makes a rattling sound when attacked.
3396. Every mammal has hair on their skin.
3397. Easter is calculated as the first Sunday after the first Saturday after the first full moon after the equinox.
3398. Neptune spins around very quickly on its axis.
3399. The six flamingo species are the Greater and Lesser flamingos, the Chilean flamingo, the Andean flamingo, James' flamingo (puna), and the American flamingo (Caribbean).
3400. A sudden short burst of a high-speed wind is called a gust.
3401. To convert degrees Fahrenheit to degrees Celsius, follow this equation: (Temperature in degrees Fahrenheit - 32) x (5 / 9)
3402. Color televisions started to become more popular in the 1970s after the premiere of Walt Disney's 'The Wonderful World of Color' in 1961.
3403. Sulfur has a melting point of 247.3 °F (119.6 °C) and a boiling point of 832.3 °F (444.6 °C).
3404. The damage that an earthquake can cause is dependent on the depth and fault type of the earthquake.
3405. Cubic zirconia is a synthetic diamond made of zirconium dioxide(Zr)2).
3406. Jupiter's moon Ganymede is the largest in the solar system.
3407. Leopards have sleek, powerful bodies that make them

great hunters, swimmers, and climbers. They can run as fast as 35.4 mph (57 kph).

3408. Dams can fail and cause much damage. In 1889 the South Fork Dam in Pennsylvania, USA, failed and killed more than 2,200 people. In 1979 the Banqiao Dam in China was destroyed by a typhoon and killed up to 230,000 people.

3409. On 19 January 2006, NASA launched the New Horizons spacecraft. It flew within 27,359 km (17,000 mi) of Charon, Pluto's largest moon, nine years later, on 14 July 2015.

3410. The Polynesians have relied on the Magellanic Galaxies to predict wind as well as for navigation.

3411. A delta rocket launched the Spitzer Space Telescope, and it weighed around 929 kg (2,049 lb).

3412. The ancient civilizations did not find Neptune. It was only first seen in 1846 using mathematical predictions.

3413. The Space Shuttle was NASA's transportation system in space. It transported astronauts and cargo to and from Earth's orbit.

3414. When they fly, bees carry a negative electrical field. As pollen has a positive electrical charge, the bee is attracted to the flowers.

3415. There can only be one queen bee in a hive. When new queens are hatched simultaneously, they fight each other, and the winner will become the new queen bee.

3416. A mother hamster will put a baby hamster in her mouth to protect it if she feels it is in danger.

3417. With a very thin and almost no atmosphere, Mercury has no weather or winds.

3418. Pluto used to be the 9th planet from the sun, the smallest and furthest planet before it was demoted to dwarf planet status.

3419. Triton is approximately 354,800 km (220,405 mi) from Neptune.
3420. Planets that can be seen at the time of a total solar eclipse will be seen as light points in the sky.
3421. Most insects have wings.
3422. Scorpions use their tail to sting their prey and defend themselves from predators.
3423. In 2008 Haumea was classified as one of the dwarf planets.
3424. Sloths live in trees in Central and South American jungles.
3425. The metal nickel was previously used to make some coins, but this ceased as some people were allergic to nickel, and cheaper metals became available.
3426. The furthest an astronaut has gone into space is 401,056 km (249,205 miles) from Earth. On the Apollo 13, Jim Lovell, Jack Swigert, and Fred Haise made this trip.
3427. Mars is often called the 'red planet' due to the iron minerals in its surface, causing it to look red.
3428. The core of Earth makes up about 30% of its mass, whereas the moon's center makes up for 2-4% of its mass.
3429. The spiraling winds of a hurricane can reach 198 mph (320 kph)!
3430. An eagle that lives in a forest has a shorter wingspan than an eagle that lives in the open.
3431. There are no longer any domesticated guinea pigs living in the wild in the world. There are, however, other types of guinea pigs still living in central and South America.
3432. Fire is a chemical reaction that gives off heat and light.
3433. Most badgers are not endangered except the hog badger, which is listed as near threatened.
3434. Flamingo chicks are born white or grey and become pink over the first two years of their life.

3435. When Phobos, Mars' largest moon, is destroyed, it will give Mars rings like other planets.
3436. Alligators are often called 'living fossils' as they have been around for millions of years.
3437. There is enough concrete in the Hoover Dam to construct a two-lane highway about 4,000 miles (2,500 km) long between New York, on the east coast of North America, and San Francisco on the west coast.
3438. An adult will blink about ten times a minute while a baby blinks once or twice.
3439. Pure gold is indestructible. It does not rust and can't be destroyed by fire. It is melted over and over again to be reused.
3440. Neptune completed its first 165-year orbit around the sun in 2011 since it was first discovered in 1846.
3441. Turtles spend most of their time in the water, whereas tortoises live on land.
3442. Penguins have a special 'preen' gland that makes waterproof oil so that their feathers are waterproof.
3443. In 1951 a monkey named Yorik and 11 mice became known as the first animals to survive a trip to space.
3444. The three varieties of peafowl are the Green, the Congo, and the Indian.
3445. While there is no water on Mercury's surface, there may be underground water.
3446. The pictures from a refracting telescope are blurrier than those from a reflecting telescope.
3447. The Hubble Space Telescope discovered Uranus' two outer rings from 2003 to 2005.
3448. Earth is the only planet that is not named after a god.
3449. The middle ear, behind the eardrum, amplifies, and equalizes sound pressure.
3450. The smallest crab species is the Pea Crab, measuring half an inch (a few millimeters) wide. The largest crab species

is the Japanese Spider Crab, which has a leg span of 13 ft (4 m) wide.

3451. Jellyfish have no backbone.
3452. The sun takes 225 to 250 million years to orbit the Milky Way.
3453. A meerkat is about 9.8 - 13.8 in (25 - 35 cm) tall when standing upright.
3454. A nebula is usually made up of hydrogen and helium.
3455. A sunflower follows the sun using an internal clock. This is called heliotropism. Genes on the east side of the sunflower are more active in the morning, and genes on the west side are more active at night. This helps the sunflower track the sun as it moves from east to west.
3456. Michael Faraday was an English scientist who was known as the Father of Electricity. He is famous for discovering electromagnetism laws, inventing the first electric motor (using a magnet, liquid mercury, and wire) and building the first electric generator.
3457. In the 1100s, Ptolemy, a Greek astronomer, recorded The Cancer constellation.
3458. A common pond frog can breed at the age of three.
3459. The Japanese macaque is a monkey that can live in very cold temperatures (5 deg F or -15 deg C).
3460. Pigeons are one of the most intelligent birds on Earth.
3461. Titan is Saturn's largest moon, out of its 62 moons.
3462. Saturn is a gas giant with a radius of about nine times longer than Earth.
3463. Forensic toxicology studies drugs and poisons found in a person for a legal matter.
3464. A dwarf planet is considered by the International Astronomical Union to be an object in our solar system that is not as large as a planet but is bigger than a small object in the solar system such as a comet or asteroid.
3465. Most of the universe is made up of dark matter, according

to scientists.

3466. Black holes are full of debris that they have collected from space. They are not empty.

3467. Blood is made of three parts - red blood cells, white blood cells, and platelets.

3468. Ganymede, one of Jupiter's moons, is named after a mythical Greek boy who, disguised as an eagle, was carried to Olympus by Zeus. He became the Olympian gods' cupbearer.

3469. A constellation begins at dusk in the east and ends at dawn in the west.

3470. The only mammal native to Iceland is the Arctic fox.

3471. Half of the total weight of a person is from muscles.

3472. H is the chemical symbol for hydrogen. It has an atomic number 1, which means 1 proton is found in the nucleus.

3473. A bee has a long tongue called a proboscis, which they use to get nectar out of flowers.

3474. The gap between lightning and thunder gets shorter the closer you are.

3475. An eagle is a large bird of prey.

3476. Our bones keep growing until we reach our mid 20's. Our skeleton's bone mass density is the most when we're about 30 years old.

3477. Because Mars' moons are not as large as Earth's moon and don't stabilize it, it tilts more towards the sun, causing warmer summers than on Earth.

3478. The front teeth of a squirrel grow about 6 in (15 cm) every year.

3479. The chameleon can move its eyes independently of each other to look in different directions at the same time. No other animal in the world has this ability.

3480. The Incas in South America built rope bridges that spanned canyons and gorges in the Andes Mountains before the 1500s.

3481. Cub leopards stay with their mother until they turn two when they can defend themselves.
3482. The nocturnal owl monkey can be affected by malaria, so scientists use them for experiments to treat malaria.
3483. The sun is our solar system's star.
3484. Toads are social animals and live in groups called knots.
3485. Not all carbohydrates are the same. Carbohydrates found in refined food such as white bread and fruit juices have little nutrition. They will give our body a temporary burst of energy. More natural complex carbohydrates such as those found in fruit and vegetables and wholegrain bread contain more nutrients and give us energy for longer.
3486. Alan Shepard was the first American who went to space on the Mercury 3 on 5 May 1960. However, the spacecraft only traveled to 186 km (113 mi) above Earth before parachuting into the Atlantic Ocean.
3487. The jaguar is the largest big cat in America.
3488. A chameleon can change its color to show its emotions.
3489. Toads are nocturnal and active at night.
3490. Turtle' was the name of the first military submarine. It was built in 1775 and held one person who used hand-cranked propellers to move horizontally and vertically.
3491. The three greatest Greek philosophers were Socrates, Plato, and Aristotle. Socrates taught Plato who taught Aristotle. Aristotle taught Alexander the Great.
3492. There is a rumor that Galileo Galilei once dropped two cannonballs of different masses from the Leaning Tower of Pisa to demonstrate that speed is not related to an object's mass. It was just a rumor!
3493. The tiger is the largest big cat, followed by the lion and then the jaguar.
3494. Water pollution results in dangerous bacterias and viruses, which is harmful to people.
3495. The most social of the cat species is the lion, which often

lives in pride or groups of females, a few miles, and they're young.

3496. Scientists believe Haumea and the sun were created about the same time, 4.5 billion years ago.
3497. Pressure systems in the atmosphere create our weather. Air movements are caused by air temperature and pressure changes, which in turn creates wind.
3498. Scientists experimented on chimpanzees in 1974 to try and develop a vaccine. When the lab closed in 2004, the remaining chimpanzees were moved to Monkey Island in Liberia, Africa.
3499. Isaac Newton stuttered, but so did Aristotle, Winston Churchill, and Charles Darwin.
3500. Magnetic objects can be attracted or repelled by magnetism.
3501. Red blood cells carry blood around your body. They are produced inside your bone marrow.
3502. Before 2016 golfers were allowed to use anchored golf putters that rested the handle against their body, giving them better control. As it was decided that it "was not in keeping with the traditional method of making a stroke," it was banned from 2016.
3503. The bicycle wheel and an axle make up a simple machine. The speed of the bicycle is determined by how fast the wheel turns. The taller the wheel, the faster they go when you turn the axle.
3504. When standing on Mars, our Earth sunset looks blue.
3505. 70% of Earth is covered with water.
3506. Birds evolved from theropod dinosaurs.
3507. Hippos give birth in water.
3508. Elliptical galaxies contain not much gas or dust, so very few stars are formed. They are often the largest galaxies and the oldest.

3509. Oil does not mix with water unless an emulsifier is used. Detergent is an example of an emulsifier.
3510. In the 3rd century BC, Aristarchus of Samos became the first person to estimate the moon's distance and size and the sun. He was also the first person to create an ancient tool called an astrolabe, which was used to solve problems relating to time and the sun and stars' position.
3511. Coins have been made from different metals, including gold, silver, copper, and nickel. Some coins have a hole in the center so they could be tied together with a string.
3512. A clownfish can change sex from male to female but not the other way.
3513. The nuclear reactor, diesel engines, and batteries provide the electrical energy to heat the submarine's temperature.
3514. Putting some chemical alkali metals, such as potassium, into the water can lead to an explosion. For that reason, they are often stored in oil.
3515. The scientist Isaac Newton was named after his father "Isaac Newton".
3516. The most famous Mayan pyramid is El Castillo, in Yucatan, Mexico. It is also called the Temple of Kukulcan.
3517. A full marathon is 26.219 miles (42.195 km).
3518. In the manufacturing, agricultural, chemical, and construction industries, magnesium compounds are commonly used.
3519. The sun is not round and is flat on the top and bottom.
3520. Titanium is a poor conductor of heat and electricity.
3521. Zebras have pigmentation in their skin that gives them stripes.
3522. Venus has a few small crater impacts than other inner planets. Its thick atmosphere, 92 times greater than Earth's, protects it from meteors and asteroids that enter its atmosphere.

3523. The darkness during a total lunar eclipse is measured using the Danjon Scale. It ranges from 0 when the moon is almost invisible to 4 when the moon is a very bright yellowish-orange color.
3524. A baby kangaroo is called a joey.
3525. The four chambers of cattle are rumen, reticulum, omasum, and abomasum.
3526. Uranium's fissile properties mean it can cause a nuclear chain reaction.
3527. The three most common forms of carbon are coal or soot, diamond, and graphite.
3528. A nebula that has no well-defined boundaries is called a diffuse nebula. The Carina Nebula is an example of a diffuse nebula.
3529. Veins carry blood to the heart. Arteries carry blood away from the heart.
3530. Au is the chemical symbol for gold.
3531. Bats carry more viruses than any other mammal in the world.
3532. In a total solar eclipse, we can only see the solar corona of the sun.
3533. Scientists believe that in the Milky Way, seven new stars are formed every year.
3534. Louis Pasteur was a French biologist and chemist scientist who discovered vaccination and pasteurization.
3535. Experimental and spacecraft systems on the ISS make up an area of around 100 telephone booths.
3536. Ganymede, one of Jupiter's moons, is the largest moon in our solar system and the only moon with a magnetosphere, i.e., it has a strong magnetic field. Scientists believe its nickel and iron core generates the magnetic field.
3537. The melting point of copper is 1,984.28 °F (1,084.6 °C), and the boiling point is 4,643.6 °F (2,562 °C)

3538. In 1914 Henry Ford further improved his production line system for manufacturing cars. He reduced the time taken to produce parts of a car from 12.5 to 1.5 person-hours by assigning each worker to a specific task or station, making the whole process more efficient.
3539. The composition of Earth is mainly iron, oxygen, and silicon.
3540. Before the invention of mathematical symbols in the 16th century, mathematicians used words.
3541. Elephants are the largest mammals on land.
3542. Your body has two types of hair. Vellus hair is the short fine light-colored hair that covers your body. Terminal hair replaces some vellus hair during puberty. It is the longer thicker hair on your head, chest, face, armpits, and pubic areas.
3543. A giraffe has a tongue covered in bristly hair to help them eat thorny plants.
3544. A woody shrub is a plant that hasn't grown tall enough to be a tree.
3545. A Mars day is equivalent to 24 hours 37 minutes on Earth.
3546. Honey badgers are immune to snake venom because they have thick, tough skin.
3547. Your tongue has about 3,000 to 10,000 taste buds or receptors.
3548. Earth could fit inside the Sun 1.3 million times due to the sun's immense size.
3549. Ducks are related to swans and geese, and they all belong in the waterfowl family of Anatidae.
3550. Oxygen makes up approximately 1% of the mass of the sun.
3551. An anemometer is an instrument that measures wind speed.
3552. Water is processed in many different ways - purification,

filtering, distillation, and plumbing.

3553. There are over 4,000 to 6,000 species of lizards in the world. Some have no legs, while others have two or four legs.
3554. Cattle do not sleep standing up; they lie down.
3555. Dinosaurs became popular, even though they died 65 million years ago, due to films and books. For example, Jurassic Park was a novel made into a movie about dinosaurs brought to life with DNA found in mosquitoes stuck in amber.
3556. Jupiter's intense magnetic field produces exceptionally high radiation levels on its moon, Europa, strong enough to kill a person in one day.
3557. The study of fossils is called paleontology.
3558. Dolly was the name of the first sheep that was cloned in 1996.
3559. A biosatellite is one used to carry living organisms for scientific experiments.
3560. Electrolysis is used to extract calcium from its compounds. Pure calcium is a soft silvery-white metal that forms a gray-white oxide and nitride coating when exposed to air.
3561. Nitrogen has no color, odor, or taste under normal conditions.
3562. Scientifically speaking, a tomato is a fruit, not a vegetable, as it has seeds.
3563. In the 1600s, astronomers once thought that the Andromeda Galaxy was part of the Milky Way.
3564. Mark, which comes from the Latin word for Mars, was the name of the character that Matt Damon played in the 2015 movie, The Martian.
3565. Venus has mountains, valleys, and lots of volcanoes. It has lots of larger craters as smaller asteroids don't make it through the atmosphere.

3566. Bats carry diseases and spread viruses that can infect people.
3567. Flamingos are omnivores i.e.; they eat meat (insects, small fish) as well as plants.
3568. The composition of the sun is 75% hydrogen and 28% helium.
3569. The earthquake in northern Japan Tohoku region on 11 March 2011 had a magnitude of 9.0. It killed more than 15,000 people.
3570. Mice have long tails, often longer than its body.
3571. A comet can break up if it gets close to the sun too many times or if it comes too close to the sun or another planet in its orbit.
3572. Calcium is necessary for our bones to stay strong and healthy.
3573. Eris and its moon Dysnomia are the furthest known objects in our solar system.
3574. On 14 February 1876, both Alexander Graham Bell and an American electrical engineer Elisha Gray filed patents for their telephones on the same day. There were many lawsuits over who should be awarded the patent with Bell winning in the end.
3575. Paleontologists believe that a very small percentage of dinosaurs that lived on Earth were found as fossils. Most animals simply decayed.
3576. There are over 2 billion pigs on Earth.
3577. Psychology is the study of the mind. A person who specializes in psychology is called a psychologist.
3578. Jellyfish have no brains.
3579. Hummingbirds only live in the Americas and mostly in South America.
3580. Crocodiles are cold-blooded, like other reptiles, and cannot generate its heat. In winter, they hibernate or go dormant.

3581. The symbol for nickel is Ni.
3582. The Triangulum Galaxy is considered a satellite of the Andromeda Galaxy because of its proximity to one another.
3583. A female giraffe has a baby standing up.
3584. The windiest planet in our solar system is Neptune.
3585. A diesel submarine can only charge its batteries on the ocean's surface or use a snorkel just below the surface.
3586. The South Pole-Aitken, the largest crater on the moon, is also the largest crater in our solar system. It has a 2,500 km (1,550 mi) and is located on the far side of the moon.
3587. It is believed that Galileo's blindness is due to looking directly into the sun with his telescope. But the truth is he became blind from cataracts and glaucoma.
3588. Polar bears have black pads under each paw, which helps grip the ice, so they don't slip.
3589. Antibiotics can be used to treat bacterial infections.
3590. A quote by Albert Einstein on James Clerk Maxwell: "The special theory of relativity owes its origins to Maxwell's equations of the electromagnetic field."
3591. An eclipse happens when the moon, sun, and Earth all lineup.
3592. The tail of a leopard helps it to balance and turn sharply. It is nearly the same length as its body.
3593. Most meteors burn up in our atmosphere before it lands.
3594. The Milky Way was also described in Greek mythology as the road to Mt Olympus.
3595. Rain and snow replenish water in dams for hydroelectric plants to create electricity.
3596. Chemistry goes back to the Ancient Egyptians. As early as 1000 BC, chemistry was used to make medicine from plants, make wine and make up.
3597. The wings of a plane are shaped to reduce the effect of gravity pulling down on the plane.

3598. Earth has one moon and two more asteroids that also orbit Earth. Earth's two co-orbital satellites are called 3753 Cruithne and 2002 AA29.
3599. Space has been growing bigger since the beginning of time.
3600. The thick shell of a crab is made of calcium carbonate and protects the soft tissue underneath.
3601. Apart from visible light that we see, the Milky Way gives out many types of energy, including infrared light, gamma rays, dark matter, radio waves, and x-rays are emitted from our galaxy.
3602. The giant panda is native to China.
3603. Lightning can strike from the cloud down or the ground up.
3604. Saturn's moons are all frozen.
3605. Much of Aristotle's original works have been lost, leaving about one third behind.
3606. On 15 December 1970, the Russian spacecraft, Venera 7, became the first successful spacecraft to land on Venus.
3607. There are about 264 species of monkeys in the world.
3608. A young female horse is known as a filly.
3609. An individual wolf will only hunt smaller prey, such as squirrels and chipmunks. However, a pack of wolves can prey on larger animals such as moose and caribou.
3610. The white rhinoceros is the second-largest land mammal. The elephant is the largest.
3611. The Leaning Tower of Pisa in Italy was restored from a 5.5-degree angle to a 4-degree angle in 1990 and 2001.
3612. The first black hole to be imaged sits in the middle of the M87 galaxy.
3613. A crocodile can stay underwater for about an hour.
3614. High altitude balloons were first used to test outer space exploration.

3615. A hedgehog rolls into a ball when threatened - its stiff, sharp spines scares off most predators.
3616. The Milky Way Galaxy is smaller than the Andromeda Galaxy.
3617. The gas that flows out of the Magellanic Clouds is being absorbed by the Milky Way and may collide or merge with it in the end.
3618. Titan orbits Saturn at a distance of about 1.2 million kilometers (750,000 miles) and takes 15 days and 22 hours to complete an entire orbit.
3619. A tornado in the southern hemisphere rotates clockwise, whereas a tornado in the northern hemisphere rotates counterclockwise.
3620. Many metals are not attracted to magnets, including copper, aluminum, silver, or gold.
3621. You can see Haumea with a good quality telescope as it is very bright.
3622. The solar system orbits the Milky Way galaxy at a speed of about 220 km/sec or 136 miles/sec, which is approximately 0.073% of the light's speed.
3623. Many astronomers believe that black holes exist in the center of all galaxies, including the Milky Way.
3624. It has been suggested that more than one supermassive black hole exists in the M87 galaxy.
3625. The methane in Neptune's atmosphere absorbs all the red light, so Neptune appears blue.
3626. Callisto, one of Jupiter's moons, is the same size as Mercury, but it is not a planet as it orbits Jupiter and not the sun.
3627. The space station completes 15.5 orbits around Earth in a day, which means that every 92 minutes, crew members onboard the station experience a sunrise or sunset.
3628. Hummingbirds sleep at night.
3629. An earth observation satellite is used to make maps and

observe environmental changes.

3630. For example, a lenticular galaxy, the Sombrero galaxy, resembles lenses and has features belonging to spiral and elliptical galaxies. They have a thin rotating disk of stars but no spiral arms. They are similar to elliptical galaxies as they have very little dust and matter, so they do not form new stars.

3631. One million Earths could fit inside the sun, which is considered to be an average-sized star.

3632. The Triangulum Galaxy is also known as Messier 33, NGC 598, and the Pinwheel Galaxy.

3633. The first vehicle to travel on the moon is the Soviet robot Lunokhod 1 pm 17 November 1970.

3634. Absolute zero, also known as 0 Kelvin, is theoretical. It is known as the coldest temperature, but it doesn't exist. However, scientists have been able to use lasers to slow down particles to a temperature just above 0 Kelvin.

3635. Three men from Yemen claimed they inherited Mars 3,000 years ago, so in 1997, they sued NASA for trespassing on Mars!

3636. A spiral galaxy is also called a disk galaxy.

3637. Scorpions have an exterior skeleton, which they molt about seven times in their lifetime. As they're waiting for their new shell to harden, they're more vulnerable to predators.

3638. Mag' wheels for cars used to be made from magnesium, but this has since been replaced with aluminum.

3639. Deers live on all continents except Australia and Antarctica.

3640. Koalas can only be found in the wild in Australia.

3641. To be able to be a NASA trainee, you must be American, pass a challenging medical and physical examination, and have 20/20 vision.

3642. The chemical element of calcium has the symbol Ca and

an atomic number of 20. It appears just below magnesium in the same group of metals that are more chemically reactive.

3643. When you're cold, you get goosebumps on your skin. The goosebumps are hair follicles standing up. If we had fur like all mammals have, or longer body hair, the goosebumps would keep us warm as it would create a layer of 'fluffy' warmth.
3644. Labradors assist in police work and are common as guide dogs.
3645. Lyman Spitzer was the first person to suggest launching a telescope into space.
3646. The red giant HE 1523-0901 is known as the oldest star in the solar system.
3647. There are more than 100 different breeds of dogs.
3648. Peacocks are omnivores and eat insects, small animals as well as seeds and plants.
3649. Pluto's moon, Charon has freezing temperatures of -220 degrees C (-364 degrees F) compared with the coldest object in the solar system, Neptune's moon, Triton, with a temperature of -235 degrees C (-391 degrees F)
3650. The official match ball of the 2014 FIFA World Cup took 2.5 years to design and test. The final result with the micro dimple textured surface improves the ball's grip, stability, and aerodynamics.
3651. Uranus is the seventh planet from the sun.
3652. An astronaut that reaches more than 100 km (62 miles) in altitude is recognized by the World Air Sports Federation (FAI). Astronauts who reach 80 km (50 miles) in the USA are awarded astronaut wings.
3653. Gold is soft and malleable and can easily be shaped. One gram of gold can be flattened into a 1 square meter sheet.
3654. Scientists believe the long black lines which run from the inside of a cheetah's eye to its mouth help them see long

distances, up to 3.1 miles or 5 km away. They also believe the "tear lines" protect their eyes from the sun.

3655. Henry Cavendish is credited for discovering hydrogen in 1766.

3656. The chemical symbol of nitrogen is N with an atomic number of 7.

3657. Apes and chimpanzees are not monkeys.

3658. Large bee colonies will divide into two to propagate their species. This process, called swarming, often means the queen bee must go on a diet to fly with half the colony to a new home.

3659. A day on Venus lasts 243 Earth days.

3660. Lightning has an average temperature of 36,000 deg F (20,000 deg C).

3661. When you cut an onion, it gives off a gas that stings your eyes. Your eyes then tear up to try and remove the stinging sensation.

3662. Outer space was first coined in a poem The Maiden of Moscow by Lady Emmeline Stuart-Wortley in 1842.

3663. When metals are recycled, strong magnets are used to sort through them.

3664. From 1656 to the time he died in 1727, Isaac Newton was the Warden of the Royal Mint, where coins were made.

3665. Hummingbirds have large brains compared to their body size.

3666. In the center of the Pinwheel Galaxy, almost no stars are born.

3667. Astronomers believe that an asteroid of 15 km (9.3 mi) diameter exploded over Siberia and caused damage of hundreds of kilometers/ miles.

3668. A meteor shower is often caused by debris coming off a broken comet.

3669. Different lizard species are carnivores, herbivores, or omnivores.

3670. Cancer is the star sign for people born between 22 June and 22 July. Cancerians are said to be devoted to their family and home and can be 'crabby' sometimes.
3671. A nuclear submarine uses a nuclear reactor, steam turbine, and reduction gearing to power the propellers.
3672. Dolphins live in groups of up to 12 dolphins.
3673. The smallest bone in your body is called the stirrup bone and found in your middle ear. It is 0.1 inch (2.8 mm) long.
3674. A scorpion's favorite meal is an insect. When there are none around, they can lower their heart rate and metabolism and survive without food for up to a year.
3675. Your lung transfers oxygen from the air to your blood for your organs. The brain uses up more than one-quarter of the oxygen in your body. Some parts of your body, such as your upper skin, receives oxygen directly from the air.
3676. Messier 87's mass is 6,600,000,000 times bigger than the suns.
3677. There are more than 300 breeds of horses.
3678. The temperature inside the sun is about 15 million deg C (27 million deg F).
3679. The space shuttle launched 135 missions in its 30 years from 1981 to 2011.
3680. A parallelogram is a two-dimensional shape. A 3D parallelogram is a parallelepiped.
3681. Zinc is essential for good health, and after iron, it is the most common metal found in our body.
3682. Alexander Graham Bell, a Scottish born inventor, engineer, and scientist, is famous for inventing the telephone.
3683. The two Magellanic Clouds, known as the Large and Small Magellanic Clouds, are irregular dwarf galaxies seen in the Southern Hemisphere.

3684. There are about 50 deer species in the world.
3685. Time does not exist in a black hole.
3686. In ancient times, astrology was used to determine the timing of specific cultural celebrations.
3687. Earth means 'ground' or 'soil.'
3688. James Clerk Maxwell, physicist, wrote his first scientific papers when he was just 14 years old. He wrote on using a piece of twine to draw mathematical curves and the properties of ellipses, Cartesian ovals, and more.
3689. Pluto was closer to the sun than Neptune for 20 years of its 248-year orbit. It will be closer to the sun again in 2231.
3690. A person or doctor who studies the heart and heart disorders is called a cardiologist.
3691. Isaac Newton's most famous book was Philosophiae Naturalis Principia Mathematica (also known as the Principia - Mathematical principals of Natural history). His Law of Universal Gravitation and Laws of Motion were described in the book.
3692. Some lizards drop their tails when caught by predators.
3693. True seals are also known as earless seals. Sea lions are known as eared seals.
3694. The surface of Mars has extreme radiation every time the sun rises as it has no ozone layer.
3695. Duck feet have no blood vessels or nerves, so their feet don't feel cold.
3696. Kangaroos are the only animals that hop as their main way to get around.
3697. A spiral galaxy is the most common type of galaxy.
3698. Rhodium is a noble element and does not react with oxygen easily.
3699. Your body takes 12 hours to digest food.
3700. Jupiter, Saturn, Uranus, and Neptune are the four gas

giants in our solar system. You would not be able to walk on them as they are made up mostly of gas.

3701. Most badgers are omnivores. The Honeybadger is thought to be a carnivore and the most vicious mammal in the world.

3702. If you want to see a rainbow, wait for sunlight to hit raindrops in front of you at exactly 42 degrees.

3703. Coal is mainly made of carbon but also contains hydrogen, oxygen, sulfur, and nitrogen. Different types of coal contain different amounts of carbon.

3704. Old World monkeys such as baboons live in Africa, New World monkeys such as marmosets live in South America.

3705. A great white shark is the most deadly shark globally and can swim up to 18.6 mph (30 kph).

3706. Hummingbirds have excellent memories and can remember where a flower is that they've visited.

3707. Water can boil and freeze at the same time! This is called the 'triple point' of water and occurs at -0.01 deg C and 0.006 atmospheric pressure.

3708. Most bones have three layers - a strong hard outer layer, a light, spongy airy part, and the middle contains a soft substance called bone marrow.

3709. Scorpions are tough. Scientists have found them frozen, and when they're put into the sun, they come back to life and walk away!

3710. Iron is rarely found on the Earth's surface in its pure form as it easily oxidizes. It is usually removed from rocks.

3711. Most telescopes can detect some sort of electromagnetic waves.

3712. Butterflies communicate mainly through chemical signals.

3713. Turtles are one of the oldest reptiles and have been around for more than 215 million years.

3714. All matter is made up of small particles called atoms. They are so small that a small object such as a button has billions of atoms in it.
3715. Snakes are cold-blooded reptiles with no legs.
3716. A scientist that studies biology is called a biologist.
3717. A horse is color blind and can only see green and blue shades, so a red apple will look bluish-green to them!
3718. Aristotle is famous for his work on logic, science and nature (physics and meteorology), psychology, natural history (animals), and philosophy.
3719. Proxima Centauri is the closest neighbor to Earth. It is part of the Alpha Centauri cluster of stars and 4.3 light-years away. A spacecraft would take 25,000 years to reach Proxima Centauri.
3720. Male bald eagles are smaller than females.
3721. Potential energy is the stored energy an object has because of the state it's in. For example, a stretched elastic band has elastic potential energy.
3722. One day the sun will become the same size as Earth.
3723. Tropical cyclones or hurricanes are measured on the Saffir-Simpson Wind scale, a rating scale of 1 - 5 of the wind speed.
3724. Research has shown that eating mangos are healthy for you. Their anti-inflammatory, anti-oxidative, anti-diabetic and anti-obesity properties lead to good brain, cardiovascular, skin, and intestinal health.
3725. Our brain uses about 20% of the energy in our bodies.
3726. Monkeys live in trees and on the ground.
3727. Astronomy is one of the oldest fields of science.
3728. With a magnitude of 9.5, the earthquake in Valdivia, Chile, in 1960 is the most powerful earthquake on Earth.
3729. The second densest planet in our solar system is Mercury. It is made up of heavy metals and rocks.
3730. Wrought iron is an iron alloy with a small amount of

carbon (like steel). The Eiffel Tower in Paris is made from wrought iron.

3731. A scientist who studies the behavior, physiology, classification, and distribution of animals is called a zoologist.

3732. The highest point of the Great Wall of China is about 26 ft (8 m).

3733. The first electronic hearing aid was made after the invention of the telephone and microphone in the 1870s.

3734. The Spitzer Space Telescope was a very successful reflective telescope and captured light images of planets outside our Solar System.

3735. A solitary bee is not as aggressive as they don't have honey to protect. The solitary male bee doesn't have a stinger, and the female will only sting if they're stepped on.

3736. Cats are usually very light. However, the heaviest recorded cat weighs 46.95 lb (21.30 kg).

3737. Neil Armstrong, from the Apollo 11 mission, was the first man to step on the moon.

3738. A male elephant leaves their herd at 13 and lives alone for most of its life. A female elephant stays in their herd all their lives.

3739. Pigs, warthogs, and wild boars all belong in the same family (Suidae).

3740. Europa, Jupiter's Earth, is covered in ice about 100 km (62 mi) thick.

3741. The Hubble Space Telescope has mirrors to capture images, so it is known as a reflector telescope.

3742. Louis Pasteur is also known as the Father of Microbiology and the Father of the Germ theory.

3743. The diameter of the Whirlpool Galaxy is about 76,000 light-years and lies about 23 million light-years from Earth.

3744. The deepest known point on Earth, at 10,916 meters (35,814 feet) deep, is known as The Challenger Deep.
3745. Lightning is the discharge of energy during a thunderstorm. Lightning can travel up to 130,000 mph (210,000 kph) and kill a person if they are hit by it.
3746. Geysers not only form on Earth. They have been observed on Enceladus, one of Saturn's moons, and Triton, Neptune's moon.
3747. A group of hippopotamuses is called a herd, pod, dale, or bloat.
3748. Neon does not join or bond with any other element to make any compounds.
3749. The most common element in the Earth's crust is oxygen, making up about 47%.
3750. In honor of Alexander Graham Bell, all telephone services in Canada and the United States were suspended for a minute when he was buried. Over 60,000 telephone operators stopped connecting calls from more than 13 million telephones across both countries.
3751. Streams of hydrogen gas and embedded stars connect the Triangulum Galaxy and Andromeda galaxies. It is suggested that these two galaxies will interact again in about 2.5 billion years.
3752. An electric current is measured in amperes (amps).
3753. Calcium is an essential element in our body, vital for healthy bones and teeth, to carry messages from our brains to our muscles and release hormones and enzymes.
3754. A shark is the only fish with eyelids.
3755. Sea otters have the densest fur of all mammals, which helps them to stay warm.
3756. Wind speed is measured in knots.
3757. On average, one meteoroid falls to Earth every year and burns up before hitting the ground.

3758. A physicist is a scientist who studies physics.
3759. Helicopters usually travel at a speed of 150 - 200 mph (241 - 322 kph).
3760. Inflation reduces the value of money.
3761. The second fastest spinning planet is Saturn. Jupiter is the fastest.
3762. You can eat a low carbohydrate diet because our body can convert proteins into carbohydrates.
3763. Space junk or space debris is any machinery or object left in space by humans. There are about 500,000 pieces of space junk in orbit that can potentially destroy or damage other satellites in orbit.
3764. As of February 2020, the ESA's Space Debris Office has identified 34 000 objects >10 cm and 900 000 objects from 1 cm to 10 cm occupying space. There are over 128 million objects of space debris with a size of 1 mm to 1 cm!
3765. Cornish chemist and inventor, Sir Humphry Davy is the first person to isolate calcium successfully.
3766. Mercury's surface is like our moon's surface, with a barren, rocky surface, and lots of craters.
3767. Nickel is one of the transition metals i.e., its valence electrons (electrons used to combine with other elements) are present in two shells.
3768. Dogs have an extremely good sense of smell. Compared to humans, they can differentiate odors up to 100 million times lower in concentration.
3769. Bees can see color, polarized light, movement, and infrared light.
3770. Trees can grow big because they can create woody tissue as they grow. This is called secondary plant growth.
3771. Ants evolved from wasp-like insects about 110 - 130 million years ago.

3772. The chemical symbol for radon is Rn, with an atomic number of 86.
3773. Lead is resistant to corrosion.
3774. Toucans are birds with large colorful bills.
3775. Platinum has an atomic number of 78.
3776. There are fewer tigers in the wild than there are kept as pets.
3777. You can only taste food once it's been dissolved in saliva in your mouth.
3778. Clyde Tombaugh, an American astronomer, discovered Pluto in 1930, but Charon, Pluto's moon, wasn't discovered until 1978.
3779. Your tongue has eight muscles. The four intrinsic muscles let your tongue change shape, roll, or tuck, for example, and are not attached to the bone. The four extrinsic muscles let your tongue change position, poke out, or move it sideways, for example, and are attached to the bone.
3780. A desert covered in ice or snow is called a 'cold desert'. The largest cold desert is Antarctica.
3781. Uranus is the smallest of the giant planets.
3782. The ISS Cupola module has a 7-window observatory area that was compared to the Millennium Falcon's 'turret' in the Star Wars movie.
3783. Vampire bats have special nerves in their face that can sense the heat of veins in their prey. They also have sharp teeth to prick the skin of their prey.
3784. Earth's crust is made up of several moving plates, Mars' crust is only made of one piece and is therefore much thicker than Earth's.
3785. The ancient Assyrians called Saturn 'Lubadsagush', meaning 'oldest of the old' as it was so slow.
3786. The platypus is an Australian mammal and only found in the wild in eastern Australia.

3787. Pigeons can discriminate a Monet painting from a Picasso painting.
3788. Auroras have been seen on Earth and other planets, including Jupiter, Saturn, Uranus, Neptune, and Mars.
3789. When an asteroid does hit Earth, a crater can be formed.
3790. Hippos have short legs, but they can run up to 19 mph (30 km/h).
3791. Recent scientific research has shown that brief faint noises such as claps, static, or crackles can be heard during auroras.
3792. The chemical symbol for silver is Ag.
3793. A satellite moves very fast, at speeds of about 28,968 kph (18,000 mph) to orbit Earth 14 times a day.
3794. Lightning heats up the air and produces a sonic wave which we hear as thunder.
3795. Mars' orbit around the sun is 687 Earth days, which is twice as long as Earth's orbit of 365 days. As a result, Mars' seasons are twice as long.
3796. Due to the amount of hydrogen sulfide in its atmosphere, Uranus may have a rotten egg smell.
3797. No one knows who discovered Mercury, but it was first observed through a telescope in 1631 by Thomas Harriott and Galileo Galilee.
3798. Most astronomers believe the Big Bang caused galaxies.
3799. The largest known galaxies are the giant elliptical-shaped galaxies.
3800. Hummingbirds are aggressive and attack other birds, such as crows and hawks, when they infringe on their territory.
3801. The melting point of calcium is 1,548 °F (842 °C), and the boiling point is 2,703 °F (1,484 °C).
3802. The HII regions of the Pinwheel Galaxy can create hot superbubbles, hundreds of light-years wide, from the high number of bright hot young stars in them.

3803. 23% dark matter, 4% ordinary matter, and 73% dark energy make up our universe.
3804. In the Mass Effect video game, Charon is a chunk of ice, not a moon.
3805. Carbon is often called the building block of life as it bonds easily to other nonmetallic elements.
3806. An archaeologist is a scientist who studies human societies by discovering and analyzing things that people have left behind in the past.
3807. Iron is an essential element in the human body. As hemoglobin, it transports oxygen around our body.
3808. Hydrogen can be gas, liquid, or solid (metallic).
3809. Vitamins A, D, E, and K are fat-soluble and can only be absorbed in our body with fats, so fats are needed for good health.
3810. Some animals become confused when it gets dark in a total solar eclipse, and they prepare to go to sleep.
3811. Scientists believe the Niagara Falls will erode over the next 50,000 years.
3812. The Noctis Labyrinthus, a region on Mars containing the largest labyrinth of valleys and canyons, means 'labyrinth of the night.'
3813. Nuclear energy has pros and cons. Pros include it's cost-effective and efficient compared to using gas, coal, or oil. Some of the cons are that power plants are expensive to build; accidents can happen and produces radioactive waste that can pollute the environment.
3814. Sloths belong to the Pilosa order and are related to anteaters and armadillos.
3815. The temperature through the Earth's core increases a degree every 18.2 m (60 ft).
3816. A bicycle has spoked wheels to strengthen it and reduce drag.
3817. The Big Dipper and the Little Dipper are not

constellations. They are patterns within constellations (known as asterisms). For example, the Big Dipper is an asterism contained in the Ursa Major constellation.

3818. A snake's skin is covered with scales.
3819. Brass is a mixture of copper and zinc.
3820. A hedgehog can 'self anoint' and hide their scent from predators. They can eat certain poisonous plants and then lick their spine with the poison in the saliva.
3821. Almost half of all platinum is used in catalytic converters in cars to reduce harmful emissions.
3822. Mosquitoes can detect heat so they can find people and animals as they get close.
3823. Red has the longest wavelength of visible light, so it is usually seen as the rainbow's most outer color.
3824. An Einstein-Rosen Bridge is better known as a wormhole. This is a hypothetical tunnel that would join two different points in space, perhaps two different universes.
3825. Uranus is known as one of the ice giants.
3826. The Andalusian breed of horse, also known as the Pure Spanish Horse, is often used for sports such as show jumping and dressage due to stamina and athleticism.
3827. Mosquitoes have been around for more than 30 million years.
3828. A hot air balloon relies on the basic scientific principle that hot air rises in cooler air.
3829. A strawberry is the only fruit that has seeds on the outside. Plant scientists or botanists believe that each seed on the outside of a strawberry is its fruit.
3830. The African bush elephant is the largest land mammal, followed by the White rhinoceros. The hippopotamus is the third-largest. All three animals are found in Africa.
3831. The Hubble Space Telescope was given its name after Dr. Hubble, famous for providing evidence of the Big Bang Theory.

3832. Three hundred fifty years after Galileo died, the Catholic Church formally apologized that the Inquisition made an error in giving him a life sentence because he believed the sun was the center of the universe!
3833. Scientists believe that a large planet-sized object hit Earth, breaking off rocks and debris, and these joined together to create our moon. This theory is known as the 'Giant Whack' or 'Giant Impact' theory.
3834. Nebulae are often called because of their shape. For example, the Horsehead Nebula resembles a horse's head.
3835. The moon's side that is visible to Earth at any particular time is called the Near side of the moon. The other side is sometimes called the Dark side even though it isn't as it faces the sun.
3836. Birds can fly, but humans rely on science to fly.
3837. Sound waves are converted into nerve impulses by our ears.
3838. The speed of light is approximately 669,600,000 mph (1,080,000,000 kph).
3839. In 2013, a huge meteoroid fireball entered Earth's atmosphere above Chelyabinsk, Russia, at 18 km per sec (11 miles per sec). It exploded 23 km (14 mi) above the surface and generated a shockwave that injured 1,600 people.
3840. A heart attack happens when an artery becomes blocked and reduces oxygen getting to your heart.
3841. Crocodiles have sharp teeth. When they lose a tooth, it is quickly replaced. They can go through 8,000 teeth in one lifetime.
3842. Nitric acid HNO_3 and ammonia NH_3 is used in fertilizers.
3843. Galileo was sentenced to life in prison for believing that the sun, and not the Earth, was the center of the universe.

The church believed this contradicted parts of the Bible. His life sentence was changed to house arrest, and he was forbidden to see friends or write any books. However, he managed to receive visitors and published one final document the year that he went blind at the age of 72. He died four years later when he was 77.

3844. Deers are social animals and travel in herds.
3845. Temperature affects the rate of chemical reactions in an object.
3846. In ancient times a sundial was used to measure time. It is simply a stick that casts a shadow across a marked surface as the sun moves across the sky.
3847. When a star explodes and turns into a supernova, it will likely turn into a nebula and neutron star. However, a large explosion may result in a black hole!
3848. Your cardiac muscle (heart) does more work than any other muscle in your body over your lifetime.
3849. Wolves are mammals and exceptional hunters.
3850. It is said that Halley's Comet started in the Oort Cloud.
3851. Lead has a melting point of 621.4 °F (327.46 °C) and a boiling point of 3,180.2 °F (1,749 °C).
3852. NASA's Hubble Space Telescope was launched on 24 April 1990, from the Kennedy Space Centre.
3853. Twelve astronauts have walked on the moon. They were all from NASA's Apollo missions from 1969 to 1972.
3854. Edwin Hubble, the American astronomer, is most well known for proving that the Milky Way is only one galaxy amongst many galaxies.
3855. A tree is a tall plant with a woody stem or trunk.
3856. Fish are vertebrates and have a backbone.
3857. Viruses are about 100 times smaller than bacteria.
3858. Dinosaurs lived on Earth from the late Triassic Period about 230 million years ago to the end of the Cretaceous

Period about 65 million years ago. This period is often called the Age of Dinosaurs.

3859. Spiders, not all, spin webs in different shapes to catch food. The webs can be orb-shaped (spider waits in the middle), sheet-shaped (horizontal web), or funnel-shaped (spider waits at the bottom).
3860. Pure titanium is silver-white in color.
3861. Kangaroos can swim.
3862. In the Himalayan mountains between Nepal and Tibet, Mount Everest is the highest mountain in the world measuring 29,029 feet (8,848 m) high.
3863. The Small Magellanic Cloud, 7.000 light-years, is half the large Magellanic Cloud size, 14,000 light-years. In comparison, the Milky Way is much bigger, about 100,000 light-years.
3864. A group of otters in the water is known as a 'raft.'
3865. There is speculation among scientists that there may be a Martian' Bermuda triangle' or a 'Great Galactic Ghoul' that has eaten about two-thirds of the spacecraft sent to Mars.
3866. Spiders, scorpions, mites, and ticks all belong to the arachnid family.
3867. In 2009, a US communications satellite Iridium 33 collided with a derelict Russian satellite Kosmos 2251 in space. Both satellites were destroyed.
3868. There are eight main blood types - A+, A-, B+, B-, AB+, AB-, O+, and O-. The antigens contained in your blood determines your blood type.
3869. Luna 9 was the first spacecraft that landed on the moon and helped astronomers understand that the moon had a stable landing surface.
3870. The Solar system is situated on the Orion Spur, an arm of the major Sagittarius Arm of the Milky Way.
3871. The chemical symbol for titanium is Ti.

3872. The International Space Station (ISS) is a sizeable human-made spacecraft that orbits Earth. Humans live and research the spacecraft in space.
3873. Despite being one of Pluto's moons, Charon doesn't orbit Pluto. They both orbit a common center of gravity called a barycentre. Due to its large size and this orbit fact, some astronomers think that Charon should be considered a dwarf planet.
3874. A famous Galileo quote: "In questions of science the authority of a thousand is not worth the humble reasoning of a single individual."
3875. More than three-quarters of volcanoes in the world are located in the Pacific Ring of Fire, where tectonic plates meet.
3876. Rainforests are forests with lots of rain.
3877. At the age of 16, Galileo started a degree in medicine. However, he was more interested in mathematics and left university without finishing a degree. He taught himself mathematics and later returned to the university to teach it.
3878. The mass of Venus is 4,867,320,000,000,000 billion kg, 0.815 times the mass of Earth.
3879. NASA's Viking 1 and 2 landed on Mars several months apart in 1976 and provided the first color pictures of Mars.
3880. A mosquito can beat its wings up to 600 times per second.
3881. Colonies of ants work together to solve problems, just like people.
3882. A cactus holds much water in their stems. People have survived in the desert by drinking water from cacti.
3883. Professional astronomers don't spend much time looking through the telescope. Most of their time is used to analyze images and data.

3884. Radiation is the movement of energy through space. X-rays, light, and sound are examples of radiation.
3885. There is a valley in Switzerland called Lauterbrunnen, which contains 72 waterfalls! Deep glacial valleys and rocky mountains surround these waterfalls.
3886. The moon has an elliptical orbit around Earth.
3887. The brightest star in the solar system, R136a1, located in the Large Magellanic Cloud, shines 8.7 times brighter than the sun.
3888. Otters keep warm by the air that is trapped in their fur.
3889. A bat can 'see' in the dark by using echolocation. It makes noises and waits for the sound to reflect off an object. If the sound doesn't come back, it knows there's nothing in front of them, and they can fly forward. They judge the distance the object is away from them by how quickly the sound comes back.
3890. Tides and weather on Earth are predictable when the moon is farthest from Earth. When the moon is closer, its greater gravitational pull creates bigger waves and more unstable weather.
3891. A total solar eclipse is rare and occurs about once every 1 to 2 years. In contrast, partial solar eclipses can happen 2 to 5 times every year.
3892. Meerkats are well-known for their teamwork. They work together to forage for food, babysit the babies, and stand guard to protect their families.
3893. Time slows as you approach a black hole.
3894. About 10,000 years ago, before money was used widely, livestock and grain were used to pay for services and products.
3895. Venus is sometimes referred to as Earth's sister planet.
3896. You can see meteors 120 km (74.5 mi) high above Earth.
3897. Gold is not as reactive as other metals.
3898. When Eris and Pluto were both demoted to dwarf planet

status, only eight planets in our solar system remained.

3899. Refractor lenses are also used in binoculars and gun scopes.

3900. Emperor penguins have a special adaptation to help them stay as warm as possible in Antarctica. They lean back on their heels and balance with the tip of their tail so that they can keep their feet off the ground. This also helps them keep their eggs warm until they hatch.

3901. The Sumatran Tiger, Bengal Tiger, Malayan Tiger, and Siberian Tiger are different species of tiger.

3902. Helium was discovered by astronomers, Pierre Janssen and Norman Lockyer, after a solar eclipse in 1868.

3903. The atomic bomb that was dropped on Hiroshima in World War II had a uranium core. Modern nuclear weapons are made from other materials such as plutonium.

3904. Snakes shed their skin in one piece.

3905. Different insects are grouped into about 29 orders of insects, including beetles, butterflies, and flies.

3906. Around 3.3 million computer code lines on the ground support more than 1.8 million lines of ISS flight software code.

3907. Before DVD and Blu-ray discs, video cassettes were used to store information. They were phased out in the late 1990s.

3908. BPM 37093, a star about 20 billion light-years from Earth, is a large diamond that weighs about 10 billion trillion trillion carats and is about the moon's size. It is also called 'Lucy' after the Beatles' song "Lucy in the Sky with Diamonds."

3909. A kangaroo can hop 22 feet (7 m) in one leap.

3910. The first mammal that was cloned from a sheep was named Dolly. She was born on 5 July 1996.

3911. The Empire State Building, located in Manhattan, New

York, has 103 floors. Its height reaches 1,454 ft (443.2 m), including the antenna spire.

3912. In traditional televisions, the signal is transmitted by radio waves which are received by the television antenna. In the 2000s, cable television became available where shows could be broadcast via radio frequency waves transmitted through cables.

3913. The capybara, two-toed sloth, jaguar, manatee, and the Giant anteater are all native animals to Venezuela.

3914. Most caterpillars are herbivores and only eat plants.

3915. A drone uses physics to fly. They use rotors for propulsion and control.

3916. An owl can fly without making any noise, which lets them sneak up on their prey, especially at night.

3917. It takes 27.3 days for our moon to orbit Earth.

3918. Jöns Jacob Berzelius discovered silicon in 1824.

3919. Platinum is rare and one of the precious metals.

3920. A group of cats is called a clowder.

3921. Astronomers do not know how cosmic rays are created.

3922. Scientists believe a huge asteroid hit Earth 65 million years ago, blocking sunlight to our planet and changed our ecology. Many plants and animals died, including dinosaurs.

3923. Some scientists believe that over 300 million years ago, Venus may have had oceans on its surface, but they dried up when the sun's rays became stronger.

3924. Stainless steel is an alloy of iron and chromium. Nickel is often added to make it more resistant to corrosion.

3925. Marble is a metamorphic rock that started as sedimentary rock limestone.

3926. Radon gives off a bright yellow light when it is cooled below its freezing point of –96 °F (–71 °C). The color turns orangey-red as the temperature decreases.

3927. Suppose you recycle old aluminum, such as cans,

bicycles, and cars. In that case, it takes about 5% of the energy needed to make new aluminum.

3928. The Komodo dragon is the largest reptile. The Australian saltwater crocodile is the next largest.

3929. The second closest star to Earth, after the sun, is Proxima Centauri.

3930. Not all fish have scales. For example, sharks have sandpaper skin.

3931. There are more than 11,000 grasshopper species in the world.

3932. A hummingbird uses its long bill and tongue to reach deep inside a flower to lap up the nectar.

3933. A chemist studies chemical elements and their compounds and properties and how they work in our bodies.

3934. Tunnels can be built for both human and animal purposes. In the Netherlands, more than 600 tunnels have been built under roads to help protect endangered animals such as the European Badger.

3935. Tulips are perennial plants and lives for more than two years. They usually only bloom up for up to a week in springtime.

3936. Some birds are very intelligent and can use tools; for example, vultures use rocks to break open hard ostrich eggs. A woodpecker finch can use a long twig to reach a grub in a tree branch that they can't reach with their beak.

3937. Pyrite is called 'fool's gold' because it looks like gold.

3938. A type of meteorite called aerolite is made mostly of silicon.

3939. A baby sheep is known as a lamb.

3940. Several million years ago, a neighbor galaxy M32 plunged through the Andromeda Galaxy.

3941. Hurricanes gather energy over water where they form.

They lose strength as they move over land.

3942. Female crocodiles usually grow up to 9.8 ft (3 m), whereas male crocodiles can grow over 19.6 ft (6 m) long.

3943. Forensic science is the use of science and scientific methods in legal cases. For example, police will use forensic science to find a robber.

3944. Muscles are attached to bones by tendons.

3945. Magnets are usually made of iron. It can only attract other metals (not all) but not glass, plastic, or wood.

3946. The Milky Way is only one of the millions of galaxies in the universe.

3947. An otter lives in a den, also known as a 'holt' or 'couch.'

3948. Galileo's discovery that Venus goes through a cycle of phases supported the theory that the sun is the center of the universe and Earth and other planets revolve around it.

3949. A monorail is a train on a single rail.

3950. The ISS program is a joint venture involving five space agencies. NASA, of USA, Russia's Roskosmos, Japan's JAXA, Canada's CSA, and ESA made up of agencies from France, Brazil, Malaysia, Italy, and South Korea.

3951. Gorillas are very intelligent. They can use tools and communicate using sign language.

3952. Queen ants have the longest lifespan of any insect. They can live up to 30 years compared with male drones that live only a few weeks. Female worker ants can live up to 3 years.

3953. A smart television is a set-top box with internet features. In 2015 when they were released, they were initially aimed at mid and high-end television sets, but they became more affordable in 2019.

3954. Sunflowers grow quickly, and under the right conditions, they can grow up to 12 feet (3.7 m) in just six months.

3955. Earth's rotation and gravity create ocean tides.

3956. In the TV show The Outer Limits, you can see the Sombrero Galaxy's black and white photographs in the credits at the end of each episode.
3957. After pollination, every little flower inside a sunflower produces a seed.
3958. The unit that measures electrical potential, the 'volt', is named after Alessandro Volta, the scientist who invented the electric battery.
3959. A hummingbird stores about half its body's weight in fat in its body before it migrates, so it has enough energy when flying.
3960. An Italian astronomer, Giovanni Schiaparelli, found strange lines on Mars in 1877. He called them Canali, which means 'channels' in Italian, but other nationalities misunderstood the translation and thought it meant 'canals.' Percival Lowell, an American astronomer, guessed incorrectly that the canals transported water from the Martian ice caps to the desert!
3961. Mars' winds can blow up to 201 kph (125 mph) and cover the whole planet.
3962. More than 50,000 meteorites have been found on Earth, of which 99.8% of them come from asteroids.
3963. Earth's core is about the same size as Mars, i.e., 7,091 km (4,400 mi) wide.
3964. The fat in our body not only helps with absorbing essential vitamins A, D, E, and K; it also protects our organs against shock, helps regulate our temperature, and promotes healthy skin, hair, and cell function.
3965. The chemical symbol of oxygen is O with an atomic number of 8.
3966. The Milky Way has two major arms spiraling out from the center bar, not four, as initially thought. The names given to these two arms are Scutum-Centaurus and Perseus.

3967. Lemons taste sour as they contain about 5 - 6 % citric acid.

3968. Uranus's names, from the center, are Zeta, 6, 5, 4, Alpha, Beta, Eta, Gamma, Delta, Lambda, Epsilon, Nu and Mu.

3969. An extra-galactic nebula is one that exists beyond the Milky Way.

3970. Platypuses are mostly nocturnal animals.

3971. A twister is another name for a tornado.

3972. Robotic engineers have studied bats' flight paths to design flying robots.

3973. Platinum is used to make pacemakers and dental implants because bodily fluids don't corrode it easily.

3974. Acute injuries account for most contact sports injuries such as American football, basketball, and ice hockey. The most common injuries are sprains and strains.

3975. Lizards can't maintain its body temperature and rely on the temperature around them to stay warm or cool down.

3976. Black holes contain the same amount of mass as their original star.

3977. A very strong tornado can travel up to 100 miles (161 km).

3978. Biochemistry, organic chemistry, nuclear chemistry, and physical chemistry are all specialized fields of chemistry.

3979. Earth rotates slower in March than it does in September.

3980. Lightning is about six times hotter than the sun's surface at about 54,000 deg F (29,982 deg C).

3981. Giraffes are most vulnerable when they drink as they can't look out for predators.

3982. The main hunter of a lion pride is the female.

3983. Tongue prints are unique to every person, just like fingerprints.

3984. Balloons with helium float as helium is a gas that is lighter than air.

3985. Some plants are carnivores, i.e., they eat meat, like the Venus Flytrap.
3986. Lunatic comes from the word 'lunar,' and the moon phases have been associated with madness. Aristotle believed that the full moon affected the water in a person's brain and made them insane!
3987. A group of stars in the middle of an elliptical galaxy can often look like one bright star.
3988. The world record for the longest helicopter flight is 2,213 miles (3,562 km).
3989. Scientists used to think that different tastes come from different parts of your tongue. This is not true, and all five tastes can be detected anywhere on your tongue.
3990. One Uranus day is equivalent to 17 Earth hours and 54 minutes.
3991. Meerkats can be found in the wild in Africa.
3992. The three zebra species are the plain, mountain, and Grevy's zebras. The Grevy's is the largest species and the rarest and endangered.
3993. A rhinoceros has a small brain.
3994. A tornado occurs when a powerful wind rotates and creates a column from the clouds to the ground. The strongest winds on Earth are found in a tornado. The USA has, on average, about 1200 tornadoes every year. It is the country with the most tornadoes in the world.
3995. You can see the Whirlpool Galaxy and its companion NGC 5195 with binoculars.
3996. Radiation exposure is dangerous to humans. It is thought that Marie Curie died in 1934 from a blood disease due to exposure to large amounts of radiation. Marie Curie was a physicist who discovered polonium, radium, and radioactivity and helped develop x-rays.
3997. Mercury is the only liquid metal at room temperature.
3998. The Lesser flamingo is the shortest flamingo species,

growing only up to 3 feet (90 cm) tall and weighing up to 5.5 lbs (2.5 kg).

3999. James Clerk Maxwell, physicist, proved that light is an electromagnetic wave.

4000. The longest tunnel in the world is the Delaware Aqueduct in New York, measuring 85 miles (137 km) long.

4001. Some foods have been genetically modified mainly to improve yield by improving plant disease resistance or improved tolerance to herbicides. In the future genetic modification can be aimed at improving nutritional content or reducing risks of allergy.

4002. Beavers not only build their homes (lodges) from trees. They also eat the leaves, root, and bark from trees.

4003. Henry Ford improved the production line manufacturing system in 1908, making cars cheaper and more affordable to buy.

4004. Hedgehogs can swim.

4005. The Triangulum has 40 billion stars, a small number compared to the Milky Way's 400 billion stars.

4006. Scientists believe that the moon once belonged to Earth, and when Earth collided with a large object, a piece broke off and became our moon.

4007. The last landing of the space shuttle was on 21 July 2011. NASA wanted to focus on cheaper methods to explore space, so retired the space shuttle program.

4008. Televisions were first sold in the 1920s, and they were in black and white.

4009. One of Jupiter's moons Io is covered in volcanoes, and its surface is constantly changing due to volcanic activity.

4010. Cats sleep for around 14 hours a day so that they can conserve energy.

4011. Giant pandas eat many bamboo because bamboo doesn't have many nutrients. If there isn't enough bamboo around, giant pandas will also eat rodents, fish, insects, and birds to supplement their diet.

4012. Calcium is essential for human life and plant growth. It is important in controlling the pH of soil.

4013. The NASA astronaut, Don Petitt, grew a space zucchini, space broccoli, and a space sunflower on the International Space Station. He wanted to make his space home more 'homely,' so it wasn't an official project. However, it has given scientists much information about plant biology.

4014. The Great Red Spot is a massive storm on Jupiter. This storm has raged for at least 350 years and is so large that three Earths could fit inside it.

4015. Frogs and toads are very similar biologically, but there are some differences. Frogs live near water and have teeth. Toads live on land and don't have teeth. Frogs are usually longer than toads.

4016. The ancient Greek philosophers were the first people to develop a model of the universe.

4017. Silver is the best conductor of electricity and heat.

4018. The golf ball used to be made from hardwood. However, over the years, different materials were trialed to improve flight performance. The modern-day golf ball is made of plastic and rubber with dimples.

4019. The eighth most abundant element in the Earth's crust is magnesium.

4020. Our body needs zinc to grow, fight bacteria and viruses, and build DNA.

4021. Dogs are very versatile and help us with hunting, farm work, and security.

4022. Charon, one of Pluto's moons, appears to have ice-based geology with active ice geysers and ice volcanoes.

4023. Giant pandas live up to the age of 20 in the wild.

4024. The furthest planet from the sun is Neptune.

4025. About 200 asteroids, bigger than 100 km (62 mi) in diameter, have been identified in the Asteroid Belt. Hundreds of thousands more are smaller than this.
4026. Your left lung has two lobes, and your right lung is divided into three lobes. Your left lung is smaller, so that there is enough room for your heart.
4027. Using the Hubble Space Telescope, astronomers discovered Xanadu on Titan in 1994, which is a highly reflective area about Australia's size. Radar images depict dunes, hills, valleys, and rivers!
4028. Scientists estimate about 200 dwarf planets are waiting to be discovered in the Kuiper belt and more than 10,000 outside of the Kuiper belt.
4029. Deimos' (one of Mars moons) temperature is about -40.15 degrees C (-40.27 degrees F).
4030. Billions of nerve cells in our brain send and receive information from our body.
4031. Gamma-ray astronomy is the use of the shortest wavelengths to study space objects.
4032. Most sharks have to swim to breathe as the water that goes over their gills gives it oxygen.
4033. A toucan will often make a nest in the hole of a tree that was made by a woodpecker.
4034. Uranium is a hard, dense metal that is malleable, ductile, and a poor conductor of electricity.
4035. The most common cause of the flooding is heavy rainfall when rivers and other watercourses don't have the capacity to carry the extra water. Other causes of flooding include cyclones, broken dams, or extreme coastal events.
4036. Scorpions are nocturnal and come out at night to feed.
4037. Infrared astronomy is the detection and analysis of infrared radiation.
4038. Cosmonauts and astronauts have conducted more than 205 spacewalks aboard the ISS since 1998. Spacewalks

are performed for maintenance and repair, as well as the construction of space stations.

4039. The largest living mammal on Earth is the elephant.

4040. Reptiles have defense mechanisms to protect themselves. These include avoidance, camouflage, hissing, and biting.

4041. The number of water molecules in 10 drops of water is equivalent to all the universe stars.

4042. The eight planets in order of their distance from the sun are Mercury, Venus, Earth, Mars, Jupiter, Saturn, Uranus, and Neptune.

4043. Jane Goodall, famous for her work with chimpanzees, lived with a group of them for nearly two years in Tanzania until Frodo, one of the chimps, kicked her out of the group because he didn't like her and became the leader of the pack.

4044. All domestic ducks came from the Mallard or Muscovy duck families.

4045. Jupiter is named after the king of the Roman gods. To the Greeks, it represented Zeus, the thunder god. The Mesopotamians saw Jupiter as the god Marduk and patron of Babylon's city. Germanic tribes considered this planet to be Donar or Thor.

4046. Haumea is the third closest dwarf planet to the sun and the fourth largest dwarf planet.

4047. The stratosphere is the second closest atmospheric layer to Earth and is about 50 km (31 mi) from the Earth's surface.

4048. About 500 active satellites are considered Low Earth Orbit satellites as they orbit Earth under 2,000 km (1,240 mi) away.

4049. Over two and a half million different insect species and 40,000 plant species can be found in South America's Amazon rainforest.

4050. The length of an adult tongue from the back to the tip is about 4 in (10 cm).

4051. In 1987, when Albert Einstein's letters were made public, we learned that he had his first baby, Lieserl, with Mileva Marić before they were married. Lieserl either died or was given up for adoption.

4052. Squirrels are omnivores and eat both plants and meat. Their favorite food is nuts, fruits, and seeds.

4053. The five most precious metals in the world are rhodium, palladium, gold, iridium, and platinum.

4054. The jaguar is sometimes confused with the leopard because of their spots. The leopard is only found in Asia and Africa, whereas the jaguar is only in the Americas.

4055. Female crickets don't chirp. Only male ones do.

4056. Rosehip is the fruit of a rose. It is often used to make tea and medicines, as it can be rich in vitamin C.

4057. The different speeds of seismic waves are used by scientists to locate the epicenter of an earthquake, i.e., the point on the surface of the earthquake.

4058. Jose Luis Ortiz Moreno from Spain claimed he discovered Haumea in 2005, but Mike Brown and his US team made the same claim in 2004. In 2008 the IAU recognized Mike Brown's discovery after determining the Spanish club may have committed fraud.

4059. The circumference of Uranus at its middle is 159,354 km (99,017 mi).

4060. The first practical helicopter to take flight was in 1939, and since then, helicopters have been used for many purposes. These include search and rescue missions, tourism, medical transport, and fighting fires.

4061. The very bright stars you can see in spiral galaxies are new large stars.

4062. Exercise requires energy. During aerobic exercises, such as running or jogging, our body uses glycogen and fat as fuel to sustain activity for a longer period. During anaerobic exercise such as sprinting, oxygen is not present, and you only use glycogen as fuel. This means you get tired quickly.

4063. Branches of forensic science include forensic pathology, forensic chemistry, DNA analysis, and forensic toxicology.

4064. The crown or top leaves of a tree shades the roots and collects energy from the sun (photosynthesis) to make food.

4065. Mars' gravity is weak, so it doesn't hold onto its atmosphere very well.

4066. The black holes located in the center of a galaxy is about a billion times heavier than the sun.

4067. Rain, snow, sleet, hail, and dew are all types of precipitation.

4068. Just like Jupiter, Saturn has oval-shaped storms.

4069. Mars has a similar size and landmass to Earth.

4070. Eight spacecraft have visited Jupiter, including Pioneer 10 and 11, Voyager 1 and 2, Galileo, Cassini, Ulysses, and New Horizons missions.

4071. Bees have five eyes, which gives them excellent eyesight.

4072. Foc-Foc in the country La Réunion holds the record for the highest rainfall in 24 hours - 71.9 in (182.5 cm) during the tropical cyclone, Denise, in 1966.

4073. Insects live everywhere except in oceans or cold places like Antarctica.

4074. Our moon has more platinum than Earth.

4075. A snowflake can contain up to 200 ice crystals in each one.

4076. As of 2013, Sergei Krikalev, a Russian, has been to space more than any other person. Including two ISS expeditions, he has traveled to space six times and spent more than 2.2 years (803 days, 9 hours, and 39 minutes) in space.

4077. With a diameter of 3,100 km (1,900 mi), Europa is larger than Pluto and smaller than Earth's moon.
4078. Granite is a common igneous rock that contains over 25% quartz. It is very strong.
4079. One of Mars' moons, Phobos, is slowly merging with the Red Planet and will crash in about 50 million years, creating rings around Mars.
4080. An eagle's beak is made up of keratin, so it continues to grow throughout its life, just like our hair and fingernails.
4081. Frogs don't drink water; they soak it through their skin. They also soak air through their skin as well as breathing through their nostrils.
4082. Neptune's climate is very active, with massive storms in its upper atmosphere and strong winds blowing up to 600 meters per second (1,968 miles per sec).
4083. The eighth most abundant element in the universe by mass is silicon.
4084. Snakes don't have the right type of teeth to chew food, so they have to catch and swallow their prey in one piece.
4085. Many creatures attach themselves to and live on the skin of whales. These include barnacles and sea lice.
4086. The mass of Uranus is 86,810,300,000,000,000 billion kg which is equivalent to 14,536 times Earth's mass.
4087. Turtles and tortoises are reptiles with shells that protect their bodies.
4088. Makemake is the second brightest object in the Solar System, and Pluto is the brightest. You can see Makemake from your home high-end telescope as it is so bright.
4089. Different countries have different currencies of money. Some countries in Europe, for example, Spain and France, share the same Euro currency.
4090. The Incas built Machu Picchu using a typical Inca building technique called ashlar. Granite stone blocks are

cut very precisely to fit together without having to use mortar.

4091. A yellow dwarf star, such as the sun, will eventually run out of hydrogen fuel and become a red giant.

4092. Scientists have unlocked the DNA of toads to help them find a way to control their population as they have become pests worldwide.

4093. The 13 zodiac constellations have the same names used for astrology plus Ophiuchus.

4094. Aristotle thought that goats could be male or female, depending on which way the wind was blowing.

4095. Steam locomotives were popular in the 19th century. Diesel and electric locomotives became popular in the 20th century.

4096. An adult leopard likes to live alone in its territory, keeping away from other leopards.

4097. Alexander Graham Bell studied the human voice and sound and worked at schools for the deaf. His mother and wife were both hearings impaired.

4098. Your eyebrows and eyelashes protect your eyes from dirt, dust, rain, sweat, and other harmful objects.

4099. Wolves are social animals and live in packs of up to 20, depending on their environment and food availability. The alpha pair are the breeding wolves in the pack and usually leaders of the pack.

4100. The wolf, dingo, and coyote belong to a group of animals called wild dogs. All modern dogs are descendants of the wolf.

4101. Alexander Graham Bell was born in Scotland and became a US citizen in 1882.

4102. An aurora is a natural display of light in the sky. It is usually green but can also be red or blue. It occurs in areas near the northern Arctic poles and southern Antarctic poles. In the north, it's known as aurora borealis or the Northern Lights. In the south, it's known as aurora australis or the Southern Lights.

4103. Jupiter's upper atmosphere is divided up into cloud belts and zones. They are primarily made of ammonia crystals, sulfur, and mixtures of the two compounds. Below the massive atmosphere, there are layers of compressed hydrogen gas, liquid metallic hydrogen, and a core of ice, rock, and metals.

4104. Charon is named after Charon, the ferryman, a Greek mythological figure, who rows souls across the River Styx to Pluto's realm in the underworld. Charon means "fierce brightness."

4105. Male and female skeletons in people are very similar except that female skeletons are smaller. The shape, size, and angle of female pelvic bones are different so they can have babies.

4106. Every time a large comet orbits the sun, it loses about 1 to 3 meters (3 to 10 feet) of its nucleus' surface. Halley's Comet will eventually lose its tail once a day and may disappear!

4107. Snails are Gastropods with coiled shells. A slug is also a Gastropod but without a shell.

4108. An owl sometimes hides its prey before returning a couple of days later to eat it.

4109. More than 30 mushroom species glow in the dark through a chemical reaction called bioluminescence.

4110. A meteor shower occurs when a planet such as Earth moves through a stream of material in the Comet's orbit.

4111. An airfoil, shape of an airplane's wing, is designed to create lift as the plane moves through the air.

4112. Charon is 19,640 km (12,203 mi) distance from Pluto, closer than our moon is to Earth, 386,000 km (239,000 mi) distance.

4113. Before Eris was reclassified as a dwarf planet in 2006, it was considered the tenth planet (after Pluto, who also lost status as a planet simultaneously).

4114. AU stands for Astronomical Unit. One AU is the distance between the sun and Earth.

4115. Sunlight can shine down 262 feet (80 m) in the ocean.

4116. The sound you hear when you 'crack' a whip is made from the whip moving so fast that it breaks the sound speed.

4117. The distance that light can travel in one year is called a light-year.

4118. Uranium was named after the planet Uranus.

4119. The Pinwheel Galaxy's star birth regions contain lots of hydrogen, so they are called HII regions.

4120. The plural of octopus is octopuses, not octopi.

4121. There are more atoms in a teaspoon of water than teaspoons of water in the Atlantic Ocean.

4122. Nearly 10 million carbon compounds have been discovered.

4123. Cardiology is the branch of medicine that studies heart diseases and conditions.

4124. A spider is an arachnid. It is not an insect.

4125. We see the stars in the sky are about 40 million km (25 million mi) away.

4126. A partial eclipse happens when only part of the moon passes through Earth's shadow. It looks like a dark bite has been taken out of the moon.

4127. The first supernova that was observed and recorded was by Chinese astronomers in 185 AD.

4128. On 18 June 1983, the first American woman went to space in the space shuttle Challenger. Her name was Sally Ride.

4129. Before Aristotle, who lived from 384 to 322 BC, the world thought the Earth was flat. Aristotle believed the world was round, and everything revolved around Earth in outer space.

4130. Like the pit viper, some snakes can 'see' radiated heat from warm-blooded animals with infrared-sensitive receptors in their head.

4131. The top layer of Saturn's atmosphere is made mostly of ammonia ice. This layer is a layer of water ice below these layers of cold hydrogen and sulfur ice combinations.

4132. In a million years, you won't see a solar eclipse as the moon is moving further and further away from Earth.

4133. The thick coat of a camel insulates them from the heat of the desert. The coat also lightens in summer to reflect the heat.

4134. Most fish reproduce by laying eggs, but some fish, such as the Great White Shark, give birth to live babies.

4135. It took Apollo 11 four days and six hours to reach the moon.

4136. Asteroids, made of rock and metal, are small Solar Systems that circle the sun. Some scientists think that the organic compounds found in asteroids created life on Earth.

4137. The Andromeda Galaxy belongs to the Local Group cluster of galaxies.

4138. A rabbit belongs to the same Leporidae family as the hare, but they are different animals.

4139. The modern cell phone or mobile phone enables people all over the globe to communicate with each other. The first mobile phone was very bulky, but modern phones are small and portable and last for hours on a rechargeable battery.

4140. There are over 60 million horses in the world.

4141. Sloths are the slowest mammal on Earth. They take them a minute to move 6 - 8 feet (1.8 - 2.4 m).

4142. Makemake, dwarf planet, has no atmosphere.
4143. A spiral galaxy is categorized by how tight their spiral arms are.
4144. NASA has three spacecraft orbiting Mars, named Mars Reconnaissance Orbiter, Mars Odyssey, and MAVEN. ESA has two orbiting spacecraft called ExoMars Trace Gas Orbiter and Mars Express. The 6th and last spacecraft to orbit Mars belongs to India and is named Mars Orbiter Mission (MOM).
4145. An alloy, such as steel and bronze, is a combination of different metals.
4146. In 1665, Sir Isaac Newton passed light through a glass prism and saw seven colors coming out the other side. A rainbow of colors was created - red, orange, yellow, green, blue, indigo, and violet. The different colors of light travel through the prism at different speeds.
4147. Eris is smaller than Earth's moon but could fit all the objects in its asteroid belt.
4148. Charon, Pluto's largest moon, has an impressive chasm, 59.5 km (37 mi) wide, named Serenity Chasm, named after the ship on Joss Whedon's cult classic show Firefly.
4149. The teeth of guinea pigs grow continuously throughout their lifetime, so they have to chew or gnaw them to keep them short.
4150. Oxygen in a submarine is replenished by pressurized oxygen tanks or an oxygen generator, which makes oxygen by water's electrolysis. An oxygen canister can also be used to release oxygen by a very hot chemical reaction.
4151. Ernest Rutherford was knighted in 1914 and became Sir Ernest Rutherford. He was also made a British lord in 1931.
4152. Modern telescopes can detect infrared and radio waves.
4153. Cell or modern phones continue to evolve to meet the

needs of users.

4154. Nebulae are enormous, often with diameters of millions of light-years.

4155. If life is found on another planet, the Office of Planetary Protection department of NASA will deal with it.

4156. Security and privacy continue to be ongoing problems with using the Internet, with confidential data, passwords, and personal information on different websites. Viruses and spam emails are major concerns for people who access the web.

4157. An alligator is a large reptile that belongs to the order Crocodylia.

4158. The center of our human nervous system is our brain.

4159. Isaac Newton became Sir Isaac Newton when Queen Anne knighted him in 1705.

4160. A red rainbow occurs at sunrise or sunset when the other colors with shorter wavelengths are scattered. Only the long-wavelength color (red) can be seen.

4161. In Greek mythology, Hercules had to fulfill 12 tasks or labors for killing his family. One of his jobs including killing a giant crab, which he then kicked to the stars, thus forming the Cancer constellation. Other versions of the story are that he crushed the crab with his foot or killed it with his club.

4162. A doctor who studies and treats disorders of the nervous system is called a neurologist or a neurosurgeon. Multiple sclerosis, Parkinson's disease, Bell's palsy, cerebral palsy, and epilepsy are examples of nervous system disorders.

4163. Venomous snakes have special glands and fangs to inject venom into their prey.

4164. A cat always lands on its feet! This is because they can work out which way is the 'right way up' as they're falling and move their head into the upright position. Kittens develop this reflex when they are three weeks old.

4165. Fire is dangerous to people, animals, and the environment. Fires can also stimulate growth in the environment.
4166. A comet comprises frozen water, supercold methane, ammonia, and carbon dioxide ices mixed with rock and dust and other debris from the solar system.
4167. A supernova explosion results in star matter being blown away to form new nebulae, making new stars.
4168. A castrated adult male sheep is called a wether.
4169. Edwin Hubble is known as the greatest astronomer after Galileo Galilei.
4170. The smell of skunks and the rotten egg smell near volcanic areas are from the compound hydrogen sulfide.
4171. There are two categories of venomous snakes, the elapids and the viperids. Cobras, mambas, and sea snakes are examples of elapids that have short hollow fangs. Vipers and rattlesnakes are viperids with long hinged fangs.
4172. An adult elephant must drink about 210 liters of water every day.
4173. The bright-colored wings of butterflies are tiny scales.
4174. No space shuttles occurred between December and January as the computer couldn't handle a change in the year!
4175. Hippos are herbivores, and their favorite food is grass.
4176. The Triangulum Galaxy received its name from the constellation Triangulum.
4177. In extreme sports, judges often are required to score players on visual and technical criteria and 'tricks'.
4178. Bald eagles are not bald. Their white head, covered with feathers, only looks bald from a distance compared to its dark body.
4179. It is more common to find a combination of chlorine with other elements than to find it in its 'free' form.
4180. Our ocean tides are caused by the gravity from our moon

and the sun.

4181. The first spacecraft to successfully land on Mars, on 20 July 1976, is NASA's Viking 1.
4182. The thin atmosphere of Neptune's moon, Triton, has tiny amounts of carbon monoxide and methane.
4183. The science of mathematics is important in many occupations, including engineering, medicine, business, and science.
4184. The Spacetime continuum is a mathematical physics model that joins space and time together.
4185. Gas giants are not all gas; for example, Jupiter and Saturn have layers of molecular and liquid metallic hydrogen.
4186. Comets and asteroids are alike, but asteroids don't have a fuzzy outline and tail as comets do.
4187. Toads, like frogs, are amphibians.
4188. Megabats and microbats are the two main types of bats.
4189. Much research has shown that parrots are intelligent birds.
4190. Scientists believe that volcanic processes created Venus.
4191. Many fish have tastebuds on their fins, face, and tail. For example, catfish are covered in tastebuds all over their body, including their whiskers.
4192. The moon is not round - it is oval like an egg.
4193. Wolves can survive in very cold temperatures of -40 degrees F (-40 deg C) because they have a second layer of fur under their topcoat.
4194. A pig has a very good sense of smell.
4195. Amber is a fossilized tree resin that can sometimes trap plants or small insects and animals inside.
4196. Proteins make up the cells in our bodies and do most of the work for them. There are over 42 million molecules of proteins in each cell.
4197. The small intestine digests most of the food that you eat and absorbs the nutrients into your blood.

ABOUT THE AUTHOR

Thank you for purchasing this book, we hope you enjoyed it!

What is your favorite fact?

Professor Smart's favorite animal is the penguin and that is why his favorite fact is number 1081.

"To stay warm, Emperor penguins huddle together in large groups."

Did you know that the Professor created this beautiful cover ... and he's only eight years old! The Professor loves all things animals, cars, science, food, and dinosaurs. And with his range of books, he hopes to inspire other kids to try new things, to learn more about the world, and to be curious!

We would really appreciate it if you have a couple of minutes to leave a review on the platform that you purchased this book from - it would mean the world to us!

www.ingramcontent.com/pod-product-compliance
Lightning Source LLC
Chambersburg PA
CBHW021828090726
47818CB00077BA/93
9781922435170